Fragments from Iraq

Fragments from Iraq

*Diary of a
Navy Trauma Surgeon*

ZSOLT T. STOCKINGER, M.D.

McFarland & Company, Inc., Publishers
Jefferson, North Carolina, and London

The views presented are those of the author and do not necessarily represent the views of the Department of Defense or the Department of the Navy.

ISBN 978-0-7864-6951-2 (softcover : acid free paper)

LIBRARY OF CONGRESS CATALOGUING-IN-PUBLICATION DATA ARE AVAILABLE

BRITISH LIBRARY CATALOGUING DATA ARE AVAILABLE

On the cover: This Marine with frags in his neck was a "melting pot" unto himself: a Tibetan Buddhist raised in northern India, who emigrated to Utah, became a Mormon, and joined the United States Marine Corps. Much to his and our relief, he had no major injuries (photograph courtesy of the author); background © 2012 Shutterstock

Manufactured in the United States of America

*McFarland & Company, Inc., Publishers
Box 611, Jefferson, North Carolina 28640
www.mcfarlandpub.com*

My wife Janna reminds me that I have to dedicate this book to someone. Besides her, that is. So here goes. To the Small Angry Man, St. John, Joey Two Bags, the TanMaster, Cookie, and Hot Lips, who kept me sane through the first half of the deployment. To Phil, Oscar Lima Pizza, the Near-Chaplain, and the Combat Proctologist—the other members of the Geriatric Group Home—who kept me sane for the second half. I probably drove them crazy, although I think Brian was feeling much better by the time I was through with him. To the Texas Rattler, for adopting me on my arrival to Iraq, and buying me steak in San Antonio. To Sensei Greg, who proved time and again that Marines do have a sense of humor. To Norman McSwain and Bernard Jaffe, surgical mentors extraordinaire, who taught me that there is more to being a surgeon than just surgery. But most important, to those who are now, have been, or will be in harm's way, both as warriors and as those who support them. We're all cogs, but cogs are what make the machine work. Even if the gears do slip every once in a while.

Table of Contents

Prologue

In these pages, you will find a view of daily life, from one surgeon's perspective, on a Forward Operating Base during a busy time in the Iraq War. The Marine Corps was actively engaging the insurgency in the Sunni Triangle as Iraq struggled to hold its first-ever elections. This is not, however, a 21st century version of the TV show *M*A*S*H*. There are no vivid descriptions of firefights, no one kicks down any doors and "gets some," although we did receive our fair share of rockets and mortars, the base chapel was blown up twice, and I almost died on the toilet. So yeah, we had excitement mixed with ennui.

This is a diary that contains reflections on the human carnage caused by war, as seen by someone who tried to mitigate its effects on the victims, and on how that carnage affected the caregivers. Some good times, some bad. We built a pool and a beach. Being doctors, we did play a little golf. We treated over a thousand casualties and performed hundreds of surgical operations, and in that area we won many more than we lost. We barbequed; held luaus and memorial services; proved at the shooting range what bad shots medical people really are; and we more than occasionally rubbed each other the wrong way and then made up. I found our psychiatrist a dog and a racing vulture. I made many friends, and hopefully, no permanent enemies (even if they do read this book). We tried to have a normal life in what is, for us as Americans, an abnormal place. But I try to remind myself that, to paraphrase Voltaire, it is the function of the physician to entertain the patient until God heals him.

Before all this began, I'd had the benefit of a protracted, misspent but enjoyable youth (well into my 30s) before joining the Navy. Eventually I went off to medical school in Birmingham, Alabama, and then to a general surgery residency at the county hospital in Phoenix, Arizona. There I had the joy of being on-call every third night for trauma cases: operating on the results of the local knife-and-gun club, the domestic disputes involving butcher knives and the occasional casualties after some drug war, and treating rodeo riders, speedway racers and drunks who drove into trees, cacti, and horses. I ran a burn unit, saw the results of an Amtrak derailment, and even saved a drunk cut in half by a train. So I thought I had a pretty good handle on trauma surgery.

As my residency drew to a close, my wife, Janna, who had accompanied me through much of my aforementioned misspent youth, reminded me that now that I had a real profession, I would have to grow up and get a real job. I pondered this revelation for a while and eventually replied that I would not have to "grow up" if I joined the Navy. Janna, in her turn, thought about this for a while, and asked whether this would mean we could travel, get based overseas, and live near water. I answered in the affirmative (there being no thoughts of sand and dust on the horizon). The beard was thus shaved, the hair cut, and we were off to the Navy and our first duty station in Okinawa.

When the terror attacks of 9/11 happened, I had just come off a ship and we were supposed to be on a plane from Okinawa to Australia for a long-planned and much needed diving vacation. However, the flight had been cancelled because Typhoon Nari had chosen to run over the island for the third time in four days. Now watching the second tower of the World Trade Center fall on TV in what was, for us, the middle of the night, we knew we would be going to war and not to Australia. I had no idea who we would be at war with but it was clear that this was no accident. I harbored no delusions that I was a fighter, but I could at least support those who would fight this war. Most of us in Navy Medicine felt the same way. However, I missed the invasion of Afghanistan as I was already slated to spend a couple of months in the jungles of Laos and scheduled to start a trauma surgery fellowship the following summer.

Despite volunteering repeatedly, I was forced to sit out the invasion of Iraq as well, as it occurred during my Trauma Surgery Fellowship at Charity Hospital in New Orleans. Charity was a wonderful place to train, one of the few remaining large public hospitals in America. The Wild West paled in comparison to the Big Easy when it came to trauma surgery, and under the tutelage of Dr. Norman McSwain, one of the "grand old men of trauma," I learned how much I didn't know. Nevertheless, I chafed at the bit. This was "The War" of my generation, and in surgery there is the truism that war trains every generation of surgeons. So when I finally returned to the Navy after fellowship, I felt that I had a lot of catching up to do.

When I finally deployed to Iraq in the spring of 2005, I sent Janna innumerable emails. I also kept a diary of sorts, which I would send to her every month or so. Although it was supposed to be a six-month deployment, we planned on my absence being much longer. The frequent emails were to let her know that, with all the things blowing up in Anbar Province on any given day, I was not among the casualties. The monthly diary was a means by which I shared my more introspective joys and frustrations with her — our way of staying connected. It also served to reassure her that I really wasn't having that much fun without her — my being of an age where a mid-life crisis was due.

Janna read it all and thought that others might enjoy it. It is entirely through her efforts that this project came to fruition. She edited out the truly mind-numbing bits, and a few of the naughty bits, to leave what is in these pages. Except for the necessary clarifications of MilSpeak and MedSpeak, and changing the names to protect the innocent and not impugn the guilty, it is essentially as I wrote it. For better or worse. (For the benefit of the reader, I've included a glossary of military language abbreviations and acronyms that one will encounter in the book.) All observations are mine alone, and I harbor no delusions that many (if not most) of my colleagues saw things differently.

Since Iraq, life has not been quiet and I have still failed to grow up. After a posting to a joint command during which I occasionally trotted the globe doing training sessions with our allies, I deployed again in 2009 with the Marines to Afghanistan. A few short weeks after returning home from that, I was off to the Haiti earthquake relief in 2010 on board the hospital ship USNS *Comfort*. As I write this, I am sitting on a cot in Kuwait, awaiting a flight to Afghanistan for yet another tour — my fourth.

Because, after all, why be a Navy trauma surgeon if you don't go where the trauma is?

Glossary

ACE	Air Combat Element (Marine Air Wing)
AOM	All Officers' Meeting
BAS	Battalion Aide Station
CAO	Civil Affairs Officer
CDR	Commander, a Navy 0-5 (Lt. Col.)
CI	Counter Intelligence
CLR	Combat Logistics Regiment (Marine Corps Logistics)
COC	Combat Operations Center (for Medical, it's really the comm shack)
CPO	Chief Petty Officer
CRNA	Certified Registered Nurse Anesthetist
CSH	Combat Support Hospital
CWO	Chief Warrant Officer
DRMO	Wrecked vehicle lot
ECPs	Entry Control Points
EHO	Environmental Health Officer
EOD	Explosives/Ordnance Disposal
EPW	Enemy Prisoner of War
ERC	En Route Care
FMF	Fleet Marine Force
FNGs	F — ing New Guys
FRSS	Force Resuscitative Surgical System (Navy/Marine Corp Forward Surgical Unit)
FSSG	Forward Service Support Group (Marine Logistics)
GMO	General Medical Officer (a young general practitioner)
Group Surgeon	General's Medical Advisor
GSW	Gunshot Wound
Hootch	see SWA hut
HM	Hospital Corpsman (HM1, HM2, etc.)
IDC	Independent Duty Corpsman; like a mini–PA on subs and small ships
IED	Improvised Explosive Device
MRS Michigan	Main Supply Route "Michigan" (from Baghdad to Syrian border)
MWR	Morale, Welfare and Recreation
OIC	Officer in Charge
OPs	Observation Posts
Orthopod	Orthopedic Surgeon
PA	Physician's Assistant

PACU	Post Anesthesia Care Unit ("Recovery Room"; "Post-Op")
PRT	Physical Readiness Test
REMF	Rear Echelon M — r F — ers
RIP	Replacement in Position
SAS	Sick As ... Snot
SJA	Staff Judge Advocate
SSTP	Surgical Shock Trauma Platoon #18
STP	Shock Trauma Platoon
SWA Hut	Southwest Asia Hut (a plywood cabin)
TCN	Third Country National (foreign worker)
TQ	Taqaddum, Iraq (home away from home)
Twigs	Navy Medical Service Corps Officers (their insignia is an oak leaf on a twig)
UXO	Unexploded Ordnance
VBIED	Vehicular-based Improvised Explosive Device

1. February 2005:
Welcome to TQ!

Sunday: Camp Lejeune Day 1.

Yet another goodbye, the third one for this deployment. And probably the best one. The first, when I initially went down to Lejeune with my unit for predeployment training, thinking I would not be back, was protracted and you looked very tearful as you drove off. The fact that we stood around the hospital gym for over an hour, waiting for a 30-second "bon voyage" from the hospital commander, hadn't helped. The second, when we revolted at Lejeune over the weeks of delay before deploying and came home for a week, was a lot shorter but also at the hospital. The third was from home, private, and definite. If you're going to do something, you may as well just get on with it.

Of course, we should be used to goodbyes after all this time. Over the years there have been months at sea, or in the jungles of Asia, or covering other hospitals in the Pacific. Ten of the preceding twelve weeks on carriers or at 29 Palms. But this was different. I am going to THE WAR, we both know that changes everything. And unless something bad happens, I won't be back for 7 months, maybe a year.

Drove down to Lejeune, got there at 1400, a four-hour drive. At 1800 we muster and are told that we are to report with our gear to our Marine unit's Headquarters, at 2030, which we then proceed to do. We then stand around, form up without the Marines, form up with the Marines, move our baggage, move it again, load it into trucks, and finally get on the buses at 2300 to go to MCAS Cherry Point, about 45 minutes away. The 191 assorted sailors and Marines then sit around in a hangar for a while, are issued four MREs that no one has any room for in their carry-on baggage — so we all strip them for the good bits and chuck the rest. Board the plane at 0400 on the 14th. Happy Valentine's Day.

Monday, February 14: On the move.

Nice airline, Delta. The crews (pilots and flight attendants) volunteer for these missions — they are paid, of course, but they turn down other trips to Europe, etc., to fly the troops. Nice of them. The officers file in last, straight into first class. I have a leather recliner that goes almost flat and has its own TV. Sweet. We are fed about once every three hours. Like the proverbial pup-fish.

First leg of the trip is to Rome, not to Ireland as we had previously been led to believe. Nine hours, we get there at about 2000 local time, still on the 14th. Happy Valentine's Day again. No chance to see the Eternal City, however; we park out on the tarmac, refuel and reprovision. They allow people out onto the stairs that have been rolled up, to smoke, but no one is allowed off the plane. Some of us stand around near the open hatches to get fresh air.

On to Kuwait, another six hours.

Tuesday: Kuwait Day 1.

We arrive at Kuwait at 0740 local time. Off the plane, onto buses, then to a large empty gravel lot where, like Barney Fife, we are issued a bullet that we are not allowed to put into our guns. Well, thirty rounds actually. We then bus to Camp Victory, an hour or so out of Kuwait City. On the way, we pass the Kuwait City Camel Racing Club. Off the bus and into a large tent, where we receive our "in-country" briefing. It's a war zone, there are bad guys, and even Kuwait gets terrorist attacks. Nothing new.

We're divided into "sticks" or "chalks," i.e., planeloads, upon arrival. About 50 per load, so we can fit into a C-130 with all of our baggage. I get to be in stick 1, and we're to leave tomorrow afternoon, sometime. We are all housed, O's and E's alike, in a single large tent. We've got cots, showers, hot food, and access to our sleeping bags. Only Port-A-Crappers, but other than that, the war isn't too bad so far. I'm sure that the bubble will burst eventually.

Camp Victory is a transit base run by the Army. Convoys into southern Iraq come and go from here, as do planeloads of personnel. Consequently, there are relatively few "permanent" residents, and very few structures that are not tents. There is, however, a Hardees, a Subway, a PX, and AT&T Phone Center, an internet café, and a coffee shop (the "Green Bean Café"). I wander about a bit and find almost nothing of any interest. There are a lot of tired-looking National Guardsmen around, but the new ones and the ones who have been here for a while all look the same. According to Mike (former Marine), they all look like "bags of shit with strings around the middle." While I don't think that they're quite that bad, they certainly have a relaxed uniform standard.

Wednesday, February 16: Kuwait Day 2/TQ Day 1.

Ninety minutes to TQ (Taqaddam). The C-130, a cargo plane with canvas seats, is as comfortable as I remember it to be. On the first approach, we twist and turn a bit in case anyone wants to shoot at us, but the landing is uneventful. We march across a pitch-black tarmac as a group of Army soldiers march past us onto the plane without a word (the start of their ride home), and eventually meet up with our luggage in another dirt lot somewhere. The Navy medical folks' gear is separated from the rest of the Marines' (who will live on the opposite side of the base), and we get on our bus to go to our new home.

First impressions are important. These people are very happy to see us, but are somewhat reserved. Vaguely reminiscent of POW camp survivors, they realize that their salvation is at hand but they don't quite believe it or know what to do.

Thursday: TQ Day 2.

Up at 0700 for chow. The food here is said to be very good, which I suppose means that it's the usual excessively greasy American breakfast foods. Which is fine once in a while, just not every day. Maybe toast and cereal this morning.

We have muster at 0830 in front of the "hospital," then a brief run-down on the various camp rules, including when to wear body armor—"but we haven't been wearing it for a while now since there hasn't been any incoming for over a month." We are told that we are "Team Indigo," replacing "Team Gold," who had replaced "Team Scarlet" (the original occupants). Taqaddam used to be a secret Iraqi base for training terrorists to send into Iran—so secret, in fact, that not even the locals knew about it. It's on a mesa

There's definitely a dress code to get into Medical—check your body armor and your ego at the door.

about 100 feet higher than the surrounding area, and the locals were never allowed up here, so supposedly they don't know the layout at all and any fire we might get is essentially random. The local town, Habbaniyah, is on the lake and used to be a resort for terrorists. No, we can't go there and shop.

We then get a brief walking tour of our little chunk of the base. Free internet café, pay (Egyptian-run) internet café, library, gym, weight room, PX, chow hall, and the "HadjiWood" (Iraqis are referred to as "Hadjis," which is actually an honorific for those who have made the pilgrimage to Mecca during Ramadan, although I don't think the U.S. Military means it that way) which sells souvenirs and pirated DVDs. There used to be a local-run restaurant, but it closed after several workers and their family members were killed by the Fedayeen. Bummer.

Interesting military-related sites, also. The "Crack House" is a three-story concrete building that houses the air guys who coordinate medevacs and do the air traffic control. It's right behind us and the tallest building on the base, so it is fairly easy to find our way home. Behind that is the "Dark Tower," a dark grey concrete block also about three stories high that houses the HQ folks. Aerials and dishes all over it, of course.

After this little tour, we fill out our paperwork to get the Navy to give us our hazardous duty pay and family separation allowance, and stop our taxes. Very important. We are

A view of our operating room from the holding area. Janna thinks it looks like the inside of a space station.

then left to our own devices—"Today is your day off, tomorrow you start work." We'll start five days of briefings and turnover stuff. These guys leave starting on the 24th.

We are wandering about when we see an armored personnel carrier with red crosses on it zip up the road toward the hospital. Even though it's our "day off" we, of course, head back over. Four Iraqis who had run a road block. One shot through the jaw, two through the neck, and one in the head. I get my first case, one of the neck guys. We then wrap them all up and they'll fly out to either Baghdad (Army) or Balad (Air Force), the Level III hospitals. As far as we know, these are just four stupid people and not bad guys. Maybe. Anyway, we patch 'em and ship 'em. Mike says that I looked pretty happy to be back in the OR, which is true.

At this point, I should describe the SSTP (Surgical Shock Trauma Platoon) or "hospital," as the road signs generally call it. It's a collection of a dozen or so tents, surrounded by barricades, that houses two ORs and a miniature ER. The "wards" are cots with minimal to no ability to monitor or care for patients. It's designed for trauma care only, that is, no sick call stuff. We have no real ability to hold onto patients or provide post-op care. No ICU, either. Limited x-ray and almost no labs.

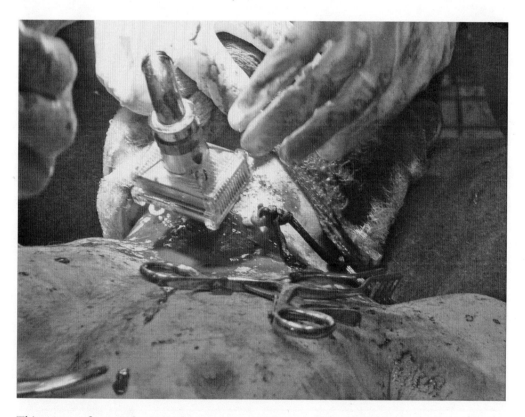

This was our first combat casualty, a gunshot in the jaw. The patient had received a crichothyroidotomy in the field. In other words, someone without an operating room, probably not even a doctor, had cut a hole in his neck and stuck in a tube so he could breathe. An excellent reminder that the unsung medical heroes in wartime are the corpsmen and medics who keep the patients alive long enough to get them to a surgeon. If they can survive that long, the odds are heavily in their favor.

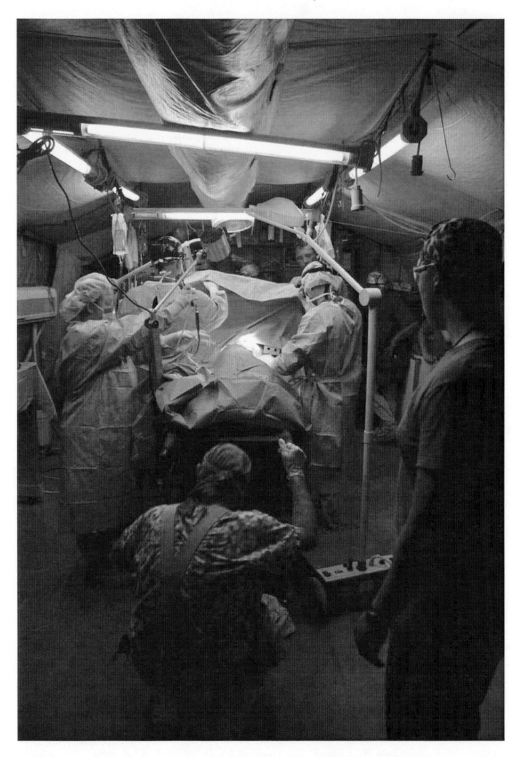

While this may look like a normal operating room, it really doesn't do justice to the amount of dirt, dust, and the occasional fly that cannot be kept out of the tents in a war zone. But it's still a great picture.

We then wander off to chow at 1700. As we are sitting in the chow hall, musing over the astonishingly bad coffee, all the Marines jump up and start to leave. We have just had a rocket attack, don't you know? Now that everyone is quiet, we can hear the siren, which typically occurs after the rounds have come in. We hasten back to the SSTP and put on our armor. We hear that more casualties are coming in, from up by the runway where the rockets hit. False alarm, fortunately.

We're told by the old team's CPO (Chief Petty Officer) that we did the wrong thing during the rocket attack. When we hear the rockets, we are supposed to get on the ground in a covered area. A few minutes after the rockets have gone off, we are to return either to our hootches or to the hospital. However, at the same time that we are on the ground, hiding, we are supposed to go and get our body armor, and also call the hospital (the number of which we do not have) to account for ourselves. I ask the Chief how we are supposed to stay put, hide, and get armor simultaneously. I get a blank look. I also ask how we are supposed to stay put when the Marines are throwing everyone out of the chow hall, i.e., dispersing the occupants so a single round won't take us all out. Another blank look. Finally, I ask what's the point of trying to get accountability during an attack, since we might become casualties after we call in but before the attack ends. Yet another blank look. I decide that it's just not worth asking any more questions.

We hear that Joe has continued to live up to the athletic reputation he earned during our predeployment exercises. He was over at the hospital when the first round hit and he got into his armor. After the second round, he dove for cover in true war-movie style. Mike now refers to him as "Snake" and I have put the Ace of Spades in his helmet band. He can supply his own cigarettes to put in there.

Nothing else of excitement for the evening.

Friday: TQ Day 3.

Up at 0700, I try to get to the bathroom. No luck, the area around it is being guarded by the Army (who supply our base's internal security). Someone found UXO (unexploded ordnance) this morning, out by the crappers. No further details on whether it has been there for minutes, days, a year...

I also learn from someone else that when Fallujah was taken down, detailed maps of our base were discovered, presumably based on intel provided by the locals who work here. The layout of the base is well-known to the Iraqis and used to be a big Iraqi Air Force installation. Gee, yesterday weren't we told that they don't know our layout and the locals are not allowed on base?

More lectures in the afternoon on the blood bank and admin stuff. Some people complain that all of this could have been done at Lejeune, but (a) these people weren't at Lejeune; and (b) out here we are going to pay a whole lot more attention, because in a week all of this will be ours.

During our lectures, I'd been told that we have no tracheostomy hook. This is a small metal hook on a long handle that makes doing trachs much easier. The Gold Team

This was the primary operating room tent, in the middle of being restocked. The OR table is just a fancy metal frame to place a stretcher on. Many nonstandard items that were acquired over time to make life easier are evident, including plywood shelves, an AC unit, and extra lights. Despite mopping three times a day, and after all surgical cases, there is still plenty of dust to be seen.

has been using a bent needle on a haemostat, which has not been very effective. I walk over to the Dental Clinic two buildings over, ask if they have any spare dental picks (which they do), file it down a little to shorten the hook, and voila! A trach hook. Seemed pretty straightforward to me...

I go over to HadjiWood and discover that they sell pirated videos like *Striptease* and *Showgirls*, the unrated versions. But we are not allowed to bring any pornography (defined as anything revealing, including "fitness magazines") into the country. I buy a sheet of Saddam money for $5, no doubt a lot more than it's worth but there doesn't seem to be much in the way of souvenirs out here.

Saturday: TQ Day 4.

Around 1400 we get word of incoming casualties. An IED was set off near a patrol (no casualties), and two guys run out from behind cover into a building. The Marines chase them, and we are getting six assorted casualties: two adult males (the bombers), a

16-year-old male, two women, and a little girl. All have fairly minor injuries, but we take one of the perps to the OR to wash out his wounds — my second case here. The wounds are all from fragments of the IED, which hurt them and no one else. Ultimately the Intel interrogators decide that the three males are all to be detainees, so they will not be released and will be sent to the famous Abu Ghraib prison,which has a prison ward and a surgeon. Wow, my first known bad guys!

I plan to go to chow at 1700 but shortly beforehand we hear that there is an incoming casualty from

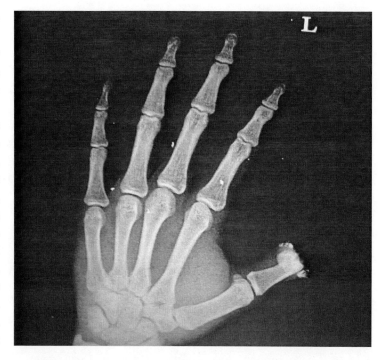

Not every injury is life-threatening, but even seemingly minor injuries can have major consequences. This soldier had the end of his thumb shot off. Think about it, how do you do something even as simple as holding a coffee cup without a thumb?

Ramadi with chest and hand injuries, no other info. On arrival, it's a Marine who picked up what turned out to be the detonator for a mine. It blew up in his hand. His chest injury is nothing, but he ends up losing half of his left thumb and index finger (fortunately he's right-handed).

Sunday: TQ Day 5.

For some reason, we all sleep late today and wake up around 0800. I suppose it makes sense, as it is a "day off." I call you on the ATT, nice to hear your voice. Learn that Moof [our Rhodesian Ridgeback] is cavorting on the new sod at home. I ask you to send me staplers; they seem to be a hot item out here.

Monday: TQ Day 6.

At noon, J.J., the Texas Army National Guard doc I've met, drives Joe and me over to the other side of the base ("Lakeside") to look around. The base is split into larger and smaller chunks by the two-mile airstrip and we live on "Mainside," away from the lake. There isn't too much at Lakeside except another chow hall, a barber, and a couple of Hadji shops, but they're a lot better than what we have on our side. They do embroidery and alterations, and sell rugs and knickknacks. I couldn't resist buying the Saddam cigarette lighter which, when opened, has little lights representing bombs dropping from an F-16 and exploding. It's inscribed, "ANXIETY PEACE WE," which I'm sure means something in Chinese (the manufacturer), but is completely nonsensical in English. I also poked around a bombed-out building and started to explore a bunker, but it had heavy steel blast doors which tended to swing shut if you let them go, so I didn't go inside. Maybe later with back-up (i.e., someone to hold the door open).

During chow we hear about a casualty coming in, a burn of some sort. When it gets here, it's a Marine who burned his hands (not badly) while burning trash. After this, a Humvee drives in with a 10-year-old Iraqi girl in "respiratory distress." The rule is that if we don't shoot them, or they don't work for us, they don't come here, but someone brought her here anyway. The problem is twofold: first, if word gets out, we could be swamped, which would use up our supplies and minimize our ability to treat our own casualties; and second, if they are really sick, there is no place we can send them for follow-up treatment. So policy from on high is to not see Iraqi civilians at

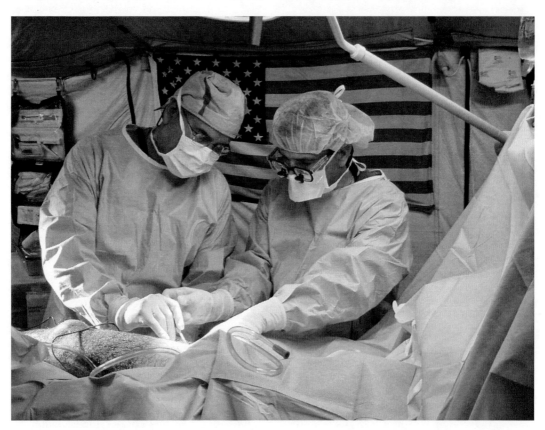

J.J. (AKA "the Texas Rattler," left), the family practice doc with the Texas Guard, lends Joe a hand in the OR. J.J. was a frequent visitor, a good friend, and a constant source of aid and entertainment to the unit. He also knew how to throw a good barbecue.

all. That said, if they get to us, we treat them and figure it out later. Anyway, she seems to be having a panic attack, calms down, goes home, and the problem is solved.

Tuesday: TQ Day 7.

I'm not sure how the diary is going to go, there will be a lot of retrospective stuff in it. I'm writing this at the end of the next day since it's been pretty busy the last couple of days.

I do remember that today (Washington's Birthday) was the day Joe chose to quit smoking. In honor of a tobacco farmer, perhaps? Of course, he reflexively smoked this morning anyway; he hadn't remembered that he'd decided to quit.

Around noon I went with J.J. back to Lakeside so we could do the tourist thing. J.J. is an interesting guy, a Family Practice doc from San Antonio who's been in the Military for 38 years, most recently in the National Guard. This is pretty amazing, when you bear in mind that his retirement will max out at 30. He is one of only six physicians in the Texas Army National Guard, all the rest having bailed out due to the deployments. His unit is armored, but retained for MP duty. We went off and took pictures of ourselves with some blown-up buildings and then explored an abandoned (and ultimately quite boring) Iraqi bunker. Even found a few "spider holes" (i.e., covered holes in the ground).

After lunch we had four casualties come in. IED with gas cans placed on top so that everything would catch fire, too. One was an 80+ percent burn who likely will not survive, and a couple of 20 percent burns. We operated on them to clean out their blast injuries (dirt and fragments in their wounds, with assorted fractures). We shipped them out along with another burn without frag wounds. So while no one died, I expect that the one big burn will.

At this point, I should explain our system. Patients come in, we operate on them to either save their lives or to do the first clean-up of their major wounds, and then we ship them out by helo. We can usually get someone out by helo ten minutes after we call; the Medevac system here is phenomenal. Helos are usually Marine CH-46s, although they say that some Army Blackhawks also make the runs. We ship them out as urgent (immediate), priority (within 4 hours), or routine (within 24 hours). They then go to a Level III facility, either the Army CSH in Baghdad (Combat Support Hospital, which has about 9 general surgeons, 1 vascular surgeon, a couple of orthopedic surgeons, 2 urologists, and 2 neurosurgeons) or the Air Force equivalent (8 or 9 surgeons) in Balad. Ultimately everyone must go through Balad to leave the country. Anyway, after we do their "damage control" surgery, they go to the Level III where they usually go back to the OR for either completion of definitive surgery (complex vascular repair, "second look" belly surgery, more "wash outs" of wounds, etc.). TQ hasn't been doing definitive repairs for vascular cases (not a single one), and the old Team says that both the Army and AF re-open every belly done at a Level II facility, so they (the old Team) don't close the belly (except for skin). Interesting and odd. I can understand not doing a vascular repair if the patient has multiple other injuries to deal with, or re-opening bellies that still need work, but the

TQ guys seem to have bought into this completely and I'm not sure why. There is no formal policy on the vascular, anyway, that I can nail down.

Wednesday: TQ Day 8.

More lectures this morning on abdominal trauma. They show us their numbers, including their deaths.

I'm planning to go to lunch and then cruise around with J.J., when word comes in that we have two casualties coming in by ground with a 45 minute ETA. Neither Joe nor I am on call, but our group of surgeons has jointly decided that everyone shows up for everything, and then if we are superfluous, we will leave. But with 45 minutes' notice, we get coffee first.

The casualties are two Iraqis shot by Marines. An IED was set off, the Marines saw the perpetrators drive off, gave chase, and another Iraqi car zipped into the crossfire.

An incoming casualty is evaluated on "the pad" outside the medical unit. Regardless of nationality, the patient would be searched for weapons or ordnance and the wounds rapidly assessed to determine severity, priority of treatment, and whether he went straight to the OR.

Not surprising; the Iraqis are reputed to drive like madmen. John and one of the Gold Team take the guy shot in the back to the OR (ends up being a flesh wound), and Joe and I take the other. This guy has two bullets through his knee, and has trashed his popliteal artery, one of the most difficult vessels to get to and repair. We wash out his wounds and put in a shunt (a temporary plastic tube to restore blood flow until a formal repair can be done). Joe hasn't done a vascular case since he finished residency (1999), so one of the old Team stands with us, unscrubbed for the entire case, and verbally walks Joe through it. I would have done it a little differently, but say little and we get through it fine (except that I found a hole with the "probing finger of death," and the part where I accidentally let go of the artery clamp and blood squirted Joe in the chest...). I would also have considered doing a graft (i.e., permanent repair), but then I have done this more recently than Joe has. Not surprisingly, Joe went back to smoking.

We finish all this up, and the Iraqis are sent to the CSH (the AF does not take Iraqis, I'm told). Joe and I decide to go to dinner but head for the showers first. I am sitting in the crapper around 1800 when I hear two tremendous explosions in rapid succession and the trailer shakes. I hit the ground, pants around my ankles, wait for about thirty seconds, and then stick my head out the trailer door, to discover a large black cloud of smoke rising from behind the SSTP. I don't know if it's been hit, and I sprint back to the hootch (50 yards or so), dive in, and struggle into my body armor while lying on the floor. About a minute later, Joe comes in — he'd been naked and about ready to step into the shower. We cautiously go out to see if the SSTP has been hit, but it turns out that it was the "Tent City," about 150 yards behind us, that got it. We wait for casualties from what I discover is a rocket attack.

The old Team runs around yelling shrilly that there are twenty people trapped in a burning building, we should expect lots of burns. Everyone is spun up. Everyone is also milling around on "the pad," the concrete apron in front of the SSTP. This happens to be right next to the buried, polluted Iraqi aviation tanks that contain 86,000 gallons of explosive "whatever." Most of the old Team have no armor on, and are telling our guys to take theirs off. Joe and I note that pretty much every other surgeon is standing in the middle of the pad, waiting around, so we keep our armor on and stand some distance away behind some HESCOs (big earth-filled obstacles), just in case.

Mike and John show up, they were about 50 yards from the explosions and both saw and felt the boom. Whoa.

After about 20 minutes, two guys are brought in with multiple fractures and wounds, all filthy, none life-threatening. A few walking wounded. An SWA hut took a direct hit, but fortunately there were no KIA (Killed In Action). Six total: we operate to stabilize and clean up three and send them off. J.J. and his guys were there the whole time, helping. I wash out a leg, do fasciotomies, and put on an ex-fix (an erector set to stabilize fractures).

By now it's 2200, and we spend the rest of the evening considering our fates. The Iraqis know that the Marines are turning over, and there are about twice as many people on base as usual. So they are shooting at us as much as they can, which admittedly is very little, but more than enough. I tell everyone that it was a good thing that I had just

This is not a burn wound. Somewhere under all that dirt and oil is a leg, hit by IED fragments. Sterility was really not an option most of the time — the patient was by far the dirtiest thing in the operating tent. Still, we did what they could to keep things clean.

dumped a load, or else I would have crapped in my pants. That is as close to dying on the toilet as I ever want to get. Mike saw the flash and explosion from about 50 yards away, as did one of our OR techs, and they were pretty rattled. It was a sobering day for all of us.

Thursday: TQ Day 9.

As I am writing this, it's so far been a quiet day. I was up at 0600, went to call you to let you know that nothing bad had happened to me, in case there was anything in the news about TQ. Of course, calling you to say that there is nothing to worry about would also make you nervous, but I decided that it's better than your seeing something on the news and not knowing.

Went by what was left of the SWA hut. A mess. A lot of debris had been cleared away to get the casualties out and to put out the fire, but it was still pretty impressive. Wood splinters everywhere, a couple of the HESCOs had busted open, and the roof of the SWA hut next door had collapsed. Amazing that no one was killed.

At our 0800-ish officers call, the STP ("ER") guys discuss how triage will be done, i.e., who is in charge of it. They waffle between the PA and the ER docs. I tell them that triage of the first wave will be by a surgeon. After the surgeons are in the OR, someone else will take over. They make it sound like the surgeon will be around for a few seconds and then leave, and after that the ER docs will just keep sending cases to the OR. No, the surgeon will be around as long as it takes to determine which patients go to the OR first, and then between cases any free surgeon will go out, see what else is there, and retriage everything. Trauma is a surgical disease. No one else has much to say at this point...

A short lecture this morning and then a brief foofurraw while a rumor about a "truck-load" of incoming casualties comes and goes. Then J.J. and I head out sightseeing in his ambulance.

We look at the lake, some bunkers, and a few stripped Iraqi airplanes. I start a trend by writing your name on one and getting a picture with it. J.J. and his driver do the same. We also visit a really cool building with all sorts of patriotic Iraqi murals on it — brave Iraqis in various poses, Iraqi forces fighting infidels, and so on. Very cool, lots of pictures. Our favorite is the one of Uncle Sam portrayed as the devil, next to a

Writing Janna's name on the tail of a junked Iraqi Mig25 fighter by the side of the road. What more could a girl want for her birthday?

A bored surgeon is a dangerous thing. Fortunately, it's only the tail piece of a parachute flare and not an actual unexploded mortar round. Still, you shouldn't try this at home.

giant snake with a Star of David on its head, menacing a mosque. We stop for lunch at the Lakeside mess hall, and I buy an even sweeter Saddam lighter at the Hadji shop (this one has the flame shooting out of Saddam's rifle). At the end of this, J.J. drops by a shipping container in the middle of nowhere, and gives me a refrigerator. Way cool.

I return to the SSTP with mythical powers. I get free refrigerators, go for rides, and buy cool artifacts. I'll never be able to live up to this.

Saturday: TQ Day 11.

We are all sitting around and decompressing. J.J. and I have been chatting about various things and one of his problems is that his corpsmen don't have adequate aid bags. When they tear up to some place in their ambulance, they then have to haul big heavy metal boxes out into the field to treat people. Oddly enough, I just happen to have a very nice, soft-sided backpack designed specifically for this... So I give him the *Sked*. He's very happy, like a kid with a new toy, and plans to show it off to all his medics. It will probably go into one of the M-113 armored ambulances.

Sunday: TQ Day 12.

It's a "day off" today, so eventually I get up and go eat. Run. Hang out. Buy a small camel statue at the exchange since I had said that I would send you a camel. We are sitting around at 1900 when an ambulance comes screaming up and starts dumping casualties off. Fake casualties courtesy of the old Team. Tomorrow's scheduled mass casualty drill is starting today. For the next two hours, we have our inadequacies rubbed into our faces. They have taken their fourteen worst patients in seven months and dropped them into our laps in 30 minutes; they won't let our 20-odd Army and ACE (air wing) corpsmen in to help, and they get in our way for everything. It finally ended at 2100. The one bright spot in all of this was the supposed "stumper." They give us a false patient who supposedly speaks only Hungarian. So I start asking him questions which neither the patient nor the examiner understand. "What are you doing?" asks the examiner. "Speaking Hungarian." "You can do that?" "Yeah." Short pause. "Okay, never mind, let's go on to the next patient." Gotcha!

We FNGs (F'ing New Guys) sit around venting and getting a little silly. I had bought

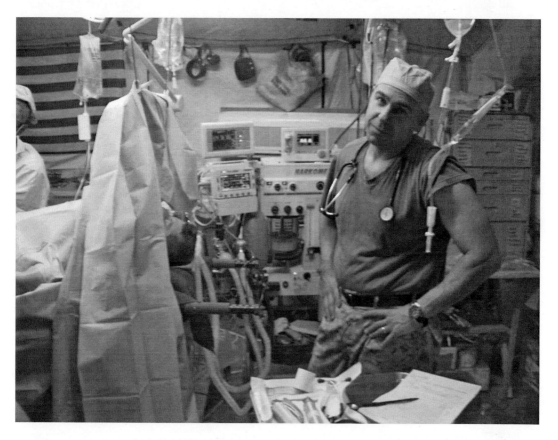

Mike, the Marine officer-turned-anesthesiologist, happy to have his picture taken as always. Dour and unflappable, he gave himself the moniker "SAM," or "Small Angry Man." An OIF 1 veteran and someone who knew what was important and what wasn't, he was a huge asset to a unit with almost no prior deployment experience.

a box of tampons at the PX to turn into a device to deliver QuickClot (a powder that stops bleeding) into wounds, but they were the wrong type — I wanted the ones with the plastic applicator tube and these were cardboard. Mike takes a couple, draws faces on them, and does an impromptu puppet show featuring the old Team. John laughs so hard he falls off his cot. You had to be there.

Monday: TQ Day 13.

At about 1400, I am getting ready to run when we hear that there are three inbound casualties from an Army Humvee that hit an IED. Two with frags to hands or legs, not too bad, and one guy who has frags in all four extremities. This last bloke has had an almost complete amputation of his left forearm, which I have to complete. At one time, John, Bob, J.J., and I are all scrubbed on this guy. He had chunks taken out of him all over, but will live. He's shipped off in the TQ "hot pocket," a body bag with a hole cut out for the face and a big red cross on it — keeps the patient warmer than blankets. They call this the "TTS" — the "Taqaddam Transport System," since "hot pocket" is someone's registered trademark. The old Team thinks this is some really cool invention of theirs (from what they say, the Team before them did nothing), but they finally admit that when the Navy Surgeon General came through last year, he noted that they had done the same thing in Vietnam.

Then a little later we get an EPW, some dude who was bopping down the road in a black coat, wearing a black ski mask, carrying an AK-47. An Army sniper shot him in the ankle so they could interrogate him. John and I wash his ankle out, the Intel guys interrogate him (he claims to be in the Iraqi National Guard), and off he goes to Abu Ghraib around 2200.

I have brought the correct tampons today; will see if I can get them to work.

2. March 2005: We Lose Our First Patient

Tuesday: TQ Day 14.

John and I spend the morning inventing. While I could rest on my laurels from the trach hook, we decide to invent the QuikClot Delivery System. After mucking about for a bit, we decide that the tampon applicator, while promising, leaks too much. We end up with two systems. The first is a chest tube (long silicone tube for draining blood out of the chest) full of QuikClot, with a clamp on each end to keep it inside and dry (it has to be dry to work). Point the tube where you want it, remove the bottom clamp, and it pours right out. The second defies gravity — it's a syringe with the end cut off, full of QuikClot, with the finger of a rubber glove on it with a hole. Push the plunger, glove pops, QuikClot shoots out. By the way, QuikClot is made of lava rock, looks and feels like kitty litter, and stops bleeding. It also is not approved for internal use, which of course is the use we intend for it. If it will save a life, we'll do it. It's a last resort, anyway.

Ran in the afternoon. Made a small detour behind the SeaBee (Navy Engineers) compound, and discovered the Iraqi tank graveyard. Well, no real tanks, but a lot of burned-out or blown-up armored vehicles. Will have to let J.J. know about this, since his unit is armored (or was, their tanks were taken away and they were turned into grunts a couple of years back; they've never gotten over it).

I have decided that we are just like zoo animals. When a new animal is introduced into the enclosure, it starts by wandering around and cautiously sniffing both its surroundings and other animals. After a while, it gets a little more comfortable and starts peeing on things to mark its territory. Finally, it realizes that it has seen everything there is to see and it is trapped with no way to escape, at which point it starts to pace the perimeter of its enclosure and thereby wear a groove in the dirt. This is exactly what we have done: we wandered around, looked the place over, and met the people. We then settled into our own little space and rearranged it to our satisfaction. After that, we all started jogging in circles. The others tell me that I watch too much Animal Planet. Which is a change; they used to say that I watched too much History Channel.

Wednesday: TQ Day 15.

At our AOM (All Officers Meeting) today, we hear that they are officially going to build our "permanent structure" for the SSTP. They have stopped referring to it as a "hardened structure" because it will be a large K-span (sort of a big Quonset hut), which is just sheet metal. It will be surrounded by HESCOs, but that's it. When we had first heard of this, I had felt obligated to point out that this structure would, in fact, be less well protected than what we are in now. At least we have HESCOs around a lot of our tents. With this new plan, we would be putting all of our stuff into plywood rooms inside the K-span, so they would be unprotected. Incurable pessimist that I am, I figure that without internal protection (e.g., more HESCOs or sandbags inside to divide it into two or four subsections), a single rocket or mortar could take out all of the OR capability (not to mention all of the surgeons).

The really annoying part of this is that the Admin officer in charge of the first team here had been offered a bombproof aircraft hangar with concrete walls several feet thick, and had turned it down because "we'll have our own hospital built in a couple of months." So the MAs (Mortuary Affairs) guys got it and store dead bodies and bits in it. Of course, the damned twig gets a Bronze Star for the excellent job he did, or so we are told. (A "twig" is a Navy Medical Service Corp officer, i.e., those staff corps officers specializing in medical administration and logistics. Their collar device is an oak leaf attached to a twig, hence a "twig.")

Went joyriding with J.J. and John later in the morning. Stopped by an Iraqi guard tower I had checked out, climbed into it, and took pictures. Then crawled around the Iraqi armored trash for an hour or so. At first John said he was pretty nervous about it, but fairly soon he was digging around, getting into, and taking pictures of everything like the rest of us. We even took some Russian labels off the vehicles as souvenirs. Then stopped by the building with the murals in it, so I could get a shot of me wearing a Hawaiian shirt next to some of the pictures. Then went by another bunker with assorted bits of trash in it, including an abandoned railway car. No rails, just the wagon. Odd. I found an expended U.S. artillery shell casing, which I took back with us so Joe could use it as his personal ashtray. In the "smoke pit" out back, everyone dumps their butts into a long (three foot) tube that used to hold the propellant for a 155mm artillery shell. Now Joe can have his own personal can.

Friday: TQ Day 17.

This morning John shows me our radio list. We have 18 radios, but only one for a surgeon and one for an anesthesiologist. All four "providers" in our ER, i.e., the two ER docs, our PA, and the Army PA (who doesn't even belong to us) have one. Three of our five nurses have one. The back-up OR techs have one, the Chaplain has one, the electrician has one, and so on, but only one surgeon has one, and it must be passed around. Interesting.

I see the Chief at breakfast. He pretty much runs the show here, and was the one who passed out the radios. I ask him why only 2 of the 18 radios go to the doctors who work in the OR, our *raison d'être*. He immediately tells me that the radios have been issued to "key personnel." Boy, was that the wrong answer. Let's see, we are a surgical unit, our purpose is to do surgery, but the surgeons are not key personnel? He then tells me that since the surgeons "all hang out together," we only need one. Of course we hang out together because we all temporarily live in one tent, right next to the SSTP, so we are always around; but in a few days that will change and if we don't have radios, you're not going to be able to find us. I tell him this is pretty jacked up, thank him for the explanation, and get up to leave. He continues to call out excuses to me as I walk out the door.

Later ... at the AOM, the issue arises. The decision is made that two radios (the Army PA's and the back-up OR tech's) will be given to a surgeon and a gas-passer. The on-call OR techs are supposed to stay in the SSTP for 24 hours anyway, and the back-up techs can't do anything without the surgeons, so what was the point in their having radios? And we never did get a good answer as to why there is a NOD (Nurse of the Day) radio, since we only have patients around when we operate.

Saturday: TQ Day 18.

Had our regular Saturday "Providers" Meeting at 0930 in the Chapel. Not much going on there. After that, went next door to the PX and bought two U.S. flags to put in the ORs to replace the ones that the old Team took with them. We now have three, two in the ORs, and one in the PACU. This way our American patients can see the flags when they go to sleep and wake up and know that they are in the hands of the good guys. And it makes for good pictures.

Sunday: TQ Day 19.

Mass at 0930, after which I go by the hootch we are inheriting, to see if the residual old Teamers need help moving their gear. Nope, the truck will pull up right next to them when they load. They are leaving at noon. They tell us they're leaving us a few things like DVDs and books. Okay.

After noon, Jeff and I go over to scope out our new home. Yeah, they left a few things. About 50 cans of tuna; empty bottles; un-emptied trash cans; literally hundreds of packs of gum, candy, crackers, soup, etc.; empty boxes; Christmas decorations; and assorted piles of laundry, including underwear. Lovely. We go back to the SSTP and I have one of our Marines (we have six assigned to us as drivers) back up a Humvee to the door, and then we start throwing trash into it. Makeshift plywood furniture, filthy rugs, it all goes. The fridge is emptied, too. Since a lot of food items are unopened, we offer first dibs to the Marine, who gets about two trash bags full to share with his buddies, and we take the rest to the MWR (movie/entertainment) tent. We then rearrange furniture, sweep, and I unplug the fridge to defrost it.

We are interrupted mid-afternoon by another casualty, a Marine shot in the neck.

Actually, he was shot at with an AK-47, which hit the 7-ton truck he was in front of, and the bullet frags hit him. A couple of small holes in his shoulder, a couple in his neck. While I'm sure that our predecessors would have operated on him to "wash out" his wounds, I opt not to. The holes are tiny, and the frags head way back behind his neck, far from any important structures. So I do an impromptu teaching on what our options are, and I opt not to operate. I really don't want to put a big hole in his neck for nothing.

Once the kid realizes that he's going to be okay, he gets pretty funny. Unintentionally, though. He has been in Iraq for all of two days, and is the first Marine in his unit to be wounded. "Will I get a Purple Heart for this?" "Yeah, you should." "Cool, I can get one of those special PH license plates when I get home." "Yeah, I suppose so. Small wounds, but you're entitled." "How about a CAR (Combat Action Ribbon)?" "If you saw the guy shooting at you, it's direct fire, so you should." "Can you guys do the paperwork for that?" "No, your command does." Later, his GMO calls up, the rumor back at his unit makes it sound like I had to sew his head back on. I pass on the info about the PH and the CAR, his GMO starts laughing and says he'll get to work on it.

I salvage a little Christmas tree from the mess we inherited, which I plan to send to you. I know you wouldn't want me to throw it away; it has little snowmen on it.

...As I write this, we hear machine gun fire in the background. The local Hadjis have been doing drive-bys on our observation posts along the perimeter the last few days. The rumor is that once II MEF has settled in, we will take down Ramadi like I MEF took Fallujah. Oh goody.

About a half hour later, we hear that there is an incoming casualty. The story, we later learn, is that the bad guys were setting up some mortars to fire at one of our OPs (Observation Posts) around the base perimeter. They were spotted and killed. However, they got off one wild round, which hit a local. He's a rather beefy Iraqi, which we wonder about, as most of the Iraqis we've seen are pretty skinny. Hmm, an older, well-fed, well-dressed, middle-aged Iraqi living in the Sunni triangle. I wonder what he used to do for a living during Saddam's regime?

Anyway, he has frags all over the place, but mostly to his legs and back. His belly seems fine on exam and on ultrasound, all that we have to go on. I take him back to the OR, wash out his legs, and then turn him onto his side to start work on his back. The problem with the back frags is that I have no way of knowing how far in they went. I can just open his belly and look, but then he's committed to a big operation he might not need. So I start cleaning out the holes in his back, and discover that one goes straight in, as far as my finger will go, heading towards Big Red and Big Blue (aorta and vena cava, the biggest blood vessels in the body). I can't feel anything bad with my finger, but how hard do I want to push?

At this point, I have a bit of a conundrum. I can put him on his back again and open his belly to take a look, but he's totally stable, nothing on exam or ultrasound again. If I open him and find a mess, he may become too unstable to move, in which case he will have to stay here, where I have no ICU. So I decide to finish up and ship him to the Army CSH in Baghdad, where they have cleaner ORs, a CT scanner, and a real ICU. Anyway, he goes. We are done by 0130.

I learn later the next day that they opened his belly (am not told why) and found nothing. Good (lucky) call on my part!

Monday: TQ Day 20.

Time for dinner when we hear that there are three more patients coming in, a U.S. soldier and two Iraqi "commandos." They were approaching a vehicle stopped at a checkpoint when it exploded, killing two Iraqi soldiers and the suicide bomber. The two Iraqi casualties are minor, would need wounds washed out, but the Army guy is a mess. He has frags and holes throughout both arms and legs, but his body armor and helmet saved his torso and head. All four surgeons get to work; we activate the "walking blood bank," and spend almost three hours keeping this guy alive. A real mess, but hopefully a save. Broken bones everywhere, repair a leg artery, and so on. Between working on the limbs, I was pulling chunks of metal out of his face.

At one point, as Mike is pouring his 12th unit of blood into this guy, our OIC (Officer in Charge) wanders up to him and says he wants to ultrasound the guy's eyeballs to look for foreign bodies...

We finish around 0130 again, still cleaning up the mess after 0200, and then to bed.

Tuesday: TQ Day 21.

Interesting AOM today. Lots of back-slapping and "attaboys." My take: we did okay. We had all four surgeons, all three anesthesiologists, and all four OR techs in the room on the same patient. In other words, two full crews. We stripped the supplies out of the second OR to use in the first. We need to be able to run two rooms at once, in case we get two such patients simultaneously. We may not always have the luxury of sending away the extras. All the OR folks are pretty much in agreement on this.

Wednesday: TQ Day 22

For some reason I fail to get out of bed this morning. Maybe accumulated fatigue. So I barely make it to breakfast at 0800. The AOM is its usual nonproductive self.

...I'm just about done moving into the SWA hut when we hear that two casualties are coming in.

They finally arrive around 1700. Two British contractors in a private car in Ramadi that was hit by an RPG. One, a Brit named Mick who is former SAS (Special Air Service, i.e., British Special Forces, I recognized the tattoo), has burns to his face and arm, so I take him straight back to the OR as this is the best place to intubate him. But he will be fine. The second, a Welshman called Greg who is a former Royal Marine Commando, has had his left leg almost completely amputated below the knee. He knew this coming in: "I saw it when I was hopping out of the car. After you cut it off, can I keep it and take it home with me, I want to put it on the mantle?" He goes to the OR next and the foot comes off with one snip. Dig a few bits of frag out of his arm, other leg, and scalp, too. We then ship them off to the Army CSH in Baghdad as the weather is bad and the helos can't fly to Balad. Unfortunately, we had no way to send his foot with him, as we have no formaldehyde.

Slept well again tonight, even though we are right next to the flightline with helos and planes taking off, landing, and flying around all night. Most of the air activity here is at night, as it's safer for the transports to fly them. Also, with all of our night vision technology, we "own the night" and make the most of it. I am getting used to this place.

Thursday: TQ Day 23.

The 2nd Battalion, 112th Armored Regiment, 36th Infantry Division, Texas Army National Guard, lost its tanks about two years ago and retrained as grunts. They have gone from DATs (Dumb Ass Tankers) to TWOTs (Tankers Without Tanks). They have replaced the 2nd Battalion, 10th Marine Regiment, who have gone home, as the base security. Consequently, their CO knows all the dope on what's going on in the area. He tells me that we are actually mortared or rocketed almost every night, but the sirens only go off if the radar projects that the rounds will fall inside the base perimeter. In theory. In practice, the sirens usually go off after the fact, and the radar is not always right. For example, two nights ago a rocket impacted about 50 yards from J.J.'s tent but did not go off, and neither did the sirens. They found out about it the next morning (sorta like the UXO behind the crapper a couple of weeks ago). Their dud was fired from about 20 km (12+ miles) away, from south of Fallujah in an area known as the "Shark's Fin." Anyway, it turns out that the machine gun fire we frequently hear at night is real (i.e., not just test-firing). However, it's so frequent that it's not even worth thinking about.

Drizzling off and on all day today, and there are mud puddles everywhere. Iraq is mostly dust and dirt, not sand.

I spent the evening doing crosswords, and putting on my body armor when the occasional boom goes off. We have "controlled detonations" (where EOD blows up munitions, UXO, or whatever) quite frequently, but they are supposed to occur on the hour. Consequently, whenever we hear an explosion, our first instinct is not to duck but to look at our watches.

Friday: TQ Day 24.

J.J. and I go "shopping" again. While running a couple of days ago, I had come across a couple of military junk piles with some useful stuff in them. We take an ambulance and pick up a large fiberglass tub with lid for OR supplies, and about 50 metal ammo cans to store surgical instruments (the cardboard boxes we use now are falling apart). There had been more of the fiberglass tubs a couple of days earlier, but the shipping containers they were in had been moved. Lost opportunity, oh well. It has been raining off

The world's largest lawn dart. No one knows how this got here, but it was a great place for a photo op or a rest in the shade as one walked around the base. Since it was sticking out of a berm next to the Navy bomb disposal unit, it was assumed to be a dud....

and on for the last two days and few people are about so, to paraphrase Tony Curtis from *Operation Petticoat*: "in confusion, there is profit." I also get a picture of me with some antitank rockets, the tailfin of a bomb, and other tourist shots.

Saturday: TQ Day 25.

Our Saturday providers' meeting has been canceled, so there is no reason in particular to get up. I eventually drag my ass out of bed at about 0900 and wander over to the SSTP for coffee. I meet up with J.J., who is also enjoying coffee in the insulated coffee mug I gave him with his name on it on a piece of duct tape. He fits right in now. I go get my body armor and we wander over to the far side of the Dark Tower, where there is rumored to be a large mural of Saddam with the obligatory hole in his head. It is everything it's promised to be, and we spend time getting various shots of us waving pistols at it. And, of course, the obligatory picture of me in my Hawaiian shirt (with pistol — it is a combat zone, after all).

Monday: TQ Day 27.

This morning, J.J. tells me that he's found out where the containers we were looking for a couple of days ago had gone. We set off after them, without any luck. After that, we decide it's a good day to go and look at the bombers again, since it's nice and sunny. While we have crawled under them and into the tail gun turret, we really want to get into the cockpits, which are about ten feet off the ground. I suggest simply parking the Humvee ambulance next to it and climbing up, so off we go. Barb decides to go with us.

We stop briefly at J.J.'s BAS to pick up his PA, who wants to come along. While we are there, I go by the trash heap out back, find another twenty or so ammo cans for the OR, and a couple of other interesting bits of junk. A pile of expended AT-4 shoulder-fired antitank missiles are there, and some blank mortar rounds. Of course we have to take the photo op of us pretending to shoot things, and I feel the urge to juggle the mortar rounds by their tail fins because they look like those thingies the acrobats use. We then head off to the old 1950s-era Iraqi bombers, known as "Beagles."

We park the Humvee next to the bombers and climb up on them. I get into the seats, have a few photo ops. They are pretty well junked, of course. Then we head over to lakeside. I get a very nice shot of the blue water in the background, the desert wadis in the midground, and the rusting junkpile in the foreground. Just lovely.

Zsolt ("Ridgeway 12") and J.J. ("Warhorse 75") next to the Saddam shrine by the old Iraqi HQ. J.J., whose military service began during Vietnam and spanned Panama, Desert Storm, and OIF, insisted that the "75" in his call sign was NOT his age.

HESCO Beach started out as simply a couple of guys on top of an eight foot HESCO barrier, trying to catch a breeze and a view of the airfield. It didn't stay that way for long.

Tuesday: TQ Day 28.

The three male medical hootches are all fairly closely together, almost in a row. We are along the outer wall of HESCOs for Tent City, so some of the guys decide to make a "beach." They level off the tops of four of the HESCOs with dirt, build a ladder, and put deck chairs on it. Camo netting is strung up between the SWA hut and the HESCOs, and Xmas lights are hung. Beautiful.

Friday: TQ Day 31.

I do a little unofficial shopping... We have discovered some NVGs (Night Vision Goggles) during the course of our cleanup, eight all told. They officially belong to the FRSS (Forward Resuscitation Surgical System), as we are really the only ones who are supposed to have them and might need them (as the only medical unit likely to be out in the dark!). They all work nicely, but there is one small problem: we have nothing with which to hold them. They are supposed to attach to our helmets with a special gadget that lets them go up and down and back and forth (for correct positioning and for swinging up and out of the way), but these are missing. These gadgets are supposed to be in the containers but are not. So during my run I drop by a nearby armory and ask the armorers if they have any of these things (since they are accessories to body armor and the armory handles this stuff). "Take all you want," they tell me. I don't want to go through official channels for these, as (1) it may take a while to get them; and (2) they may decide that we don't need the things and take them away. I want to give them to our ERC nurses to use in the helos, since they are basically in the dark for the trip due to light-related security. Every light they have used so far is the wrong color, too bright, or something, and the helos fly usually at night and with the doors open so the gunners can see (we use "designated" helos, which are armed, do not have red crosses, and can be used for other things, as opposed to the Army, which uses unarmed "dedicated" helos with red crosses and can carry only the wounded). If the nurses could use no light at all, that would be even better.

When I get back from the run, I learn that someone has trashed the boys' beach. The camo netting and Xmas lights were taken down and the ladder onto the HESCO was stolen. It's rumored to be the work of the Camp Commandant's office...

I play with the NVGs this evening. They are really cool, you can see almost like daylight with them. I want some.

I am sitting in the COC tent, checking my email, when a Marine bird colonel comes in. It's the CLR 25 (Combat Logistics Regiment) CO, and therefore our boss. He says he's just stopping by. I introduce myself, we chat a bit. "This your first tour with the Marines?" "No sir, eight deployments with the 31st MEU on the gator freighters out of Okinawa." Some discussion about Asia, diving, and so on. He then asks me about what a general surgeon does. He tells me that he knows there are various kinds of surgeons like ER surgeons, orthopedic surgeons... "Uh, sir, there's no such thing as an ER surgeon." "Sure there are, doc." "There are ER physicians, but they are not surgeons. They don't operate." I then proceed to fill him in on the division of labor in the SSTP. He seemed very surprised by all this. Either he has been working under some incorrect assumptions, or someone hasn't been telling him the real deal. Hmmm...

Saturday: TQ Day 32.

...About ready to start my 1000 "Grand Rounds" talk for the medical folks on the base when the radios go off. Single GSW (gunshot wound) to the abdomen in an Iraqi citizen. We all pack up and head over. The patient eventually shows up; the bullet has passed right through his belly. Off he goes to the OR. John is primary, Joe is his back-up, and I scrub for the ride. The guy has two holes in his stomach, the bullet magically misses injuring anything else important, and exits by blowing a hole through the back of his pelvis which oozes up a storm (as it always does with this sort of injury). However, the case goes well and we are done in an hour or so. Rather than send him to Baghdad immediately on the ventilator, we get him off the vent and watch him for the afternoon, planning to send him on as a stable patient that night (when it would be safer to fly). The Air Boss told me a couple of days ago that the locals have been firing SA-7 man-carried ground-to-air missiles at some helos recently, so the fewer trips they do during the day, the better. At night, with NVGs, the bad guys show up really well and have no excuse to be wandering around in the desert, whereas in the daytime they have reason to be out.

I am sitting around with J.J. at the hootch, drinking coffee, when Joe comes by and tells me that we are wanted up at the SSTP. The patient's belly has gotten big and he is oozing a lot out of the bullet hole in his butt. So off we go, back to the OR. Still lots of ooze, really not much that you can do about it but pack it tightly, and we are done again. This time he goes out on the vent. We think about what we could have done differently, not that much really. We feel bad about his needing the second operation (always a possibility with this sort of thing), but are glad that we kept him and did it, rather than send him elsewhere and have someone else do it.

So much for my post-call day off.

Sunday: TQ Day 33.

We lost our first patient today. It had been pretty quiet all day, just reading and running. Around 1600, word came in that there is a GSW to the back, Army guy, coming in from Ramadi. We head up to the SSTP and get the update that he is hypotensive as they put him on the helo. Eventually he gets to us, and as he's brought off the ambulance from the airstrip, he has no pulse. Never a good sign — I wrote a paper on this very subject, CPR in trauma, that came out in the *Journal of the American College of Surgeons* a year or two back.

He goes straight back to the OR, where we find that he has a carotid pulse. He has been shot low in the back on the right side and was paralyzed from the waist down when he got to the aid station in Ramadi, suggesting that the bullet hit his spine. He has a chest tube in that is not putting out much blood, and he was intubated in Ramadi while they waited for the helo to arrive. When we get him on the table, he has a pulse but a lousy blood pressure, so we quickly open his belly to look for the bleeding source. While the bullet has bagged his right kidney and his liver, there is not much bleeding there and his blood pressure is continuing to go down. Still not much blood coming from the chest tube, so at that point I suggest to Joe (who is on duty today with me as his backup) that he open the left side of the chest (not the side that was shot) to check the heart and clamp the aorta — this will send all of his blood flow to his head and not his belly and maximize his odds of survival, which are almost zero, anyway. We do this, the heart is uninjured but empty and the clamp is placed on the aorta. So he has "bled out," but to where? Belly is unimpressive, left chest/heart are okay, no blood coming out of the right chest tube. The right chest is the only place left to look and at the exact moment that I say this to Joe, Tim, our CRNA, says he can no longer ventilate the patient. Arterial blood is coming up the ET tube, never a good sign. I can see the left lung is uninjured (since I had to lift it out of the way to get my hands around the heart to do open cardiac massage), so we quickly extend our left chest incision all the way across to the right. Not much blood in the chest, but the right lung is a huge, blood-soaked sponge. He is bleeding into, not out of, his lung. We try for a couple of minutes to resect the injured lung segments (a good half of it), but the gas passers can't ventilate the guy. I tell Joe (as I perform cardiac massage with both hands again) to just clamp off the entire lung, vessels, airways, and all, and take it out. Doing this will stop the blood loss, and stop the blood getting into his trachea

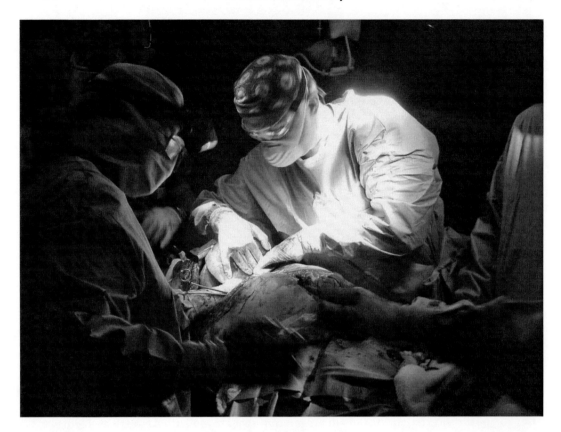

Joe (left) and Zsolt's first resuscitative thoracotomy in Iraq — we "cracked his chest" just like the doctors do on TV. Unfortunately, unlike the doctors on TV, we couldn't save him. His death cast a pall over the unit, and really brought home the fact that they weren't in Kansas anymore. This case was the one I wrote up for a piece in the *Journal of the American Medical Association*.

where it is blocking the ET tube and preventing ventilation. Joe does this while I do cardiac massage off-and-on, but ultimately his heart stops and we call it. A helluva case.

As you can imagine, everyone is pretty somber at this point. Even I'm a bit glum, although I've had my share of trauma patients die on the table. Our first death here, and a very graphic one at that. I think that a lot of our folks, whether corpsman, nurse, or doctor, had never seen anything like this.

I apologize to Joe for telling him what to do even though he is the "surgeon of record." Not only did he not mind, he didn't even notice it. I'm glad, because I like Joe and he's a damned good surgeon, albeit a touchy one at times.

We all get called together in front for a powwow. I say my bit: "I am a trauma surgeon by trade; this is what I do for a living. Before coming here I spent two years at the third largest trauma center in the United States. You all need to know that there is NOTHING that we could have done there that we did not do in that tent. Nothing. We did everything that was humanly possible. Every one of you did it right tonight, all of you. You need to understand that. That's all I have to say." Silence. Nods.

After that, dinner. I discover that Joe has never lost a patient on the table before—

or at least one that he was the primary surgeon for. Ever. A new experience for him. So in the last two days, John got to do his first ex lap in Iraq, and the first take-back for bleeding. Joe got the first thoracotomy and death. My turn next, I assume... On the plus side, several people tell me that the corpsmen needed to hear what I told them.

Monday: TQ Day 34.

The Marine electricians are busy fixing our power issues today, they are replacing generators. The power had gone off during our case yesterday, although it didn't really matter since the lights and vents all have battery back-up. Some asshole had come by while the electricians were working and told them that the reason why the guy died yesterday was because of the power outage, and that they had therefore killed him. When I hear this, I (in full battle rattle) head over there and immediately straighten it out. I tell them that if they find out who said this, they need to tell me and I will "adjust their attitude." I don't care who it is, that is not right, and I tell them that the guy's death had nothing to do with their work. The staff sergeant in charge looks freaked out but after a bit he asks me who I am. When I tell him, he looks at me and says, "You're not a Marine, sir?" I suppose that he doesn't expect the Navy to act this way.

As I am heading back to the SWA, I run across Barb, Carmen and Eileen. We talk a bit about the OR death. They tell me that I am a completely different person in the OR: calm, patient, focused, and "incredible to watch." So outside the OR I am...? "You don't know how to take a compliment, do you?" "No, so don't compliment me."

Tuesday: TQ Day 35.

I ran across J.J.'s battalion XO. He's an interesting guy, the CEO of some corporation in Texas. He goes out of the wire at night to sneak up on his unit OPs so he can give them hell about not being alert. Me, I would worry about getting shot.

Anyway, I have a little chat with him about the perimeter and base security. He tells me that we can go all the way down to the lake if we want, we can even go hang out at the little palace that is down there on the water's edge, which has been cleared out and is not in use. Cool! In fact, if I contact one of his patrol leaders, they can put on an extra truck and a bunch of us can go on a field trip.

Wednesday: TQ Day 36.

At the AOM one of the nurses brought up the issue of photography in the OR. I think she's still a little freaked out (upset doesn't really cover it) over the death a couple of days ago, and she thought that the photos were morbid, gruesome, what have you. Yes and no. I use them for teaching and publication purposes, with the faces blanked out. I am assuming that the other docs will do the same. We are not letting the corpsmen take pictures, although on occasion we ask them to take pics for us with our cameras. She is still leery of it, and thinks it gets in the way. This latter I agree with in part — a couple of people become oblivious to everything else and become a hindrance. I tell her that pictures will continue to be taken, but propose that ONLY physicians may take pictures (or occasionally their designees, with the physician's camera). A sign will be put up in the ORs to that effect. She still doesn't look happy. I do feel bad for her but she's going to see a few more dead people before all of this is over.

Our road trip to the lake is not on for today, we couldn't work out the extra vehicle. We will try for Friday or Saturday. I learn that Saddam gave Lake Habbaniyah to his son, Uday, and that the house we want to go look at is rumored to have once belonged to him. Can't wait to see it. I also learn that just outside the perimeter are two small towns, nicknamed "Trailer Town" and "Tourist Town." The latter was a party town for Baath party members, and had a hotel with a pool on top and all sorts of goodies. The former housed all the prostitutes, many of whom were East European. Of course, it's off base and now populated by the local Iraqis. Would have been interesting to see, but not worth trying to go outside the wire.

We do, however, go out to see the ECPs (Entry Control Points), the two gates where all vehicles go in and out. I can see MSR (Main Supply Route) Michigan, home to many IEDs. The ECPs are pretty interesting and take up a lot of space, with primary and secondary barriers, bermed-off areas for vehicle inspections, and so forth. I even get to see an Iraqi come up to the first gate, arms outstretched, to talk to someone (these guys usually want to talk to the Intel guys). Don't worry, I was way, way back from where they were.

Thursday: TQ Day 37.

After chow, my reputation as the "nonoperative" trauma surgeon evaporates — we had all noticed that on my call days, we didn't do many operative cases even if we had casualties. We get a call for "All Ridgeways" (that's our call sign) to come to the SSTP. No other info, but I gird my loins for battle (meaning I change into PT gear and skuzzy sneaks). When I get there, I hear that we are in for a grand old time. VBIED (vehicle-based improvised explosive device) in Ramadi — a suicide bomber drove into the middle of a convoy transporting Iraqi policemen. Twenty casualties, all coming our way. Damn my radio, number 13! I make sure we can run all three of our ORs, talk to the other docs about how I want to run triage (I'm the duty doc) and then go pee. When I get back, I hear that the 20 will be split between three locations: us, Balad, and Baghdad. Okay, a little better. We will be getting three U.S. by helo, three Iraqis by ground. A few minutes later, I get a call from the GMO at Combat Outpost in Ramadi (who happens to be a cardiologist), who sounds a little freaked out (can't really blame him): 23 casualties, 9 KIA, 14 WIA (wounded in action, five seriously); he's not sure which ones will be coming our way so I get info on all of them. A few minutes later, we hear that the helo is bringing us four, not three.

Then the brown stuff hits the whirling blades. It's like a *M*A*S*H* episode as an ambulance arrives. I look at the four with the PA as they come off the rig. Send one of

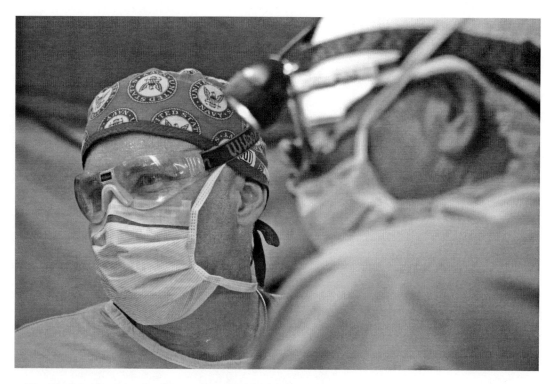

Hot work in the OR, which was kept at 90 degrees or above at all times to prevent hypothermia in the patients. A low body temperature keeps blood from clotting.

the first (U.S. Army) straight to the OR with Joe, he needs to be intubated and has pulseless legs. We get another guy with a head injury, who also needs to be intubated, but I shunt him to the STP tent while I look for more urgent cases. Nope, nothing else emergently surgical in the ambulance. I go to look at the Iraqi needing intubation; he has blood on his head and is unresponsive. Tom is about to intubate him. I quickly look at his head, which has a big hole in the right side of it with a greatly depressed skull fracture that feels like mush. His pupils are blown. Lots of talking, orders flying everywhere, they are getting the intubation gear. I stand up and yell, "Everybody stop! I am declaring this patient 'expectant.' Move him to a different tent." Tom looks at me. "Open skull fracture, blown pupils, no CT or neurosurgeon, and plenty of other cases to do. He's dead." He agrees, we move him out.

Later it occurs to me that this is the first time I have ever declared a patient to be "expectant," i.e., still alive but unsalvageable, a case where we can do nothing. Sure, I have had patients that I knew would not survive, I have stopped treating patients who were hopelessly dying, but I have never had to make the decision to not start treatment based on our resources. It was not difficult to do, maybe because I didn't have to think about it. Logical decision, one I had trained myself for.

Someone sticks his head in and says I'm needed. I walk out just as four more ambulances pull up in a row. We are not receiving six or seven, we are getting all fourteen. This really is a mass casualty scenario. Back to triaging. An Iraqi with evisceration (guts hanging out), still breathing but going down. I tell John to take him to the other OR while I keep looking at the others. My plan is to make sure that I haven't missed anything more serious, then go back to the OR to see how Joe and John are coming along and jump in where I'm needed the most. I see the rest as they come off the rigs (max of fifteen seconds each), decide they are less urgent, then go to the COC and check with the Chief to confirm that we are not expecting anything else. Negative.

I then head back to the STP tents to see what more info we have. Everyone has frags, of course. One guy with a broken humerus (upper arm) and no pulse, another with nasty calf fracture and no leg pulses. They need surgery to get blood flow restored, within the next couple of hours, but they are otherwise stable. Life over limb. One guy has multiple frags to his neck and face, is bleeding profusely from them, and Tom is intubating him. He is urgent surgical, also, more so than the other two. He will be next. Everyone else will need surgical exploration for various things, but not emergently. I tell Tom and the OIC to get on the horn with the Air Boss and find out if we have the ability to send any of these folks elsewhere. Could Balad and Baghdad take any of these?

I go back to the OR. Joe and Bob are looking at multiple x-rays, their guy is intubated. No pulses in his legs, he has frag wounds throughout both as well as his belly, both arms, and neck. He will need a few hours of work but is currently stable. Go in to see John, he is standing there scrubbed before a mass of flesh. The guy has a chest tube, bowel

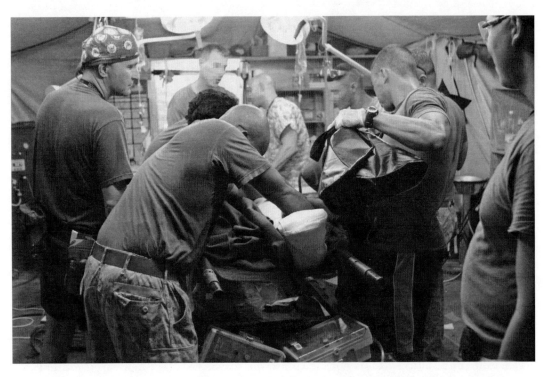

Unlike a regular hospital, patients could not be taken to an intensive care unit after surgery — there wasn't one. Critically ill patients would have to be transported to a higher level of medical care, usually by Marine helicopter. This meant careful packaging to ensure that breathing tubes, IVs, chest tubes and other things were not pulled out en route. This was usually accomplished by putting the patient, and all the gear, into a body bag with a cut-out for the face. In addition to keeping the gear under control, it also kept the patient warm.

hanging out all over. Blood pressure is so-so. Can't ventilate him properly. I gown and glove without scrubbing, and we get to it. John starts to replace the chest tube, which helps with ventilating him, while I look at his belly. He has a hole about a foot across the middle of the abdomen, so I can put my hands straight in. I can smell the holes in his colon, there is blood everywhere. As I put my hands in, I feel a six inch chunk of metal and pull it out of his bowels. Reach up to his liver, spleen and diaphragm — intact, so I know that the ventilation problem is not that his chest is open through his belly. Weak aortic pulse. His bowel is mush, and his legs are trashed with tourniquets on them because he had been bleeding in the field from his wounds. So he will need his belly and both legs worked on. I make the hole in his belly bigger with large scissors, and lift his guts out to look around. He has a wad of metal bigger than my fist right in his aorta. At this point, Jeff says he has no blood pressure. His aorta, which I can see, has no pulse. He is trying to die.

My second "expectant" decision. We now have 12 more patients, this guy will take hours to fix (if we can fix him), and he is trying to die already. Countless units of blood, hours of surgery (assuming that we can even resuscitate him), and still almost certain death. I call it. Jeff asks what he should do since he's intubated. "Give him a big slug of narcs, pull the tube." I whip-stitch his belly shut so the mortuary guys will have an easier time, about a minute. He is dead before I am done.

While I am doing this, John has been talking with Joe. Same story, will need vascular repairs on both legs, plus a neck exploration, and that doesn't include ex fixes (erector sets) to stabilize his legs, and cleaning out his wounds. This is a "two-team" guy, i.e., we need two sets of surgeons working simultaneously. I go to the STP, and am told that Balad can take all of these patients, now. Great. Send the three urgents ASAP (arm, leg, and bleeding face), we will start on Joe's guy, which will still leave us an OR in case something else bad comes in emergently. Since they will need more than one helo trip to get everyone out, if we are done in time we can keep a couple of the more lightly injured patients back and do them here.

I go back to the OR and we get to work. John and Bob work on the first leg, while Joe and I do the neck exploration. While Joe closes that, I move to the other leg. Both legs get filleted open, ex fixes placed. I move to the arms and the guy's face. Surgical poetry in motion, we are all moving and working simultaneously.

As we finish him up, I hear that an oral surgeon wants to bring a patient into the OR. Oral surgeon, do we have one? Which patient? It turns out that we had received five more patients, Iranian refugees involved in another IED. They drove up to the gate and the Army brought them back here, about thirty minutes after the big batch of fourteen. The visiting oral surgeon from Dental was working on some of the facial lacerations, but he can't seem to get the bleeding controlled on one guy and the patient is getting antsy, in Farsi, of course. I go out and take a look, say "hi" and we go back to the OR.

After he's asleep, I put on gloves and a few minutes after that I've tied off the facial artery and we are moving right along. I get all sorts of relieved looks. But, of course, it's not that easy. The guy's EKG starts to look bad and he is dropping his pressure. Looks like he is having a heart attack. Great.

We finish up and ship him off. I am told it's to Baghdad, so I email them (their preference). Then I'm told Balad, so I email Baghdad and cancel. As I'm calling Balad, the Air

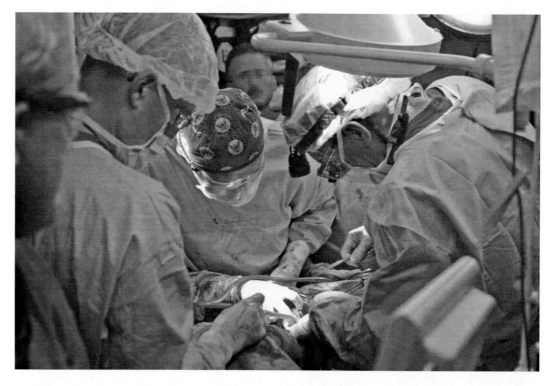

Three surgeons working simultaneously on one patient. This was the preferred way to do business—more surgery could be done faster, with the best assistance possible. During multiple or mass casualties, however, each surgeon was usually on his own.

Boss calls to say it's really Baghdad. Put down the phone, email Baghdad for the third time. Later, I hear that he really went to Balad, and they were pissed because no one had called...

I think back over what happened this evening. We were done faster than I had anticipated. Could we have kept more patients to operate on? In retrospect, yes. It bothers me that I sent patients up to the Level III, assuming that they would be able to get them into the OR faster than we could. Something to ponder and to discuss with my colleagues. Nineteen patients in less than an hour, only two Americans, though.

Good cases, lousy hours, bad outcomes — the life of the trauma surgeon.

Friday: TQ Day 38.

I get my official, permanent radio, number 12, which actually works.

Saturday: TQ Day 39.

I go to Easter Mass at 1900; we did the candlelight thing, the whole works. After that, what I thought was going to be a quiet evening.

It's 2200. Wham. Wham. Wham, wham, wham. At least six, some say maybe ten or twelve explosions, spaced out over two minutes. Code red, some sort of attack (mortars? rockets?). A few minutes later, we hear that there is an EPW coming in, "bleeding uncontrollably from a GSW to the abdomen." Neither Jeff nor I, the only two in the SWA at the time, are terribly excited about going to treat an EPW during a rocket attack, but we head out. Scurry from HESCO to HESCO (well, not really, but we do walk briskly and stick close to fortified areas). We get there, mill around, hear that the guy is stable and will go to Baghdad instead, and eventually we stand down to code green. Back to the SWA for the night.

A couple of days later, I learn the real story on all the explosions. Some mortar rounds came into our camp, hitting nothing. We did counterbattery fire with 155mm howitzers onto the Iraqi mortars. The Iraqis then fired mortars at our 155s. We then fired our mortars at their mortars. They then fired rockets at our mortars. Our howitzers then simply carpeted the point of origin for the Iraqi fire, and that was the end of that. Big boys, big toys.

Sunday: TQ Day 40.

No particular reason to get up today, so I lie around in bed until almost 1100. Finally, a critically low caffeine level drives me from my lair. After that, a long run and some gym time.

After concerns were raised by the Base Commandant about people falling off or getting sunburned, the Beach grew stairs, railings, lights, music, shade, flagpoles, and even artificial turf! It became a favorite hangout after surgery, was used to impress visitors, and even became a random "photo op" for visitors to the base. It was the one Beach the USMC never took!

When I get back, I help the guys work on improvements to HESCO beach. The Safety Officer had come by and said we needed a handrail, so one was constructed. There is also a driving range — another HESCO with a flat top from which you can hit golf balls across the road into a big gravel parking lot. There is a metal pole sticking up, rumored to be about 130 yards away. I walk over with the GPS: 303 feet/101 yards. Sorry, boys.

Easter dinner is ham, turkey, cranberries, mashies, stuffing, pecan pie, ice cream, and so on. Really good. The disconcerting part is that all of this stuff has to be trucked in to us, and every convoy is at risk. So people are dying to bring us ice cream? Makes you think — how many fewer convoys would there be if we had water, MREs, basic food, instead of all this really fancy stuff. Is it really worth it? The flip side, who would stay in the Military if we didn't do this and, of course, the politicians want our boys to have the best...

Monday: TQ Day 41.

Yesterday, we had received the unit t-shirts that we had ordered while in Lejeune, with SSTP/FRSS on the back and the 2nd Med Bn's logo on the front. We had already trashed the "Damage Controllin', Death Cheatin'" signs the old Team had put up, so we have been working on a new slogan. I had suggested "TriQare Middle East: no paperwork, just people," and while the sentiment was agreed with heartily, it was decided that any visiting medical dignitaries might not think it as funny as we do. Mike offers: "We're just bein' here, man," which we all love but probably won't look cool on a t-shirt. So it has been suggested that we just use the 2nd Med Bn motto, "We Fight for Life." Brief and to the point. However, I noted that on the t-shirts, the Latin on the 2nd Med logo is, in fact, gibberish. "Nos pugna pro vita" translates to "We (as opposed to you) (order you) fight! For life," or "We the battle for life." It appears to me that someone who knows no Latin grammar lifted an English-Latin dictionary off the shelf and pulled words out of it. Sort of like *Life of Brian*: "People called Romanes, they go the house?" "It says, 'Romans go home.'" "No it doesn't..." and so on. So I suggest either the more grammatically correct "Pro vita pugnamus," or even better (and to borrow from the Navy Seabees' "Construimus, batuimus" — "We build, we fight"), "Pro vita batuimus." Motion accepted, the signs will be made, more t-shirts will be ordered.

Thursday: TQ Day 44.

Another lovely day, up at 0900. Not much going on today, more refinements to HESCO beach. There is now a sign on the wall, 'HESCO Beach Club'; the golf course has a 'Par 3' sign; and a hole has been made in the HESCO wall across the road (so we can walk straight through to pick up the golf balls) that has been christened "Hamster Pass" in honor of Tommy who looked like he was going to gnaw his way through the HESCOs to get his golf ball back.

3. April 2005: "There's a grenade in his pocket..."

Friday: TQ Day 45.

I give a trauma lecture to the Casevac (helo) corpsmen with the Marine wing at 1700. They have been living about 100 feet from the Saddam mural for the past two months and didn't even know it. They also think that there is only one entrance into and out of their squadron area, which is guarded; yet I still managed to walk into the place without going through the gate, while carrying a laptop, projector, and wearing full body armor. My mythic powers grow, but all I did was take a short-cut through a bombed-out building. Maybe they need to secure their perimeter better.

Saturday: TQ Day 46.

An eventful day, but not entirely in a good way. Up in time for breakfast, and at 0930 I give the lecture for the "providers' meeting" in the chapel, on extremity vascular trauma. At the end of it, Mike stands up and tells us a few things, like the rumor/possibility that there will be a push into Ramadi (supposedly 10 battalions of Iraqi troops supported by us) in June or July. Of course, the Iraqis do not have our training, body armor, or medical assets, so we can expect lots of casualties if this happens. Mike says that they are working with the Iraqi Ministry of Health on figuring out the Iraqi medical support for this. Yeah, right. We're heard that there is one hospital in the entire country that Iraqi soldiers can safely be sent to, Baghdad City Hospital. They "disappear" or "die of complications" at all of the others, but somehow these guys will be cared for at local hospitals?

...Around 1900 we hear that we are getting eight casualties by ground, at an unknown time. By the time I get to the STP, the patient is already there. Yup. Patient. The radio call said "a patient," our comm Marine heard "eight patients." An Iranian Kurdish contractor was doing something with UXO and it blew up, blowing a hole in his leg. Ugly but not serious, I clean it up in the OR. I have the Catholic chaplain, Father Tim, scrub in to help me. Unlike the Baptist chaplain, he doesn't faint at the sight of blood. Former Navy Corpsman, donchaknow...

Back to the hootch by 2300.

Sunday: TQ Day 47.

We get an interesting patient at around 1500, a GSW to the arm and flank. Probably a single AK-47 round from a sniper; it went through his forearm and into his side, in the gap between his front and back body armor. The snipers are getting good out here, but it also tells you that we are taking fewer casualties if they have to be that good. The kid is lucky; the bullet tracked along his back and missed everything important, we didn't even have to open his belly. Broken bone and bruised nerves in his arm, but those should heal. The interesting thing is his name, which sounded Nepalese to me, so I ask him about it. Nope, Tibetan. Right mountains, wrong country. He is a Tibetan Buddhist Mormon U.S. Marine born in northern India who lives in Salt Lake City. Quite the multinational force we have here. A melting pot of one.

Monday: TQ Day 48.

We were going to do our usual AOM this morning, but instead we get a GSW to the foot, supposedly accidental, on an Iranian Kurd who is a security guard for a contractor. The guys drive up in their white South African armored vehicles. This is the second Kurdish contractor with these guys this week who has been shot in the leg. Joe (the duty surgeon) and Bob operate on him. Afterwards, the Tibetan (who did not fly out yesterday due to bad weather) is taken back to the OR to rewash his wounds and put wires through his elbow fracture, since that is usually done with the second washout if it is clean enough. This way he can go straight through to Landstuhl, Germany, instead of being admitted to Balad for the second operation.

At 1400 I go over to J.J.'s BAS to give his medics a trauma lecture. This is the one I had planned to give last week, except that we had "transportation problems," i.e., the Army JAG's insurgent confiscated car wouldn't start. Lasts almost two hours, it seems to go over well. I get back to the hootch and go eat dinner, after that to the PX. As I'm leaving there, learn about more casualties — we'll be getting four Marines from an IED blast. When we get to the SSTP, the Air Boss is there and tells us that the first two coming in were actually picked up by a Huey gunship, not one of the Medevac birds. This is the third IED of the day, but the first casualties to come in. When the wind and dust are bad, like last night, the helos don't fly and the Iraqis plant IEDs under the cover of bad weather.

They arrive and both have almost complete leg amputations, but they aren't dying, due in no small part to the placement of tourniquets by the field corpsmen. We start to resuscitate (blood, fluid) these two in the STP ("ER") tent while we wait for the other two to arrive, but when they get here we find that they're much less seriously injured. Joe (duty surgeon) and John head to the OR with the first guy, who has both legs and arms messed up, while I head to the second OR with the guy with one leg and hand messed up. I complete his left thigh amputation without much trouble, and clean all sorts of dirt, debris and frags out of his stump, while Bob cleans up his hand (left pinkie blown off). Bob then goes off to help the others while I finish up the case.

Joe, John and Bob are still working on the other guy when I am finished with everything.

His right leg is off below the knee (same as my guy, a couple of snips and it is gone), and his left arm has multiple chunks taken out of it. When they are ready to start working on his left leg, I stay unscrubbed and help get that leg ready. Put on an adjustable OR tourniquet, then take off the field tourniquet (bungee cord) and the shreds of clothing it held on. Hmm, there is a lump in his clothing; let's take it outside and see what it is. Lookee here, there's a grenade in his pocket, a 40mmm. The guy had been searched on the pad, his clothing had been cut off in the STP tent, but the clothes near his tourniquet were left on, along with the grenade.

I give the grenade to one of our Marines to pass along to EOD. It's actually a grenade for a grenade launcher, not nearly as dangerous as the type where you pull the pin and throw it. This is basically like a really big explosive bullet, you have to actually put it into the weapon and pull the trigger to fire it; then the warhead doesn't arm itself until it has flown a distance and spun a number of times. Still, not the sort of thing you really want to find in the OR after you've already been operating for an hour.

But it gets better. While Joe, John and Bob are working away, I do the OR paperwork for the cases and take pictures of x-rays. When I get to his, there is a very nice x-ray of the 40mm grenade in his pocket. Ooops!

As the only surgeon not scrubbed, I also talk to this guy's unit. My guy's sergeant had been sitting in the vehicle right next to him; his only injury was a scratch on the nose. He is somewhat freaked out and feeling pretty guilty about being okay. I talk to him about his buddy and the other guy still in the OR. When his LtCol shows up, I talk to him, too. Later, so do Mike, John, Bob, and one of the psych guys. The LtCol was pretty badly shaken up, apparently.

It's about midnight and while I'm ready to go back to the hootch and hit the sack, we hear that two more are coming in. Everyone regroups but it turns out to be a false alarm. Lightly wounded, will go to Baghdad. Our two patients (mine awake, Joe's on the vent) fly out to Balad, Carmen with them as the ICU nurse/vent-meister. To bed at around 0100.

Tuesday: TQ Day 49.

No chance to sleep in, out of bed at 0800 for another casualty. GSW to the leg, an Iraqi "good guy" of some type. We wait around discussing what he will have. If it's the morning, it's a GSW to the leg, and if it's an Iraqi/Kurd, we are betting that the big white South African vehicles will drive up again. All sorts of comments are made about how the contractors are training their Iraqi contractors, the best one being, "What do you say to an Iraqi contractor shot in both feet? Nothing, you've already told him twice."

Wednesday, April 6: TQ Day 50.

First up at the AOM today is the Intel brief. Lots of interesting and supersecret stuff. Well, not that much actually. The locals in Fallujah are getting tired of the insurgents and are starting to turn in both them and their weapons. For a fee, of course. The rockets being lobbed at us are being aimed by laying them against berms and eyeballing it, so no surprise that they fly 10 miles and fail to hit us. Still lots of bad guys out there.

After that, a briefing from a visiting environmental health guy from Al Asad, where the Marine HQ is. Not much exciting, except that they are trying to track down some unusual bugs that are showing up in wounds. Not biological warfare, just strange stuff in the dirt.

Afterwards, we learn that the Camp Commandant (i.e. the guy who runs the base facilities, the "apartment manager") wants HESCO Beach closed. There seems to be no good reason for it, except that in all likelihood we are having more fun than he is. You know the Marines, if they see a beach, they want to take it. So we must marshal our forces to fight the enemy, it seems. The Air Boss, Comms Boss, Civil Affairs Boss, and various other people think the Beach is great and have been up on it. I suggested getting Gen. Hagee, the Marine Corps Commandant (who happens to be visiting the base today), to pose on the green, teeing off with a cigar in his mouth, but no one else wanted to try that one out in case he doesn't like it.

Not much else going on today, just reading and puzzles. At around 1900, the boys all get together to watch *Animal House*. About an hour into it, "All Ridgeways" are called, and we head up to the SSTP. Four Iraqi civilians, coming by ground from the field, with conflicting stories. Patrick, our Marine CI (counterintelligence) guy, spoke to the unit that picked them up; they were supposedly in a car that was either driving by, or setting up an IED, when it exploded. The field medics say that some of them have been shot. Then, much later, we hear that they were actually digging around in one of the numerous Iraqi junkyards when UXO went off. Ultimately, it is decided that they are not EPWs, our main concern.

We get four, total. John is duty doc, so he tells me and Joe to head back to the OR with the first one who has frags to all four extremities, his belly and chest. While some of these look like GSWs, they aren't. We ex-lap him and discover that, while he does have a frag in his belly, it didn't hit anything. Debride his chest wounds, none of which made it to his lungs. Work on both arms and both legs. Meanwhile, John and Bob work on another patient with similar injuries, a 12-year-old.

At one point, someone sticks a head into my OR (okay, they stuck the rest of their body in as well) and says that John wants me to look at something. I go over there, just as John is explaining to Bob (who is helping him) how to do a Whipple which, in the general surgery world, is *The Big Operation*. His kid has a duodenal injury and he wanted advice on what to do for it. I walk over, take a look, and say, "Whipple? Hell, you haven't even Kocherised the duodenum properly yet!" (This is the first part of a Whipple procedure, and the only part of a Whipple that John would need to do for this injury.) I give him some advice on it, mock him roundly for stealing all the good cases, and go back to my case with Joe. Damn it, a good case, too. For the surgeon, if not the patient…

Joe and I finish first, at around 0200. Just then, we hear that two Marines are coming in, from a vehicle rollover. We decide to wait and see what they have before scrubbing in to help John and Bob. Then we hear that they are going to Fallujah instead, it's closer. Finally, we hear that it was not a vehicle rollover. A four-man Marine sniper team was crossing the road when it was run down by recon Marines in humvees. Great.

Joe and I are about to scrub in to help John when we are called out. Our patient has soaked through his right arm bandages. Back to the OR, all of about twenty feet away. One of the good things about working here. In the OR, we find that he is bleeding from the brachial artery in his upper arm. The strange thing is that we had looked at the artery earlier and it had looked fine, no bleeding at all, and great pulses in his hand. Now, it's bleeding, and he has no pulse in his hand. We can't explain it; maybe there was a hole with a clot that had come off. But we had looked for something like that and found nothing. Anyway, we fix the artery and both patients are flown straight off to the CSH in Baghdad.

Friday: TQ Day 52.

There was an "incident" at Club TQ on Thursday night. Club TQ is the dance club on base — no booze, just dancing, and everyone must be in uniform. It is mostly frequented by the junior enlisteds. An Army guy got drunk. He admitted to twelve shots of *Jaegermeister*, which is some sort of liqueur, apparently. He went outside and started hassling several Marines, who told him where to put it. At that point, he went to Condition 1 on his M16 (locked and loaded) and aimed it at one of their heads. So the Marines beat the crap out of him. His Army CO wants to court-martial him. They've been trying to get along with the Marines on a Marine base. He wants everyone, Army and Marine, to know that this sort of crap is not tolerated. Especially not with loaded weapons. The guy is probably Leavenworth-bound.

Saturday: TQ Day 53.

Spent the day working on some PowerPoint talks for corpsmen, and watching DVDs. Didn't feel like reading or crosswords today. I am interrupted by our OIC who says that things are getting more involved regarding HESCO Beach. The directive has come from the head of TQ Base Operations. The OIC "talked" to the man (dunno if this means actually talking, or e-mail), who seems to be mildly against it but says that he won't argue about it if the Chief of Staff (i.e. our Commanding General's #2 man) says it can stay. The COS supposedly likes it but says that this should be handled at a lower level... We shoulda snagged the Marine Corps Commandant when we had the chance...

The Boys are rather glum; it's not looking good at all.

Sunday: TQ Day 54.

It's our fourth straight day of no casualties. What's going on?

Monday: TQ Day 55.

A disappointing breakfast. We have banana milk, strawberry milk, and chocolate milk; but no milk. I have tried banana milk with cereal in the past, it doesn't work. We have two flavors of cream cheese but no bagels. I settle for an English muffin with PB and orange marmalade, and some water.

At the AOM we hear that "they" (they? Who is "they?") are thinking about sending half of the ward-holding capacity from Fallujah to here. That would be ten "beds" and some nurses and corpsmen. What do we think? I'm first out of the gate with that one. It sounds like more "mission creep" to me (this is the phenomenon where a unit or force is sent to do something, and then little bits keep being added to it, until the unit is now doing things it was never expected, and is ill-equipped, to do). If we are a Level II facility (patch 'em and ship 'em), what do we need more holding capacity for? Adding beds will not increase our ability to do surgery. In fact, if the surgeons have to do post-op care as well, it will diminish it. If we have "holding capacity," it may give Balad and Baghdad an excuse to not take our Iraqi patients, with the rationale that we can look after them here. In the dirt. And if the Iraqi Army starts to take over as we are told that they will, and they have no medical capabilities as we have been told that they do not, then who is left holding the bag? Us.

"They" say that we could be getting ICU capability with this, as we would be getting extra nurses. I jump all over that, too. Personnel is the least of our problems with an ICU. "What do you mean?" We need monitors, proper ventilators, invasive lines (which would be placed in a dirty environment, thus assuring infections), additional types of drugs, proper lab capabilities, a real blood bank, and real ICU beds (bed sores would develop in a day on cots or stretchers). And oh, by the way, all of this would have to be in a place we can keep clean, i.e., NOT a tent. A real building, with real ventilation and a real floor that we can keep clean.

In other words, mission creep. If they want a Level III, they need to talk to "Big Navy" (i.e. BUMED) and get them to send one. What they are doing is calling it a "Level II plus," which is reinventing the wheel, badly, and not providing the support it would need.

After my run, I'm ready for a shower when we hear about two casualties coming in. I am duty doc, so I will get first pick, cool. We also hear about a heat stroke patient coming in by helo. When the "heat stroke" arrives, he is awake, talking, has a normal temperature, and literally begs us to not insert a Foley (bladder) catheter. Cured.

The other two are Army guys who were out at the base range. They were lying down, shooting, when an Iraqi mortar round comes in and frags them. One has almost no injury, is patched up, and can go back to his unit. The other is peppered but has no major injuries; the worst is a broken foot from a frag that went through his boot. A couple came close, though. He gets his ticket home.

We also get word that we need to have our "battle rattle" with us at all times. The Intel guys have concerns that there may be a VBIED attempt on base in the next few days. A week ago there was an organized attack on Abu Ghraib prison, when three VBIEDs were exploded at all three entrance checkpoints in a short period of time, thus stripping away the Quick Reaction Force. This was followed by a concerted attack with small arms, rockets, and mortars on the prison itself, reportedly with twenty or so casualties, fortunately none killed. They are worried that the same will be tried here; two or three VBIEDs at the ECPs, and separate perimeter attacks by 50 to 60 insurgents. Great, the rockets and mortars aren't enough?

Tuesday: TQ Day 56.

Up at around 0830, coffee and crosswords. Around 1000 I go check my e-mail and get ready to run. As I am stretching out back of the SSTP, we get the call that there is a casualty coming in, GSW to the neck to an American civilian, a DOD contractor. Good timing, otherwise I would have had to run back. Twenty minutes later, we are told that he has died. I am stretching again when we are told that, no, he is in fact still alive and headed our way. Another twenty minutes and no, he has died. We get confirmation and stand down.

I learn from our other Mike, the GMO/Flight Surgeon with the Casevac squadron, that the ERC nurses were given their flight suit patches with their official call signs on them. Carmen is "Cookie" because she grins so much when offered any. Corey is "Junkyard Dog" because he will eat anything. Barb is "Tank Girl" because, well, she is. Tim is "Gaylord Focker" since he is a male nurse. And Eileen is "Hotlips." I suppose it's because she's blonde and the same rank, although Mike thinks that maybe it's because the squadron thought she was very "military," which she isn't. Mike doesn't know that, even though he has been referred to as "Buck-buck," I know that the pilots have given him the call sign of "Tampon." He once made the mistake of describing Navy Medicine during a briefing before a general as "we are like a tampon, no one wants us around until they need us, and once they are done with us, they want to disavow any knowledge or responsibility."

Wednesday: TQ Day 57.

As I'm leaving the AOM, both Barb and Mike accost me to ask my opinion about something. We put all of our patients on wool Army blankets in the OR, since they are sturdy enough to lift patients with and can soak up some blood. The problem is that they are expensive and apparently cannot be washed by the base laundry; so we will need to come up with some substitute or possibly use nothing at all. I say that "nothing" is not an option, as sliding people on the stretchers will actually cheese-grate their skin off, they are not designed to be lain on naked, and they will get pressure sores. And besides, why can't the laundry wash our blankets? I hear several versions on why not, none of which make sense, so I tell them I will simply go over to the base laundry and sort it out. What a notion!

After coffee with J.J., we head out on the laundry errand. Lo! And behold! It's not a problem. I talk to the guy who runs the entire laundry facility (a huge warehouse) for the base and he says that they can wash whatever we want, whenever we want it, with a two-day turnaround. Just send the stuff over in a crate with our regular laundry drop-off on Mondays and Thursdays, or if those dates are not good, pick another day. No problemo. It seems that the whole laundry issue was actually yet another item of misinformation from the old Team. On the way back, we stop by DRMO (the wrecked vehicle lot) and get a few more pics of assorted things blown up by mines, IEDs, what have you. Some of them burned so fiercely that they are partly melted.

J.J. also fills me in on more goings-on around the base. Since his unit provides the base security, he hears it all. Yesterday the ToiFor (Toilet Force) subcontractor's compound was raided by the MPs. These are the guys who manage the showers and shitters. They have lots of TCN (Third Country National) workers like Turks, Indians, Nepalese, and so on. During the raid, they confiscated 225 cans of beer, ten bottles of Jack Daniels, plenty of porn, and a large number of digital cameras. The last provided some interesting viewing: step-by-step photos of how two Romanians built and then hid their still, and a number of pics of assorted people enjoying themselves in various ways.

I spend the afternoon sorting out several hundred photos that J.J. has given me (no, not from the raid), some from the OR (he is our unofficial photographer for cases when he's not scrubbed), some from our trips. I also get a box from you that was nice. Mmmm, Brussels cookies!

At dinner, a few of us are sitting around when the psychiatrist walks in and sits at the next table. John has to duck his head into his hands to cover up his laughter. His head has been butchered — he has hair sticking up next to random bald patches — it looks like he has mange. I ask John if someone should tell him, he laughs and says "yes." So I look at the OIC and say, "I would think that it would best come from a peer, someone of the same rank, but whom can we find to do this noble deed?" He looks at me and says, "I'll ask the Group Surgeon the next time I see him." Me: "Okay, I'll take the bullet for the team." So when he gets up to find dessert, I walk up to him and ask, "Go to the barber today, sir?" "No, I clipped it myself. It's a little uneven, I was going to work on it again after dinner." "Uh, sir, do you just want to stop by the hootch after chow and I'll buzz it down for you?" "Would you? That would be great." So I start my career as a barber, and get him cleaned up. To do that, I had to run the clipper over his head without the guard, so it's just stubble. I point out my "do" and tell him that I have been cutting it myself for years — you just do it with a blade guard. He says he'll try that next time.

Thursday: TQ Day 58.

Mike and I discuss making a going-away plaque for J.J.. It has to be something incredibly cheesy, of course; you can't make it look professional at all, otherwise what would be the point? We discuss some options, centered around the lid of an ammo crate with a Kabar Marine Corps knife attached to it. I'll get to work on it over the next couple of weeks, as he leaves on the 30th.

As we are finishing dinner, we get the word that there is an "urgent surgical" patient headed in, ETA unknown. I drop my brownie and we head back. Before we get there, we hear that the patient has died. No idea what injuries, nationality, anything. I try to feel guilty about wanting to go back and finish my cookie, but can't. I'm too jaded, I suppose. Jeff and I had discussed this very issue this afternoon, about various people's reactions to our first (and so far only) U.S. death. For me, I have seen enough trauma patients die that it's no longer a shock, even if it is one of the "good guys." I am sorry that he died, but do not take it personally, or to heart. I think of it as significant because it was a milestone for our unit: most of our people, including the physicians and nurses, had never seen anything like this before, and it brought the message home that this is serious and real. For Jeff, it's because he's never lost a "good guy," even one he didn't know. Other people's reactions I have mentioned before. Like the Kurosawa movie (the name of which escapes me), we all saw the same thing and yet saw something different.

Saturday: TQ Day 60.

Another day written in retrospect, it was quite busy. After the 0930 Providers' Meeting, I go for a run. I need assorted bits and pieces for J.J.'s plaque, like some wood stain or clear varnish, a branding iron to inscribe the wood, maybe something to etch the plaque with. During my run I go by the Seabees (no luck), the Engineers (no luck again), and the EOD unit (no luck, but I am invited to watch them blow up UXO on base, don't worry) when they get back from Fallujah in a couple of weeks. I then stop by the 2/112 gym to use the weights, and on to the new BAS they are still building, to see if maybe they have what I'm looking for.

I tell his guys it's for J.J.'s going-away plaque. "Gee, sir, I guess you'll get working on it pretty fast." "Why, is he short-timing it that bad?" "Well, he is now." "What do you mean?" "You didn't know? He fell off a table hanging a clothesline and broke his leg. He's over at your place now." I run over to the STP to find him.

Yup, he broke his right leg, just below the knee. The x-rays are not too bad but the ligaments in his knee may be torn, too. He'll be heading home for definitive surgery. Apparently he was standing on some rickety table, tying up cord for a clothesline, when the table started to give way. He jumped off the table and, as he hit, he heard his leg snap. Ow. He was in the back of the officers' building that the Texans have nicknamed the "Alamo" because of its look and shape (and they are Texans, after all). So he had to crawl out of the building and across the parking lot to get help. Double ow. By the time I see him, he is splinted and on morphine. He's had time to work up a great story about how two hajjis came through the wire, he had to take them out with his Kabar that was held in his teeth as he low-crawled his way to safety, etc., etc., can I have my Purple Heart now? Well, of course there are no bodies; they carry away their own dead. Yes, it was a daylight raid, so they must have been Saddam's Special Forces. Yup, same old J.J..

Bob is not sure when J.J. will fly out; his guys are trying to work something for him so he can go straight home to San Antonio for surgery, instead of the usual Balad-to-Landstuhl-for-surgery-to–Walter Reed-to-home deal. This sounds pretty doubtful to me, but what the heck. Bob says he will probably leave tomorrow evening with the daily "milk run."

I furiously start to work on J.J.'s plaque with what I have. It ends up being a Kabar wired onto the lid of a .50 cal ammo crate with Iraqi barbed wire. I carve a suitable inscription into the wood with my Gerber tool, color it in with a felt tip, and glue an "OIF" coin from the Exchange onto one corner. It is, as one of my colleagues puts it, "quite ghetto." I suppose that's good, and it is certainly unique. Later that afternoon, I hear that J.J. will, in fact, be flying out at 1015 tomorrow morning, straight on to Landstuhl, Germany, after transferring plane in Balad.

In the evening I am up at the STP, arranging a satellite phone call for J.J. to his wife. He gets dozens of visitors and bad jokes are flying (many of them mine, regrettably). "You know, J.J., you're not the first Mexican to fall at the Alamo, but you may be the last." His XO likes that one so much, they plan to make a plaque and put it on the wall of their building.

At around 2100 we get word of three incoming casualties. The helo was flying from Ramadi to Balad when one of the patients "crashed," no further details. In the end, the full story is that a mortar hit an ammo dump, 4 killed and 3 wounded. One of the wounded is 60 percent burned. He was "crashing" because he'd started "bucking" on the ventilator while in the air. It was due to his not having a proper IV in so none of the drugs to keep him calm were going into him. In other words, stupidity. He is sorted out fairly quickly. Another patient has a head and eye injury, whom we intubate. These two go back on a helo and are out of here. The third patient has no pulses in his arm, so he goes to the OR and gets a brachial artery repair.

Sunday: TQ Day 61.

I put the word out that we're having a "going away" ceremony for J.J. at 1600. Some of his folks are there, many of ours also. There hadn't been much time for the word to get out, although I had spread it pretty widely. At one point, J.J.'s "Surgical Internship Program Director" (i.e., me) steps up. After long deliberation about his dereliction of duty on his last night of call, I took a vote among "myselves" and decided to award him his internship certificate, anyway. Our psychiatrist looks at it and says it looks too real; patients might get the wrong idea. Then, in front of the crowd, I retell J.J.'s story of the Hajjis in the wire, the Kabar lost in the struggle, and so on. "But before you think it's just another one of J.J.'s stories, I am here to tell you that it's true. I found the Kabar in the wire, and here it is." J.J. thought it was really cool; it's going into his office at the VA. You'll see the picture eventually.

A little later I hear about yet another problem with HESCO Beach. Tim was teeing off and almost beaned the Marine SJA. The Staff Judge Advocate. The General's lawyer. The guy whose job it is to tell the Boss how to avoid problems. Just the guy we don't want to have against us. Tim had teed off; the ball bounces right in front of the SJA and then right past his head. He walks over to where Tim is peering down and says, "You are coming down here to apologize, aren't you?" Tim comes down, at which point the LtCol asks for his name, his unit, who he works for, his OIC and CO, and then reams him a new one. He then also asks who the senior officer up on the Beach is, and Bob comes down. He and Bob are the same rank, but he reams Bob a new one also, for not being able to control his people.

J.J. shipped out at 2200. The OIC and I were there to see him off; I helped carry the stretcher to the ambulance. A final picture of him waving from the back of the rig, and he was gone. As the boss and I stand there, chatting, Greg, the Marine Civil Affairs Officer, comes by. We learn from him that of the five people you don't want to piss off on this base, the SJA is three of them. He is very by-the-book, which can make him a bit difficult at times; but at least you know where he's coming from. His main job is to keep the General out of trouble, and allowing people to hit each other in the head with golf balls is probably fairly high on the list of things he would suggest that the boss not allow. I suggest to "our" boss that, as the OIC, he might want to make a preemptive visit to the SJA (i.e., before the "Dark Tower" staff meeting at 0800) to tell him that: (a) he is right, no golf ball head whacking; (b) he, as OIC, has closed the golf course so it won't happen again; and (c) he heard that the SJA reamed his boys some new ones, good on him. In other words, that he agrees that it is a problem and has taken appropriate action (but not closed HESCO Beach). The boss doesn't really want to do this until Greg chimes in that it's an excellent idea, and that since he works with the guy, he would bet that the SJA will leave it at that.

Tuesday: TQ Day 63.

Today the OIC and I are supposed to head over to Camp Manhattan, our first trip "outside of the wire." It is a death-defying 45 second trip from ECP 1, across the continuously-patrolled bridge over the canal, to the main gate of Camp Manhattan. We are heading over to check out the BAS there, as we get a fair amount of business from it, and possibly coordinate some training with their medics. Also, and a complete coincidence of course, they have some cool planes, bunkers, and a reputedly excellent Hajji restaurant. The Texas CAO (Civil Affairs Officer) has said that he will take us over in an armored Humvee, at 1100, after he gets back from an early morning road trip.

1100 comes and goes, without word. At 1200 the boss and I drive over in the SUV to see what's going on, and we discover that the CAO is off-base on a mission, apparently escorting some detainees. Oh well, another day. I do con two Iraqi National Guard recruiting posters out of their JAG (aka "Habeeb" or "Matlock"), which are very cool.

Since we are in tourist mode right now, we poke around a lot in some bunkers and take assorted pictures. I find a roll of maps, which turn out to be military maps of Iran. Excellent — and perfectly legal as war trophies. Go up to the abandoned Iraqi guard posts overlooking MSR (Main Supply Route) Michigan, have an entertaining time for about an hour, and then head back.

Wednesday: TQ Day 64.

...I'm heading back on the final stretch of my run around 1130 when I hear the radio call that two casualties are coming in, frags to the head. I'm the duty doc (although we all show up anyway) so I race back to the hootch, which is on a direct line to the SSTP, and get my stuff (I wear a belt with a camera pouch, ammo pouch for writing gear and flashlight, and something to hook my radio to, since I operate in PT gear). When I get to the SSTP, we hear it's two Marines who took frags to the head from an IED. One dies in the helo on the way to us, the other doesn't look good. Actually, the vital signs are great, but he has a hole in the left side of his head with bone and brain sticking out of it, and little remaining brain function by clinical exam. I stabilize him, shoot x-rays that show his head is smashed like an eggshell, and then consider what to do. This kid is going to die, or worse. His brain is already mostly dead; the rest of his young body just hasn't accepted it yet. The only reason he's still alive is that, with his broken skull, his skull can expand as his brain swells, prolonging the inevitable. But his vital signs are still great. If I send the kid to a Level III, I will put a helo, its crew, and one of our nurses at risk for a daytime flight. Of course, theater medevac policy is that head injuries do not go to Level IIs anyway, as we have no neurosurgeons or CT scanners, so they didn't do this kid a favor by sending him here, something that will need to be discussed at a higher level. I try to call Balad and talk to the neurosurgeons there, but there are no doctors currently at the hospital and the neurosurgeons are out jogging. They can give me their pager numbers, though... Uh huh. I call Baghdad, where both neurosurgeons are scrubbed in on an "important trauma case" and won't come to the phone, so I relay info to them. They say send him anyway, but since they're busy, send him to Balad. Uh huh. But he's not entirely brain dead, so away he goes, and as expected he dies about 30 minutes after he gets there.

For some reason, Mike has gotten onto some sort of Indian kick. He refers to me as the "Great White Chief with square head" (I was wearing the octagonal Marine cover) and talks about how I "do ex lap, save many braves." He has been doing it all day, and has referred to himself as "Squanto."

We all go off to dinner at 1700 as always. We discuss my reputation as the "NOTS"— nonoperative trauma surgeon — that on the days that I'm on duty, even if stuff comes in, we don't operate. Still true to form. At 1800, we hear that we are getting five casualties; an Iraqi pickup truck has driven up to ECP 1 with them. It turns out that these guys are from the same tribe (yes, the Iraqis have extended family tribes) as the Iraqis that showed up last week after blowing themselves up in the junkyard and, yes, they were doing the same thing but this time their truck flipped over. Three are kids about 10 to 15 years old, one of whom blew a toe off last year and was treated here. They have lots of bumps and bruises but nothing serious. The fourth has a couple of broken ribs; we will watch him overnight. The fifth has some pretty impressive facial lacerations and took a pretty good hit to the face. He really needs a head CT before he is put to sleep to get his face cleaned out and sewn up. So he's to Baghdad for that. My nonoperative reputation remains intact. I consider doing the case anyway, but it's really safer for the guy if he is CT'ed first. He will go after nightfall, in an hour or so.

Mike tells me that I need to do something, he's been up here twice for seven patients today, and we need to do a case. I say, "Great White Chief tell Squanto 'be careful what Squanto wish for.' You go, hunt buffalo now."

A half hour later, another incoming. Iraqi EPW, GSWs to chest and flank. I talk to the sending doc in Ramadi; he was setting off a VBIED and was shot. Bad vital signs. He comes in getting CPR, I take him straight back to the OR. John is my back-up today, so I ask him when was the last time he did an emergency thoracotomy. "Residency." "Go to it, boy." We get to work, knowing that the guy will probably die (if he isn't dead already — Mike and Jeff haven't even hooked him up to monitors yet). As we open his left chest to get to his heart, dark blood is squirting out of the hole below his ribs on the right, presumably from a massive liver injury. We finish up the thoracotomy to control the aorta, get to the heart for open massage, and call it. John learned a lot from it. Our corpsmen learned a lot from it, as I called them all in to give them an anatomy lesson. A bit morbid, but it's by learning on guys like this that you develop the skills to save people later. And every once in a while you do save a guy like this.

The atmosphere for this thoracotomy was very different from our last one about six weeks ago. Most of the crew had never seen anything like it, it was a U.S. Army soldier, and we had not had a patient die on us. Now, we've seen a lot more, it was a confirmed bad guy, and we've had other deaths. Who he was should make no difference, but of course it does. This is a war, after all. And as we know, war is insane: we attempt to kill people by shooting them, but if we do a bad job of it, we do everything we can to save them. I guess that's what makes us the good guys.

We are done with this at about 2230, time for a nap. I told Squanto to be careful about what he wished for...

Thursday: TQ Day 65.

Up at 0800 to drop off laundry, the clean stuff that I put on yesterday before the EPW came in is now rather dirty. Then wait around until 1100, when the SUV is back from a staff meeting at Lakeside. The boss and I plan to go touring again today with Kevin, the psychologist. We'd heard that there's a free coffee shop and some unexplored (at least, by us) bunkers out by Spring Lake. Kevin is nowhere to be found, however, and we finally discover that he's with a suicidal patient who will be medevaced out. I get vague directions over the phone from him, and off we go. Also along for the ride are Eileen and Mike, the flight surgeon with the Marine Cobra squadron. As we pull out I start with, "Let's go see the castle." Drive over to the Engineer detachment with the Marine squadron, and sitting there on a pile of HESCOs is a beautiful wooden castle, complete with drawbridge. Very nice, good photo op. As we turn around in the gravel lot, I see something else to go look at, a large mural in the MP compound dedicated last year to a fallen MP. Nice mural of an armored Humvee and the "band of brothers" quote from *Henry V* (no attribution, though, and I was surprised that none of the others knew it).

Then off to Spring Lake. On the way, we pass some old fighting holes and gun emplacements; wander over to those for a look but nothing exciting. Then over to Spring Lake and the coffee shop. The "Black Sheep Coffee Shop," free coffee and pastries, run by an Army Reserve logistics unit. It's built into a large bunker, and it was almost like being home. They have a big screen TV, tables, chairs to sit on, several flavors of free coffee, a few pastries, dozens of boxes of Girl Scout cookies, a card table, and the pool table in back is almost set up. They also own the pool next door.

Yes, the pool. The Army reservists at Spring Lake worked out some deal with the Seabees (the SeaBee we talked to was a little vague on the details) to build them a six foot deep, 20 by 20 foot pool surrounded by a deck. Clean water and everything. We all posed by it, were dying to jump in, but had to be back by 1330 because we were expecting some non-urgent casualties (DOD contractors) to fly in around then. Besides, no swim suits (although I always wear PT gear under my cammies; that way I can strip down with impunity).

Proof positive to the unbeliever that yes, there really was a nonlicensed pool built on base. A 25,000 gallon water bladder, a water purification unit, some decking, and netting meant a good time for all. Well, for those who knew where the pool was hidden, anyway....

I spend the evening putting together a quick slide show for our Wednesday meeting. This is the weekly AOM where we discuss the patients from the previous week and do follow-ups. Every week for the last few weeks, John has presented some sort of mockery at the start. The officers all mock each other regularly here, we even take pride in being "equal opportunity mockers," and a standard question here is, "Are you mocking me?" Anyway, the first time, it was a shot I took of Mike and his characteristic scowl in the OR, labeled "Don't judge me, just love me." The following week, a picture of Bob operating but looking like an obstetrician from the angle of the shot. Then a shot of me from the weekly providers' meeting, lecturing in the chapel behind the lectern, labeled "the Reverend Stockinger sermonizing."

At around 2300, as I'm reaching to turn out the light and go to bed, the call comes that we have two wounded Marines coming in, victims of an IED. When they get here around midnight, one is pretty straightforward, a few frags in his leg. The other is a lot more impressive. His neck has been filleted wide open and he was intubated before he got to us. There is some initial confusion about his status; he is getting CPR as he comes off the ambulance and we rush him back to the OR. When we get there, his vital signs are actually pretty good; he was probably getting CPR because they couldn't feel a pulse in his neck since the anatomy had been distorted. We work him up for other injuries and then look at his wounds. A couple of frags in his leg and ass, but the neck is the impressive part. It's been laid wide open under his chin, and his jaw has been smashed. His tongue is sitting there in the middle of all of this, flapping in the breeze as it were. Everyone is very excited, but having seen a similar case at Charity Hospital in New Orleans of a shotgun to the chin, I realize that it's actually not as bad as it looks. The major blood vessels in his neck are spared, his jaw can be rebuilt, his tongue is intact (very important for speech and swallowing), and he has very little skin or muscle loss (so he'll have scars but no deformity). Eyes, nose, upper teeth all okay. We spend some time cleaning him up, give him a tracheostomy (hole in his neck to breath through), and then the two of them go out at around 0400.

Friday: TQ Day 66.

I eventually crawl out of bed at around noon and go running, but as I missed breakfast, I only do about 2 ½ miles and the weights. Then I sit up on HESCO Beach, read for a few hours, and then watch the boys pitch horseshoes (the horseshoe pitch replaced the golf course), and eventually shower and eat. The power is out most of the afternoon in tent city, so there are no lights or AC in the hootches. We sit up on the Beach, reading and chatting as the sun goes down.

At about 2000, two more casualties. Army patrol in Habbaniyah was fired at, two guys shot in the hands. When they get here, one has a hole through the end of his left thumb, the other through the side of his left hand. Having just finished reading my African World War I book, I realize that in another time and place, injuries to the left hand would have been considered a sign of cowardice until proven otherwise. The assumption has always been that, in wartime, gunshots to the foot are self-inflicted, but historically it is to the left hand: you aim with your dominant (right) hand at your nondominant (left) hand, become disabled, but can still run away. However, those are usually to the palm. We wash their hands out, but they are too late to go with the milk run tonight, so they'll have to wait until tomorrow night to leave unless there is a "flight of opportunity."

Saturday: TQ Day 67.

At the providers' meeting today, a lecture by the psychiatrist on Combat Related Stress. The bottom line: treat the "shell shock" victims close to the front with the expectation that they will return to their units after a brief rest ("three hots and a cot"), and over 90 percent will do so.

After this, Joe and I go over to Lakeside in the SUV so he can get a haircut. On the way back, we stop at the Black Sheep Coffee House again. Where I have a real raisin bagel, lightly toasted, with cream cheese, and watch the History Channel. Almost like the real world again.

When we get back, we discover that the power is out. Again. On top of that, the

OIC has told everyone that they'll need to get off HESCO Beach for a week. It's breezy and 108 outside, airless and 98 inside. If I'm going to be hot and miserable, I may as well get something out of it, so I go for a run. Don't worry, only as far as the 2/112 gym (about ¾ of a mile), then I use the treadmill and weights. When I get back, mail call, one of your parcels arrived. Golf balls (too late, alas, as the course is closed), wall thermometers, cookies.

Sunday: TQ Day 68.

Dragged my ass out of bed around 1030. Made some coffee, and got ready to run. As I was putting my shoes on, the call comes in that we have four inbound. My coffee and I head over to the SSTP. Eventually, four Marines with frag injuries, none particularly serious, arrive. They had been doing an ammunition moving detail when they were hit by a mortar in, of all places, Hit, Iraq. They were supposed to fly to Al Asad but it was "dusted" in, the helos couldn't go there. So they came to us instead. We work on them until about 1500 and then head back to the hootch.

No power, again. Our row of huts is the only one without power today, just like yesterday. Is this a conspiracy to punish those naughty medical people? As Joe says, it's not a question of if you are paranoid, but if you are paranoid enough. So we sit outside reading until chow. Too damned hot to run today, and a little late for it.

Eat chow at 1700, and when we walk out of the DFAC (what the chow hall is called — it stands for Dining Facility in contractor-ese), things are different. The wind is blowing, it's dark, and visibility is down to less than 100 meters. A dust storm has settled in. Of course, we still have no power and it's still 100 degrees, so I sit outside in the dust, reading with goggles and a dustcover over my mouth. At least the wind and flying sand keeps the flies off of me...

Monday: TQ Day 69.

The usual 0800 AOM, where literally nothing happens. That was a good waste of time. Barb and I look at some surgical instrument sets, and then I wander back to the hootch and do crosswords for a while. Jeff and I sweep out the dust that blew in yesterday, it covers everything. At 1130 I go running. It's a nice day, overcast, around 80 degrees, and it's actually trying to rain. By that, I mean that there are water droplets falling from the sky that, upon contacting the ground, disappear in little puffs of dust. I run about 5 miles; it's so much easier to do when the weather is not infernally hot.

I've been back for about five minutes when we get the radio call, "Attention all Ridgeways. Emergency in the COC." I sprint out the door to the STP, where a white pickup is on the pad and a bloke is lying on the ground in a pool of blood. But it's not as bad as it first looks. This is a KBR contractor, one of those oddball security guys, who was "riding shotgun" in the pickup when he managed to shoot himself in the leg with a flare pistol. Correct, a flare pistol. We get several detailed descriptions of how this actually happened, all blaming no one, and none convincing unless this guy is a contortionist (which he clearly is not, just by looking at him).

The flare pistol shot straight into his outer thigh, burning a hole about an inch-and-a-half across and six inches deep. The hole is deep black, crispy-crittered, and oozing slowly. The inside of the truck cab has blood everywhere, it's pretty impressive, but the patient is not. No broken bones, but the wounds will need to be washed out.

A problem occurs to me. "What sort of flare was it?" "A red one." "No, what was it made of? Is it phosphorus?" No one knows, including the EOD guy when we call him and have him come look at the expended flare cartridge. Here is the problem: phosphorus burns spontaneously on contact with air, so if we take him to the OR and open his leg up, and air gets to the leftover phosphorus, we will have a serious problem. Not quite as exciting as removing UXO from someone's body (which I hope never to do), but more than enough for me. This needs to be done underwater.

Joe and I take him to the OR, which normally has all sorts of hangers-on and observers, but not today — only one Looky-Lou, the EOD guy, who is holding the sand-and-water can that we will drop the phosphorus bits into if we find any. Extra fire extinguishers are placed conveniently, in case other stuff catches fire (phosphorus itself must be immersed in water). I get Mike to run the case without extra oxygen and away we go.

Some independent security contractors came in one day in a "armored" SUV, after a "negligent discharge." In other words, a flare went off in the truck. The truck, and the leg the flare shot into, were both a mess.

While constantly pouring water over it, we open up his leg, remove all the obviously dead tissue, wash everything out, and do fasciotomies so that when the leg swells up the nerves and vessels won't be compressed. We find no obvious bits of phosphorus, but all the bits we wash or cut out of him are put into the EOD's bucket. Surprisingly, he has no vascular injury at all, even though the hole goes down to his popliteal artery.

While we're doing this, another patient comes in, a guy shot through the wrist by a sniper. John and Bob take him to the OR. Very bad fracture, and looking at the x-rays, if I had wanted to shoot myself in the radial artery, that's exactly where I would have aimed, but again, the artery is intact. Another lucky guy, although his wrist joint is a mess.

Tuesday: TQ Day 70.

Went to bed at around midnight, but for some reason I had trouble sleeping, dunno why. No bad dreams, and I'm used to all of the nighttime aircraft noise. Then at 0430 the radio starts with its incessant "low battery" beeping, even though I'd changed it before I retired. So I went to get a new one, did e-mail, and went back to bed. Until noon.

It might only rain a couple of days a year, but when it rained, it poured. Even bike rides were cancelled. The dirt (there was no sand) turned to thick, sticky goo.

After that, the usual run around 1400. Not much going on today. Chow. Some Army Casevac Blackhawks (helos) dropped off blood for us, got a couple of snaps. The Army uses dedicated helos for medical missions, so they have big red crosses and no armament. The Marines use designated helos, which can still be pulled for other missions, so they have machine guns and no crosses. Since the Iraqis have blown up ambulances in the past, the red crosses obviously don't count for much around here except provide a nice aiming point. In general, the Marine Casevac people are a lot happier than the Army folks. At least the Marines can shoot back.

Around 1900, after dinner, fortunately, it actually started to rain for real. Torrents, in fact. The water was cascading in around our poorly fitting back door, but this is the door farthest from where our beds are, so it wasn't too much of a problem. Until the large puddle started to accumulate. So I knocked a hole in the plywood floor with a nail in the middle of the puddle, enlarged it with my Gerber, and let it drain out. Voila! Instant plumbing.

Then the power went out. Again.

Wednesday: TQ Day 71.

Still no power when I arose at 0700. Had brekkie, a bagel with OJ as there is a milk shortage again. Our 0800 AOM started with the FSSG Group Surgeon, a Family Practice doc, giving us a medical intelligence lecture for Iraq. We plan to let the Iraqis take over. When they do, they will have no medical facilities to speak of. Yes, we have identified all of the hospitals in Iraq, we don't know which ones are open or what they can do, but maybe they will be able to help. Yes, there are a number of hospitals shown on the map as Iraqi military hospitals, but we don't know if they exist anymore. They used to be there, but even though we have been here for two years we don't know if they are still standing. Yes, there is one listed as being right here on base where we are, but we don't know where it is. Bloody brilliant.

Thursday: TQ Day 72.

No reason to get out of bed again, finally do around 1000. We still have no power. Mike tells me that only one of the three generators for Tent City is working, and even if the others were, the power distribution is fried, and the needed parts are in Dubai. I hear from another source that all of this is run by contractors, who have left it all to a Hajji electrician who is chasing his tail. The most powerful military in the world and we can't get power...

HESCO Beach is closed again. A 'talk' was had with the OIC last night for about twenty minutes. All sorts of rumors about what was said, including that the COS was amazed that we had all disobeyed a "direct order" from the Base Ops Commander. What direct order? Last we had heard, he and our OIC were discussing it, and we never received any order from anyone. Of course, this is the same COS who was up there last week smoking cigars with the boys.

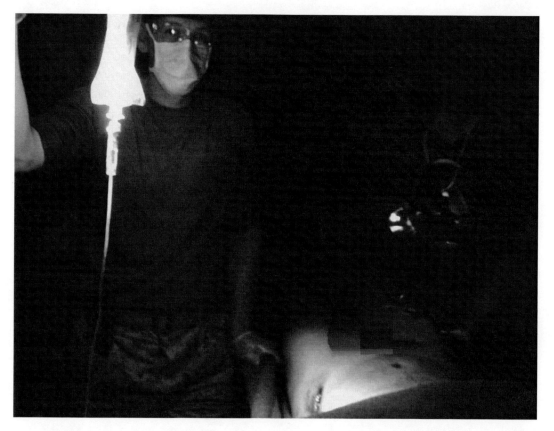

Despite having a back-up generator, there were occasional power failures. When the power went out during a rocket attack, this soldier was operated on under the light of battery-powered lamps.

We get one patient after dinner, a U.S. Army guy shot in the penis. Bullet went through the base of his old feller and came out his inner thigh. We had to operate to put a catheter into his bladder surgically, since his urethra was transected. There were two equally implausible stories as to how this happened. In the first, the guy dropped his M16 and someone else's 9mm pistol went off (huh?). In the second, he had unloaded and cleaned his 9mm, put it down, one of his buddies picked it up and "messed with it," and it went off. If "messed with it" means loaded a magazine, chambered a round, took off the safety, and pulled the trigger, then yeah, I suppose I'd believe that.

Just before midnight, another case. There's an explosion somewhere outside the base, a roving patrol goes out to check on it, and then 17 people show up at ECP #1 wanting medical attention. The same tribe that has blown itself up twice since we arrived while looking for things in the junkyard off base has done it again. The Army medics check them all out at the ECP and bring one in to the Texas BAS for a better looksee, and they send him over to us. He has a frag (a rock, probably) in his ankle, we open it up and wash it out, and ligate the small artery it had transected. Nothing broken, though. He will be sent back out into the wilds to follow up with some Iraqi doctor somewhere.

4. May 2005: Outside the Wire

Monday: TQ Day 76.

Oh boy! Our two month anniversary since we took over (although it's 2½ since we arrived, but what the hey...). Muster at 0930 for a group photo which doesn't happen. MWR has brought out a bunch of chairs, a couple of BBQ grills, and a couple of picnic tables, as we plan to have a "wetting down" for Tom, who puts on CDR today. The Master Chief reads the list of our accomplishments for the month: 25,000 square feet of camo netting put up, 35 HESCOs filled, 125 sand bags, 250 feet of comm wire... Is he joking? Are we really going to list this? Jeff mutters, "800,000 steps to and from the chow hall." No one actually mentions how many patients we treated, though. Several Letters of Appreciation from the OIC. Then the photo at last, a group picture with the ambulances nicely obstructing the view of the SSTP.

At 1900 we have Tom's "wetting down"—basically a BBQ/cigar/near-beer party at the SSTP. Unfortunately, the weather is turning bad. Wind blowing, dust is picking up a lot. But still tolerable. Jeff and I head over. I don the swim mask I have with me (for the OR, but even better for this as it's completely impervious to both dust and water). Between that, the OR tool belt (in case anything comes in, 1800–2400 hours being "prime time"), the HESCO Beach t-shirt, shorts, grungy OR sneakers, indescribably beautiful Hawaiian shirt, and floppy Marine Corps hat, I am quite the sight. Even better, when I get there I have the good fortune to get laid by both Sharon and Eileen—well, "lei-ed" actually. They are wearing green plastic grass skirts and strap-on coconut bikini tops. Lots of pictures all round. Several people have Hawaiian shirts, a number of parrot hats, pink flamingoes dotted about tastelessly. And really good BBQ steaks and chicken. The Texans were invited and they said they would bring beer, but they fail to show up, presumably due to the weather. The Marine Corps Inspector General (a major-general, i.e., a 2-star) is coming this week, and his aide (a bird colonel) was there. Air Boss, mini Boss, Marine Civil Affairs Officer, some of the Army guys. Anyone wandering by was invited to join in—even the Turkish guy who cleans the toilets out back came over. A fine time was had, and the dust storm actually worked out well since it gave us a good excuse to terminate the festivities smartly. Yes, got some good photos.

As I start to head back, it also begins to rain. Rain plus dust equals mudstorm. Lovely little droplets of mud land on me as I go back to the hootch. Inside, no rain, but I could see the dust drifting around, which then proceeded to set off the smoke alarms.

Zsolt with Greg (right) at the unit's luau. Greg was the Marine Corps civil affairs officer who spent much time off the base working with the local populace on nation-building projects. Greg summed his job up as "It's like being in the Mafia. I have to find a way to make them deals they can't refuse."

Tuesday: TQ Day 77.

Nothing happened today. Nothing at all. I slept until 1000, when I could sleep no more. Ran, did weights. Read. By 1600, despite having risen only six hours beforehand, I could barely stay awake. Ate dinner. Did crosswords. I spent an hour writing a "Piece of My Mind" article for *the Journal of American Medical Association*, a page description of our first death here. It has some touchy-feely stuff in it; *JAMA* likes that sort of thing. I hope. If not, it was only an hour.

Wednesday: TQ Day 78.

Since we've had only one patient this last week, not much to talk about at the weekly patient conference. We get an Intel brief on what's gone on in the last week in our neighborhood. Some really big arms caches found (hundreds of rockets, mortars, artillery rounds, etc.). That will put a dent in the Hadjis' war effort, albeit temporarily. Also a warehouse full of medical supplies, which probably won't make much difference at all, as the insurgents have few or no doctors. We've had no mortars or rockets fired at us in 37 days, probably because they have very few big ones left and consequently they won't shoot at a target like us — one that they can't observe (because we're on a plateau) and aim at properly.

The Intel guy takes the opportunity to mock me at the start of the briefing. He shows a map of TQ that indicates one "indirect fire event" on Monday; fired from a range of 20 to 30 yards. Looking carefully at the map, its right about where we are! He then shows the approximately 30mm diameter improvised projectile, which looks suspiciously like a golf ball. Finally, he shows a picture of the suspected perpetrator, which is me playing putt-putt golf at the 2/112. A double mock, at both me and Tim, the infamous staff JAG-beheader.

Thursday: TQ Day 79.

I'm gotten out of bed by Tom for a surgical consult. An "Iraqi commando" (whatever that means) came in from Ramadi by convoy with a felon, which oddly enough is the medical term for a fingertip abscess. I look at it, yup; it will need to be drained. By now, Bob, the orthopod, happens by and he agrees. However, it will need a couple of washouts and IV antibiotics, and it really shouldn't be done here. So once again, we are caught. The Level IIIs will refuse to take him as the problem is not life-, limb-, or eyesight-threatening. The same rule applies to us, of course, but we are a lot easier to get to. So once they're here, we're stuck with them. On paper, this guy should be treated at a local Iraqi hospital, which is the same line the guys at Baghdad and Balad have given us. Naturally, they are also the ones who have told us that there is only one Iraqi hospital (in Baghdad, where else) that will treat these folks and not result in their death or disappearance. Bob says he will talk to the Group Surgeon about this issue, again, predicting that he will tell us to treat the guy and handle it here while he "drills down on the issue and gets granularity on it," whatever the hell that means. In other words, SS, DD (same stuff, different day.) We plan to take him to the OR at 1330, so everyone can get lunch.

There have been some rumors flitting around about J.J. and a magazine so I go and check the *People* magazine website, where I find his smiling face with Jessica Simpson in Germany. The old dog! I save copies of the pic and plan to distribute the link to his guys. The rumor is true after all.

At 1330 we go to the OR to open the guy's finger, a five minute case. I help Tom do it. As a non-surgeon, he thinks it's pretty cool to watch the pus squirt out. The guy will need to stay for a couple of days getting antibiotics. On Saturday we will wash it out again and close it, and then he can go back to Ramadi for inadequate follow-up care and a recurrent infection. Great plan, but there isn't much else we can do. A little later we hear that we have a broken leg flying in, but then hear that it's coming in an hour, and then that it's going straight to Balad. Whatever.

Friday: TQ Day 80.

Off for a run. I stop by the Texas JAG's office. I tell "Habeeb" to type a web address into the computer. He does, and J.J.'s picture with Jessica Simpson pops up on the *People* website. "That rat bastard — he's going down. I'll make him pay." Habeeb's number one priority now is to write up a fake line-of-duty investigation on how J.J. was injured (no, not "clothesline of duty"), and a fake JAG investigation to boot. He's also going to put pictures of this into his nightly staff meeting. "They're gonna love this." I sit in the back while he plots, field-stripping an AK-47 they have confiscated from an Iraqi National Guardsman who turned out to be a bad guy. It was surprisingly clean. "Doc, where'd you learn to do that?" "Well, you have to know these things if you're going to be a surgeon."

Run almost five miles, do weights. Get back and hang out, get another package in the mail. This one's from Karen, it has ten boxes of Oreos in it and a pile of gummy bears. Just what I don't need, but it was really nice of her, nonetheless. I will share them so that I'm not forced to eat them all...

Tuesday: TQ Day 84.

A restless night, mostly because between 0200 and 0400 there were numerous calls between Ridgeway Base and Ridgeway 13 (the ambulance drivers), asking about whether the milkrun bird had arrived yet. Which is pretty silly, since (a) we can hear it land, and (b) the ambulance drivers have nowhere else they can go until the bird lands, after which they come back to base to drop off the ambulance and then go to sleep. But they kept us awake anyway. "Are we there yet?" "No." "Are we there yet?" "No." "Are we there yet...?"

Thursday: TQ Day 86.

...A dust storm settles in, which normally would mean no more casualties (the Hadjis don't like bad weather). We then learn that another patient is coming in by ground, a gunshot wound to the abdomen. Since I'm the only one not scrubbed, it's mine, a "gimme" case straight to the OR if the report is to be believed. The story is that a pickup truck with eight Kurds in it drives up to ECP 2, drops one guy off, and leaves. He tells our interpreter that he was shot by the U.S. Army, which is unlikely because the Army would have then brought him in. Later, from our counterintelligence guys, we learn that the likely scenario is that he was involved in a business dispute over junkyard foraging rights and lost the negotiation. However, if we shoot him, he gets $2,500 compensation from Uncle Sam; if someone else shoots him, nothing. Anyway, I take him straight to the OR and get started. It's just me and Phil, the PA, who I have asked to scrub with me as everyone else is in the OR. I do the case the typical trauma way: one long slash down to the fascia, another long slash through that, and I'm in. Joe pops in (John and Bob are finishing up another case) and asks how it's going. I tell him he's welcome to scrub but he has time to get some water, smoke, and pee if he wants. He leaves and comes back in about five minutes, during which I look around, stop the bleeding from the retroperitoneum (behind his kidney), run the bowel, check liver and spleen. Even get Carmen to take a couple of pictures. When Joe scrubs in, I'm ready to mobilize the colon (detach it from the abdominal wall) to fix the holes in it. Joe starts to help me by lifting up a little piece, just like you would for an elective colon cancer operation. I make a nick in the attachment, unzip it with scissors, stick my fingers in the space and peel it right up. The trauma way. In elective surgery, bleeding is kept at a minimum; in trauma surgery, the patient is already bleeding so "haste makes speed." We fix the holes and Joe scrubs out while I whipstitch the belly shut. The packs by his kidney will need to come out in a day or so.

I'm done with the whole case in 35 minutes, skin to skin, pretty much by myself. Carmen and Mike couldn't believe it. There was no magic to this, really. I've been here before and, more importantly, he didn't have any really big injuries.

We are done right at 1700, time for chow. After eating, I stop by to make sure my patient is okay. I'm told that he's being very difficult, he keeps trying to get out of bed, he wants to eat and drink, and so on. I use Yasser, our Jordanian interpreter, to read him the riot act. You had holes in your guts. I saved your life. If you eat or drink too soon, the holes will leak, and you will die a slow, painful death. If you want to die, you should never have come here. He cooperates. Does surgery make people assholes, or do assholes naturally gravitate to become surgeons. Chicken, egg — you decide.

The dust storm has ended, so the helos can fly again and he will go out tonight.

Saturday: TQ Day 88.

Nary a dull moment today... Jeff did not really want to run or lift weights today, but felt guilty, so he went running with me. We swung by the junkyard so I could get some shots of him with various blown-up bits of Iraqi ordnance and airplanes, which he thought were pretty cool. We finish up 4½ miles, about 2 less than he normally runs. I then get a call to see a 9-month-old with a scald burn that Tom is looking at. Another patient who has somehow made it in the gate, despite all the rules to the contrary. I can hear the kid screaming as I walk up to the SSTP and, when I get there, Eileen, our peds clinic nurse manager, sent here as an adult ward/ICU nurse and doing a damn good job of it, is trying to stick an IV in her. The kid's burns are minor and require no treatment except bacitracin a couple of times a day. "Why are you starting an IV?" "The Commander told me to." "Tom, why do you want an IV? These burns are so small, the kid doesn't need fluids." "Antibiotics." "We've been over this before, there is no role for prophylactic antibiotics in burns." "Okay, morphine then." "Give a single dose IM (a shot in the muscle) if you want, but an IV is unnecessary." So Eileen stops, and once people stop poking the kid and holding her down, she stops screaming, puts her hands out to her daddy, and wants a drink of water. Most of the kid's pain was from being tormented, not from the burns. Another save.

Off to dinner. As I sit there drinking my milk and contemplating whether I want ice cream or not, we get a call that there is a casualty coming in. That answers that. By the time I get changed and up there, it is three U.S. Army casualties. When they come off the ambulance, no one is dying but they are messed up a bit. A friendly neighborhood Iraqi dropped a grenade in the hatch of an M1 Abrams tank, and it went off as one of the crew was trying to throw it back out again. One guy has a smashed jaw; frags in his head, arm and leg; a dislocated/mangled left hand (I assume that he's the grenade thrower, trading his hand for three lives); and frags that on x-ray could be in his heart. While there is certainly surgery I can do on him, he would be better off getting his head and chest CTed first to evaluate where those frags really are (we can't tell where they are on plain x-rays). So he will need to fly out ASAP. Much to Mike's and Tim's relief, I bring him back to the OR to get him intubated for the trip out, "in case he needs a crich if his airway is compromised by the broken jaw," i.e., so the ER guys don't do it. As I've said before, we who work in the OR are all on the same page with this stuff, this is not a game.

Next guy has a ruptured eyeball; he will need an eye surgeon ASAP. He also has frags in his side, peppered with lots of tiny bits that could have gone somewhere, maybe even into his belly. Short of opening his abdomen, I have no way to know without a CT. With the eye and his being stable, I already have a reason to send him up ASAP, so he will go with the jaw guy. The third guy, the least injured, has a bunch of frags in both legs. I'm duty doc today and John's my back-up, so John had looked this guy over while I handled the first two. By the time I'm done packaging up the two to fly out, John and Bob are in the OR with this last guy. We could have sent him with the first two, but then he would sit around waiting for his surgery behind the others and whatever else the Level III might have going on, so we kept him as we can do all his evaluation and initial surgery here, without detriment. The other two needed CT scans we don't have. I stand by and mock to my heart's content while they work. My reputation as the "NOTS" remains intact. Another day on duty when I did not operate.

Sunday: TQ Day 89.

The day started off well enough. Got up at 1000, got in the SUV with Barb, Carmen, and Greg to go to the coffee shop. Coffee and bagels, yum. After that, we went over to two different sets of blown-up bunkers that overlook the river, Habbaniyah, and Camp Manhattan, since the girls had not seen them before. Photo ops for them, they had fun. After that, I dropped them off at DFAC (aka the chow hall) while I went to shovel pigeon crap. Yes, pigeon crap. Our amateur gardeners (John and Tom) have run out of fertilizer and the compost heap is progressing very slowly, being fed mostly by coffee grounds. During my travels, I have discovered where the pigeons roost (no big deal, inside the abandoned guard towers on base that no one ever goes into), so I have brought a bucket and shovel and, in about a minute, I have twenty pounds of the stuff. It's not as good as bat or seagull crap, because they eat bugs and fish which have more nitrates in them, but it'll have to do. We are definitely NOT going the nightsoil route.

Around 1500, two casualties come in from an IED blast. One has a little hole in his neck; Joe takes him, while John and I double-team the other one. Our guy goes straight back to the OR, where he's intubated while I stick a chest tube in him and put a central line (huge IV) under his collar bone. He has had most of his left hand blown off, holes in his neck, multiple frags into his left chest and flank, and some over his right hip and arm. Lots of work. Ultrasound shows blood in his belly, so we start by opening that and taking out his spleen. The blast shattered his spleen, but no frags actually penetrated his abdomen, so that's good. Meanwhile, Bob has been working on the left hand. At this point, his life is saved, a dust storm is coming, and we want to ship him out before we are closed down. So I go shower and get ready for dinner while John does the paperwork and makes the transfer call.

Unfortunately, the dust really came in quickly and between here and everywhere else, the helos can't fly safely, so our two patients aren't going anywhere. So, before I get to dinner, John and I go back to the OR for more work: leg, neck, and side. We are pulling various bits of metal up to an inch in size out of the guy for a couple more hours, finally finishing around 2100. By then, the weather is better and the two patients fly out around 2300.

I'm in the hootch, getting ready for bed when I notice that the boss is having trouble with his pistol. He can't figure out how to take it apart, and is blowing a spray can of EnDust for Computers (which is flammable) down the barrel. The Group Surgeon has invited him out on a trip to Karbani, the local fishing village, because the Civil Affairs guys have finally worked out a deal with a local Iraqi physician to provide medical care there. Anyway, since he will be "outside of the wire," he will need to be armed. In the three months that we've been here, he's never cleaned his weapon and doesn't know how to use it. Actually, in his twenty years in the Navy, he has never been issued a weapon, since he has never deployed, he tells me. Scary. Tempted though I am to let him lie in the bed he has made for himself, I can't, so I teach him how to strip and clean his weapon and his mags. He still keeps using the EnDust, though.

Monday: TQ Day 90.

I hear back about the little girl with the scald burn that I treated a couple of days ago. Her father had never changed the dressings, but the kid was looking fine. What Greg, the Marine CAO, later realized is that Dad is not going to do it, and Mom doesn't know how, so they will do nothing. So next time a female nurse needs to go, to teach Mom how to do it, since she is the caregiver. But a doc will still need to go, to ensure that the wounds are okay, and the blisters will probably need to be popped and debrided at that point. Of course, I volunteer for the job (well, I tell the boss that since the kid is my patient, I should be the one to go), and Greg wants Eileen since she treated the kid before, so we'll probably go out on Thursday morning. Cool.

Tuesday: TQ Day 91.

Up at the crack of 1000. At around 1130, we get a radio call that we have to turn in our radios to be re-encrypted (someone in the Engineer unit lost one), which we then proceed to do. This gets, of course, buggered up, as our radios are placed on the same net as AGDAG, the air terminal. There's some confused "What are you doing on my net?" "Your net? What are you doing on MY net?" before it's sorted out after a few hours.

We hear that we have an incoming gunshot to the thigh, so while we wait, Bob tells us that he's tired of all the "assistant OIC" stuff. He needs a deputy assistant OIC, which is an O-5 job. No volunteers. I ask if the D-A-OIC gets an executive assistant. John offers to be the Under-Deputy Assistant OIC for Excellence and Granularity. I see a definite mock in the making here.

Before the thigh guy shows, we hear that there are two more GSWs out there, who will probably arrive in an hour or so. When thigh guy shows up, I take him straight back to the OR to get started on him. Hopefully we can be almost done before the other two arrive. Unfortunately, the other two get here about five minutes after we start the first case.

All three are Iraqi "Special Forces Commandos." From what they say, they were sitting around eating lunch when they heard gunfire and next thing you know, the three of them have holes in them. So much for situational awareness, and these guys are SF? Anyway, thigh guy has a nice hole in his leg that I clean up, tie off a few bleeding veins, nothing major. The other two need no surgery at all; Joe checks them out while John and I are working the first one. One has a nick on his flank; the other was shot in the ass but the bullet is still there and didn't go into his belly. Wash the wounds in the ER and they can go back to where they came from.

I'm ready for chow when I get a phone call from one of the docs in Ramadi. He tells me that the Iraqi commander of the unit our three "commandos" came from is not happy with the care his people received. He feels that, because two were sent back to Ramadi, they are not getting the same care as the Americans are, and he's considering filing a complaint about it. I tell the doc that (a) they have no injuries requiring either hospitalization or follow-up care with us; (b) they certainly do not need to be sent to a higher level of care; (c) all they need is for their wounds to be checked every couple of days for signs of infection; and (d) if the Iraqi commander wants to complain, he should complain directly to his own Ministry of Health, whose policy is that the Iraqi people want to look after their own soldiers and that they are supposed to be treated at local civilian hospitals. There is a pause on the line and then the doc says, "Okay sir, never mind." We'll see what happens at my court martial when the international incident hits the headlines...

After dinner, I'm back at work on tomorrow's mockfest. I've created an in-depth organizational chart for TQ Surgical, complete with three Deputy Assistant OICS, six Under Deputy Assistant OICs, five executive assistants for same, and at least four special advisors to the OIC. As I am putting the finishing touches on this, another casualty rolls in at 2000.

Young Marine, shot through the thigh with a broken femur but intact blood vessels. I ask him who he is and he says, "The worst sniper in the Marine Corps, sir — I'm supposed to shoot them, not the other way around." Good kid. He is part of the various teams trying to take out the Chechen male-female sniper team reported to be moving around Ramadi. Dangerous business. He's finished up in time to make the "milk run" out to Balad at 2300.

Five patients today, three cases. But I'm supposed to be the NOTS (Nonoperative Trauma Surgeon). I had been looking forward to being on call today so I could have a day off!

Wednesday: TQ Day 92.

We had a good AOM today, possibly the best so far. I explain the Table of Organization for TQ Surgical. There is a Special Advisor for Tonsorial Affairs (the psychiatrist whose hair I fixed), a Special Advisor for Wildlife Management (Shannon, aka "Bugs," the Environmental Health Officer), a Liaison for Legal Affairs (Tim, of SJAG beheading fame), and so on.

I run across the Texas Civil Affairs guy, now back from leave to San Antonio. We get to talking about various things, one of which is that, as the U.S. pulls out and the ISF (Iraqi Security Forces, the replacement for the disbanded Iraqi National Guard) picks up the slack, we can expect to get more casualties with fewer people available to treat them. No one seems to be working this, and he says that there is one so-so (even by Iraqi standards) hospital in Fallujah and one craphole in Ramadi. I tell him that, while the bunkers he had shown us would not do for our hospital, they might do well for an Iraqi one, since it is secure and close to the MSR. We get to brainstorming about "what ifs," like what if Civil Affairs (which gets its money from a whole different pot) rebuilt it as a basic trauma hospital for the Iraqi military, and then staffed it with some Iraqi surgical people, whom the U.S. could then train up. Security would have to be U.S., of course, for the protection of all, but it would be a beautiful thing. We bat this around for a while, and then he says sure, he'll take it up the food chain. This man has initiative! If this could get off the ground, I would even consider staying around for a few extra months. It won't, but it's a sweet idea.

Go over to Lakeside, where I buy an inlaid wooden backgammon board. It will make a nice conversation piece. I had seen it weeks ago, but I needed something to look forward to, so I waited to buy it.

Spend the evening getting ready for my little trip tomorrow. Don't know if it will actually happen, but I get my battle rattle set up, clean my weapon, and so on. It's supposed to be early in the morning and I haven't heard anything back yet.

Thursday: TQ Day 93.

Had a fairly interesting day today. Up at 0800 to drop off laundry, nothing on the trip, so back to bed until almost 1100. They know how to find me if they want me. Went running, it was only 112 degrees today. However, I did put on suntan lotion, at least on my head. Stopped off at the Texas HQ to find out if or when we are going out, discover it's at 1800. I have some misgivings about this, since we were supposed to go early in the day and 1800–2400 is our peak trauma time, but I plan to bring that up with Greg when I see him. I also work out the comms issues (for how we can be recalled if multiple casualties come in) with their S-6, in case no one has done that. After that, hung around the hootch reading until 1530, then go over to the Dark Tower to meet up with Greg (Marine Civil Affairs) and Eileen (peds nurse) for the patrol briefing. While I'm waiting in the foyer for them to show (I am early, of course), who should pop out but the Marine Commanding General. "Pretty high-ranking guard you got here," he says to the Corporal of the Guard jovially. "Say Doc, I hear you're going out on the town today. That's good, real good. You folks should get out from time to time and see what it's like out there. See what the troops do." So much for my misgivings about going out late...

Greg and Eileen show up and we head over to the HQ of Alpha Company, the folks we'll be going out with. They will have their usual four "gun trucks," which are up-armored humvees with machine guns. Greg will be using a Marine gun truck from the General's PSD (Personal Security Detachment), which he has access to whenever the general is not using it (the PSD, not just the gun truck.) Greg says we will do the brief, grab dinner and our battle rattle, and then head out.

Straightforward briefing starting at 1600, discusses the route, comms, security, IA (immediate action) drills (i.e., response to attack), and so on. Yes, we will be driving down MSR Michigan for a couple of miles, the one running from Fallujah to Ramadi that has all the IEDs on it. But they rarely put any IEDs so close to our base because of all the patrols, so it's "pretty safe." After that, we will get off the highway and go down to the lake, where the village of Karbani is located. The village is basically on a dead-end road that no one has any reason to go to unless they have business there, and the Muqtar (headman) and his family have been known to shoot at strangers. In short, it is secluded and there has never been any trouble there. Best of all, it's at the bottom of the escarpment that our base is on, so our OPs overlook it for added security. Eileen will be in the Marine vehicle (Greg's idea, he wants to keep her happy), I will be in one of the others.

Unfortunately, they want to push the mission forward to maximize the daylight, so we will leave at 1715. So much for dinner. I grab two Harvest granola bars along with my gear and eat them in the car on the way back to the jump-off point. I also discover that one of our interpreters is a jovial, chunky, middle-aged lady who is my favorite interpreter. She is Iraqi, raised in Baghdad, left in the early '80s, went to Australia, then England, and finally to the U.S., settling down in Detroit. Her family used to come here on vacation when she was growing up — Lake Habbaniyah really used to be a tourist area before Saddam took it over. First the Iran–Iraq war, then Desert Storm, and now OIF have really knocked it for a loop, apparently.

We have some comms snafus that eat up a half hour: the Marine Humvee can't talk to the four Army humvees on the tactical radio but only by the Motorola handheld (which is the back-up for comms within the patrol). It can't talk to the Texans' HQ, either. Apparently the Marine vehicle has new comms encryption loaded (the radios are computerized), the Army has the old set and were planning to load the new stuff tonight after they got back. Oops. But the Army can't change the Marine vehicle back to the old ones. However, if they change to the new ones, they can't talk to their TOC, either. Eventually, things are worked out and we head out at 1800 as originally planned. Drive through ECP 1, across the bridge, and onto MSR Michigan. Just a little nervous as we drive down the highway, looking at all of the rubbish at the side of the road. Hell, there could be IEDs almost anywhere! I keep the peeps open, well aware that three of our bulletproof glass block windows do, in fact, have bullet marks on them. After a few minutes, we pull off the highway, down a secondary road, over a bridge (after stopping to check it for mines and IEDs), and down to the lakeshore. We are in Karbani. The vehicles form a "coil" (all facing out in different directions), and at least two men stay with each vehicle, including the driver and machine gunner, while the rest of us get out.

It looks like so many other rundown villages I have seen over the years, in Laos, Thailand, the Philippines — poverty is poverty everywhere. Cinderblock or adobe boxes with flat roofs, trash all over, animals wandering around, free range children everywhere.

The kids come over as soon as we arrive, with the usual "gimme, gimme." The women stay way back, out of the way, peeking from afar or out of doorways. After a few minutes, Greg, Eileen, our Marine guard, the translator, and I go to the house where the burned baby is. This house stands separate from the rest, on a little rise, has a fan built into the wall, and electricity, so the owner is obviously important in the village, although we don't find out exactly what his status is. He had come with his daughter when the patrol had brought her to the SSTP last Saturday, though. The only other decent-looking building in the village is the Muqtar's, which is quite nice and right next to the small mosque they have.

Adding to my impression that the father is relatively important here, we learn that he had gotten an Iraqi doctor to come look at his daughter today, which is just what we would want to happen. The baby is fine, although Eileen freaks because she sees that the baby's belly is dark brown, as are some of the bandages. I ask if the Iraqi doctor gave them anything to put on the burns, and yes, he did, something dark brown in fact. It's in a dish with saran-wrap on it, and looks like mercurochrome. Which is okay, but painful. Still, I make it very clear to them that this is all well and good. I don't want to give the impression that we are better than their doctors. What I am worried about is that the women are not there, and that it's the mother who actually cares for the child. So I suggest that Eileen and our translator take the baby in the back room with the women, so they can teach the mother what to do. Which they do, while Greg, the Marine bodyguard, and I stay in the front room and keep the men from interfering.

We put up with about thirty minutes of pestering by the Iraqi boys. I have a pen and a flashlight attached to the front of my battle rattle, and the whole time I get the same spiel from every little boy there (accompanied by gestures, of course)—"You give me that, I be your friend." No, thanks for the offer. When Eileen comes out, she has had a pretty good time all told, once she got over the initial mob scene (the women are a lot less inhibited when the men are not around, apparently, and played with her blonde hair, looked at pictures of her kids, and so on). Mission accomplished.

We go for a walk through the village and meet up with the mission commander, an Army captain, who is doing some sort of site survey. After another half hour or so, they are done and we are ready to head back. Into the humvees and away we go. In through the "CA [Civil Affairs] gate," which is a locked gate in the perimeter fence, and then home at 2010.

Having missed dinner, I check back in to the SSTP and then go over to Greg's hootch for a near-beer. Super Dave, a long-time resident contractor, is having a cook-out, so we go over and I have a really good hamburger with BBQ sauce, pineapple-raisin tuna, spaghetti, and cashews. One of the best dinners that I've had since leaving home.

Friday: TQ Day 94.

As I am putting on my running shoes, we get a radio call. Army guy, frag to the neck. When he arrives, he has an impressive chunk of metal sticking out of his neck, but

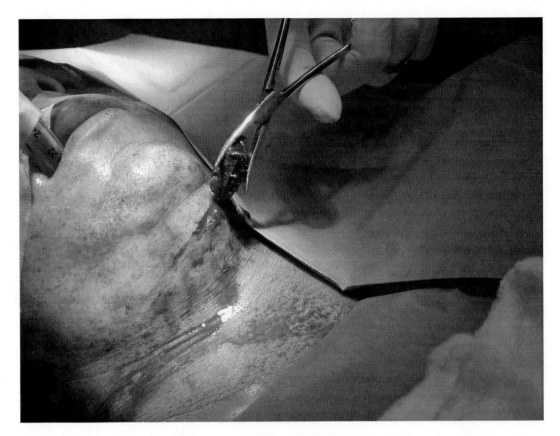

A metal fragment from an IED is removed from a soldier's neck. This frag was resting on his carotid artery, but did not injure it. Talk about luck.

he's completely stable. Extremely hoarse though, suggesting an airway injury. So I bypass the STP tent and take him straight back to the OR, where we intubate him nicely and calmly. No hurry, no fuss, just get the job done. Shoot some x-rays; find out that this thing is about 3 × 2 × 2 inches, buried in there. "The tip of the iceberg," as it were. There are, of course, the usual jokes about his mother telling him not to pick at zits...

Very nice case, dissect out all the blood vessels in his neck. The thing is sitting on top of them all but, besides creating a gaping hole, has injured nothing. Hardest part of the case was pulling the damned thing out, which I did at the end after I had checked everything else. After all, this thing could have been the cork preventing his bleeding to death.

Monday: TQ Day 97.

John and I play the inaugural round of bocce ball, it was especially challenging on the uneven packed dirt and gravel. I squeak out a victory, 12–10, after being down 1–6.

At about 2300, we get a call that there is a "U.S. civilian with a GSW to the abdomen, intubated," coming in. As I put on my shoes I say to Jeff, "Intubated? This doesn't sound good." Since I had just given Grand Rounds on "ACLS in trauma: why bother?" which included the tidbit that by some reports, over 90 percent of patients intubated in the field die, he agrees. Thirty seconds later, we hear that he has "DOW," died of wounds. I take my shoes back off. Jeff asks me if it's a burden to be so damn smart. I wish.

Wednesday: TQ Day 99.

A relatively brief AOM/patient conference today, as we haven't seen too many cases in the past week. Learned that our "Hump Day" party, originally scheduled for Day 100 on Thursday, has been pushed back a couple of days for I'm not sure what reason. Go back to the hootch to ponder whether to run (it looks like a nice day, a little breezy and overcast) or just sleep for a couple more hours. I am leaning (reclining, actually) towards the latter when we hear that there is "one incoming U.S. military casualty, coming in right now!" Put on sneaks without socks and run over.

It's a guy from our Texas buddies. They were on patrol a mile or so from the gate when an IED went off. One vehicle had two flat tires from frags, but the vehicle gunner (the guy sticking out of the top with the machine gun) was hit in the left shoulder with a frag and is squirting blood all over. Almost certainly a subclavian artery injury, probably the hardest artery in the body to get to. His medic managed to put pressure on it and get him to us ASAP, thus saving his life (I am writing a formal recommendation for him to their CO). His uniform is completely red, he's yelling, and blood is squirting all over when I walk into the SSTP tent. Joe is primary, and as he walks in I tell him we need to go straight back.

As we head back, Joe tells me that he's never seen or done one of these. Me, I have done one, seen one, and written a paper on one we managed at Charity Hospital with a stent (i.e., without an operation)—I guess that makes me the expert. More importantly, even though I have little experience with it, I know the approaches. I tell Joe we will look at where the hole is when we get to the OR and decide on approach — through the clavicle, through the anterior chest, through the sternum, depends on how proximal (i.e., close to the middle of the chest) the injury is. When things calm down a little, I see that it will be proximal, so I suggest to Joe that we do a sternotomy (i.e., right up the middle of the chest); that way we can control the artery right where it comes off the aorta. A "trapdoor" incision, basically making a flap out of part of his chest and swinging it out of the way, is another approach, but it can be difficult to retract.

After the guy is intubated and blood is hanging, we get to work. My hand is in the hole, controlling the bleeding. Joe decides to do an anterior chest incision, which is a little low but workable. He gets his hand in there and manages to compress the vessels with his fingers. Unfortunately, his hand uses up the entire incision and now what? We extend this into a trapdoor and struggle with this exposure for a bit, eventually simplified by my pulling REALLY hard on the flap, breaking two ribs, and folding it out of the way. Crude but effective. Now we can get a little better exposure. We get clamps on the various ends of vessels, since we discover that both the subclavian artery and vein have been destroyed for a length of several inches. Nothing like the usual simple stab wound or pistol bullet that either makes a nice hole or nicks it. This will be a bitch to fix, assuming we can do it.

By this time, the patient is getting his 20th unit of blood (including blood from our "walking blood bank," which we have activated). Joe looks up at me with "Now what?" in his eyes. I say simply, "Life over limb." The hole in this guy's chest is hamburger, the vessels are shredded, and the blood vessels (assuming we can find good ends to sew to, which we have not yet) will take an hour or more to repair. He is oozing from everywhere because his blood will no longer clot, even though we have the major bleeding under control. And the brachial plexus, the extremely complex network of nerves that go into the arm and which surrounds the vessels, looks bad, so even if we can fix the blood supply, odds are so-so that the arm will ever work again. So we get to work tying off all of the vessels. You have to be alive to have a complication...

When we are finally done, he has received 30 units of banked blood and 10 units from the walking blood bank. He is oozing from everywhere. But he has a blood pressure. At this point he needs further resuscitation, let his body catch up with the insult, and in a few hours, if he's lucky, he can get round two of surgery (vascular repair or amputation, depending on how things look). But not here. He also looks like he may need his belly opened for abdominal compartment syndrome, like that guy a couple of weeks back, but Joe decides that he's good enough to get out of here now. He heads out on the helo to Baghdad.

The Texans' Physician Assistant has shown up with their CO. I tell them what is going on, that the guy is alive but SAS (Sick As ... Snot).

At one point during the case, Joe was asking for something to be put into his hand (he wears loupes or magnifying OR glasses and so has a restricted field of vision), and the OR tech kept telling him that he already had it. Yeah, it was lying there, but Joe needed it put into his hand. After the fourth time asking for the same thing and getting an argument, Joe just lost it and started screaming at the guy. While this was very uncool, I have to admit that it's not surprising; perhaps surprising that it doesn't happen more often. Why is the OR tech arguing with the surgeon?

And oh, by the way, the Commanding General happened to be in the OR when all of this was transpiring, and thereby seeing first hand that the surgeons here do, in fact, have tempers. Between this incident and some other small crap that's happened with him standing nearby, maybe he figured that if he closed HESCO Beach, we would REALLY go off the deep end!

The case is done around noon. Debate with myself for a while, but decide that I will run anyway. I go by the Texans as usual, they are all pretty shook up, this is the second of their guys in three days to get hit and the worst so far. The medic who looked after today's guy is not there. I wanted to stop by and tell him that he saved the guy's life, which he did.

After the run, I start working on a memo to the Texan's CO, recommending that the medic get some sort of recognition for the day's events. If the guy lives, it will be because this medic had the wherewithal to grab the guy's chest and put pressure on it and not let go for anything until they got to us. He's the same medic who brought in another of their guys three days ago with a fragged arm and face. After dinner, I head back over to the Texans (this time in uniform and SUV) and meet the guy. He tells me what happened.

They were driving past the site of a burned-out car from a previous VBIED, which still had trash everywhere, when another IED went off. Front tires in the second Humvee are flattened. Normally, the guys get out, secure the perimeter, do a sitrep (situation report on the radio), and then eventually call the medic (a couple of vehicles back) to come up and look at the injured. Instead, about fifteen seconds after the explosion, he gets the call to get up there pronto. When he gets to the Humvee, the gunner is hanging in the straps of the turret (there is no real seat), looking like he's dead. He cuts the straps, the guy drops into a pool of blood. He finds the hole, puts pressure on it, and doesn't let go. He is holding the guy from behind in a bear hug, pressing on the hole in the front of his chest with both hands. They get in the next Humvee; he is sitting on the floor with the guy cradled between his legs, still giving the bear hug. The patrol leader says they need to wait for the gun truck (SOP) but he tells him it can catch up — if they don't move their guy is dead. So they burn rubber back to base, the gun truck following, and come screaming into the SSTP. Joe now has a new criterion for going straight back to the OR with a patient: if the Humvee corners on 2 wheels, it's serious.

So I write up a memo to their CO about this — if the guy lives, it's because their medic got him to us. We're the trauma surgeons; we're supposed to save lives. This guy is a factory worker, his only medical experience is with the Texas Army National Guard, which is basically weekend drills and not even sick call. A helluva thing.

Joe, John, and I debrief in the evening, looking at my trauma books to decide what we could have done differently. Besides starting with a sternotomy, nothing, and the sternotomy would not have changed the outcome. We also have added a "4" to the BIS score. "BIS" is a scoring system in anesthesia to decide how asleep someone is, based on EEG. Our B ... Injury Score is named in honor of Joe (or "Joey Bag-of-Doughnuts"):

BIS 1: Jacked up.
BIS 2: Really jacked up.
BIS 3: So jacked up that I wish someone else was doing the case.
BIS 4: Jeff asks for blood.

Jeff is notorious for asking the surgeons whether additional blood transfusion is needed during cases, so today when he was telling the blood bank tech to bring him "any blood, I don't care if it's frozen, walking blood bank, whatever," you knew it was pretty bad. Jeff finds the BIS 4 hilarious, fortunately.

Thursday: TQ Day 100.

Day 100. I celebrate by sleeping until 1100. I get up, drink coffee, do e-mail, read your book. At around 1400 I run, about six miles today. I also stop by and chat with my Texas buddies.

When I get back, I get an update on our guy from yesterday. He's still alive, and has made it all the way to Germany already — Baghdad moved him right along to Balad, which shipped him to Landstuhl this morning. Hot potato! But if he has survived this long, he will probably make it.

Have dinner with Greg, we talk about going out to the range to shoot. He says that he can set it up since it's on base. Mostly we want to get folks who have the potential to go "outside the wire" up to speed: that would be Barb, Carmen, Eileen from our group (Mike, Joe and I can shoot already, but would love the practice), and then there is also Shannon (EHO who base-hops) and the two members of our "combat stress team," the psychiatrist and Kevin.

Friday: TQ Day 101.

Up at the crack of 1030 today, then off for a run. Afterwards, I check e-mail. Not much exciting except that *JAMA* accepted my vignette on our first death here, without editing. Don't know when it will come out, though.

Our "Hump Day" bash is scheduled for tomorrow afternoon, and I discovered that Eileen, who has decided that she wants to organize this thing, has not gotten any near-beer for the party. Lots of soda, but near-beer is better if you want to have near fun. There is plenty of soda at the chow hall, but near-beer you have to buy, and most of the juniors don't want to spend the money for it. So I get up a quick collection and I go buy four cases.

Apart from that, not much going on again today, either. I guess the second half of the deployment will all be downhill...

Saturday: TQ Day 102.

Got an email from J.J.—he's doing well. Still hasn't figured out e-mail access at his house so he has to go to the library to do it. He is convalescing while still on active duty. He gave us some follow-up on one of our first patients, a guy with both legs messed up and his left arm taken off—they are doing physical therapy together. The kid is learning to play golf with his prosthesis as part of his therapy!

The party was supposed to start at 1600, but few people had shown up by then, including our own folks, although plenty of food had been cooked. Eileen was pretty pissed off, since she had worked all week to make the arrangements: lobster tails, bratwurst, burgers, hot dogs, she even had some smoked salmon. Jeff and I had picked up four cases of near-beer yesterday, since that had been forgotten. I know for a fact that the officers knew about it, since I had told them of the start time, and then reminded them at 1630 when they had not shown up. But it was the usual attitude of "the party won't start until I get there." A bunch of Texans (officers and senior NCOs) came by after 1730. They had a very good time and were extremely relaxed. Some of the CLR 25 guys came by, as did assorted other associates: Jevdet and Shendet, the Turkish contractors (brothers) who clean our showers, and who we have sort of adopted; the Air Boss; Mike, the Marine Flight Doc; Fireman Joe (contractor from the TQ fire dept); just to name a few. We know a lot of folks around here.

Greg was also there, along with a former patient of ours. At the start of March, we had a Marine LtCol, another JAG, come through with a frag in the chest from an IED. The chest x-ray showed the frag overlying his heart shadow, but that didn't tell us if it was in front of, behind, or inside of his heart. He was stable, so we had shipped him to Balad, where they CTed him, then opened his chest. He had recuperated in the States and then volunteered to come back to finish his tour. He was thanking us all for looking after him. I told him that we can't take credit for the thoracotomy; he should thank Balad for that. By the way, the guy is stationed in New Orleans, so we had a nice chat.

5. June 2005: They Came by Pick-up, Humvee and Bradley Tank

Thursday: TQ Day 107.

I go off and run, stop by the Army guys. We are still on for Camp Manhattan tomorrow, the "30 second ride of death." I also pick up a nice little leaflet from the IO (Information Ops) guy, a PsyOps flier that has lots of writing and some fuzzy black and white photos. I don't need a translator: if you are caught digging holes in or near the road, your friendly neighborhood Iraqi Security Forces are authorized to kill you — and have a nice day.

While I'm in the gym, doing weights, a couple of the Texans come in, we chat a bit. Turns out it is the H&S (HQ and Service, i.e. "head shed") Company CO and their company 1st sergeant. When they find out who I am, they tell me that it's really cool that I wrote up that letter for their medic, its part of the PR packet they have released to the guy's home town. Not only that, but the guy had been fired just before deploying. His wife got on TV about him being a hero, the warehouse he used to work at was getting all sorts of nasty phone calls and press, and now it looks like he has a job for life. Cool.

Make it to dinner about 1945, just before they close. Get back to the hootch and at 2030, a case comes in. While we are waiting for him to show up, we hear two really loud explosions — the insurgents fired two rockets at Camp Manhattan and missed, apparently blowing up other insurgents living in Habbaniyah, instead. When our casualty arrives, it's an Army guy from Ramadi, shot by a sniper — he had gone out to brush his teeth when a vehicle stopped on the road outside their perimeter 600 meters away, fired a shot, and screeched off. The bullet went in and out through both thighs, hitting no nerve or vessels but making some nice holes. The wounds get washed out and we talk AJ, the Air Boss, into scrubbing on the case. He has some fun. AJ often comes down from the "Crack House" (the Air Control Tower) to the SSTP to wait with us for patients to arrive. Another of our SSTP buddies.

Friday: TQ Day 108.

Off we go to Camp Manhattan — yes, the same Camp Manhattan that they were aiming at yesterday. But the rockets only come in at dawn or dusk there, so we should be fine. I am in the back of the armored Humvee (real Class I armor, not the homemade stuff that we used to see when we got here), and we have a gun truck with a machinegun also. We go through ECP #1, race across the bridge at high speed, and screech to a halt in front of Camp Manhattan's checkpoint.

Iraq was invaded by the British in 1915, when it was part of the Ottoman (Turkish) Empire. In one of my British army books about World War I, there were three great quotes about Iraq. The first was an old Arab saying that when Allah created hell, it wasn't terrible enough, so he made Iraq — and added flies. The second was when a Gurkha regiment (Nepalese mercenaries in the British Army since 1815, who love fighting more than anything else in the world), the first unit into Baghdad, arrived there, they said, "This wasn't worth fighting for" and immediately marched back out again. The third was a quote from a Scottish soldier, who described Iraq as "miles and miles of fook-all."

Anyway, what we now call Camp Manhattan was built in the town of Habbaniyah as a Royal Air Force base by the Brits in the '20s and '30s. It is still full of British military colonial architecture — big barracks with high ceilings, lots of fans, well laid out around square parade grounds or gardens. Very well built, but of course fallen into significant disrepair between the ravages of the Gulf War and OIF. When Iraq became independent in the '50s, it was still a major base until Saddam built TQ in the late '80s. Apparently there was an incident at some point when an Iraqi AF pilot flew his jet to Saddam's palace in Tartar and bombed it. He was shot down and captured alive. Saddam personally tortured him for several days, and then brought him back to the base at Habbaniyah, where he was burned alive in front of all of the AF officers on the base. Saddam then executed the base commander and all of the squadron commanders in front of them. Or so they say...

Wandered through the old barracks, which were full of piles of Iraqi uniforms and boots, trash, broken furniture, etc. Found one room full of ruined books — all from the 1920s and 1930s, British, including one by the author of Biggles! Too trashed to bring home, unfortunately — if it had been a Biggles book, I would have done it anyway. Saw an old French pre–World War I field gun with 1907 Russian markings on it, a British war trophy I assume.

We stopped off at the Army BAS there. Nice spacious building, tiled floors. They had a decent painting hanging on the wall of some Bedouins by a tent with a camel and some hookahs. Wasn't for sale, damn it, they plan to take it with them. Not a great painting, but it would have been a great souvenir: "Oh, that's just something I looted from Saddam's Air Force..."

Around 1200 we went to the Hadji restaurant, which was set up like a real restaurant. I had lamb kabob, falafel, hushpuppy-like things, salad, and tea. Good food, not great, but nice for a change.

Went to the "New Iraqi Store" next to it, but they didn't have much. The only thing I wanted to buy, they wouldn't sell me: an oval sign that said "Tiger Energy Drink" with a cheesy-looking tiger and a lot of Arabic on it. Very kitsch.

Back to the SSTP around 1300, we hadn't missed anything. Since I just ate lunch, no PT for me today, darn it! I go over all of my pictures from the trip.

...On the subject of extending out here for another tour, got some great e-mail replies. The C.O. of 2nd Med says that while he, his CPS (Chief of Professional Services, his top doc, whoever that is), and the Group Surgeon sit down to decide what is needed where, and then who goes there, it's ultimately up to the Group Surgeon. The Group Surgeon says that he doesn't know who is going where, and that it's not up to him. He also says that getting two weeks of R&R would be difficult to handle logistically, and he's not sure it could be done (even though I know through other channels that the Marines guarantee it). Figures.

We have our weekly rooftop get-together with Greg. The sunset, the orange glow of counterbattery artillery fire on the horizon, there is nothing like it.

Saturday: TQ Day 109.

Up a little earlier than expected today, at about 0620. Two huge booms, then a couple more. A split second later, Chief's unmistakable voice on the radio: "COC, talk to me." So much for proper radio comms. Hmm, let me see, Chief: the insurgent–COC psychic hotline is down right now, you will have to wait more than 35 milliseconds to find out if they plan to fire any more. But we don't need to wait long, a minute later the Big Voice siren goes off. That answered that. We do the radio accountability thing; I put on my body armor, and go back to bed.

Wake up again at 0800, incoming patient. Guy shot in the leg, a nothingburger, no surgery required. He gets patched and goes back to his unit at Camp Manhattan. Guess I won't be heading over there again any time soon. Barely have time to get coffee and dress for the 0930 providers' meeting, which of course everyone had hoped would be cancelled. Such apathy, and we have three months to go.

We are in heat condition red flag today, I'm not sure why. It's 118 degrees, not our hottest day by far. I go running, stop by the Army to ask about the explosions. Four rockets (two duds), barely inside the wire, in the middle of nowhere. They were expecting something like this; the local sheikh's nephew (his favorite one, I'm sure, he only has twenty or so) was arrested yesterday afternoon. He was caught walking away from a freshly planted 155mm artillery round by the side of the road, carrying a cell phone with wires hanging out of it. No, couldn't possibly be an IED...

Sunday: TQ Day 110.

I run about five miles today but get sidetracked. The loop I run usually has a lot of empty space on it, but today a large number of vehicles in various states of disrepair appear — including a tank! Of course I go over and crawl all over it, get inside, etc. Pretty beaten up but not blown up. I suspect this is a "parts" tank — the least reliable machine in a unit, be it a tank or a plane, which is typically stripped for scarce parts when other machines need them. There were also some armored cars, and two blown-up humvees. The humvees are pretty interesting, I got pics of the dented armor and smashed (but not penetrated) armored windows... We see the human carnage, not the mechanical.

Spend the afternoon sorting the various pics I got today and at Camp Manhattan on Friday. During the course of the afternoon, the power goes out five separate times. It's going to be a long summer.

I have an odd discussion over dinner with John. He had a strange thought today, that he is an epiphenomenon of a dream I'm having, where I am in my perfect place. For some reason, he thinks that this is my paradise: surgery, things to play with, and little trips. I tell him that he has it wrong; this is nothing like my perfect place. However, unlike some people, I am trying to make the best of it and make my stay here interesting. So I go looking for things to do. It's interesting what people do to keep themselves occupied: some PT for hours a day, some read, some talk. One of the ER docs plays a road-racing videogame for 6+ hours a day (why doesn't that surprise me?). Me, I read, do crosswords, write, play with slides and pics, and take every opportunity to do something different. While some days are longer than others, I fill up each day. Although I would rather have other things to do, I am not bored. I don't think that most of my colleagues can say the same.

Tuesday: TQ Day 112.

Today was a little busier. I'm the duty doc; get up at the usual 1030. At 1100, we get in three casualties, Iraqi contractors in a convoy hit by an IED. One has frags to his head, the other to the middle of his chest — they are stable but need CT scans so we send them to Baghdad. The third has a nasty broken upper arm and frags in his ass so he goes to the OR for an ex fix and wound washouts.

Done with him around 1300. I get set to go running, am about twenty yards out the door, when we hear that two more are coming in. These guys are more contractors, one Iraqi, one Irish. The Iraqi has a frag in his eye and a gunshot to his shoulder that tracked up over his collar bone. He needs to go out ASAP to the eye guy in Baghdad. The Irish guy has minor wounds to his thigh and elbow, and a big chunk sticking out of his cheek. A case. However, he also has a ruptured eardrum with blood in it, suggesting that he has a basilar skull fracture, which could mean bleeding in his brain, which means he needs a CT. Damn, thought I had a case... He probably has nothing, but what is the excuse to not be sure? As I'm examining him, I notice his tattoos. So I ask him, "FFL?" (French Foreign Legion.) "Yeah, got out in 1997." "Thought I recognized the Legion Etrangere insignia. Morocco and west Africa?" "Yeah, the weather here is better but I was never fragged before this." Of course, no one else has any idea what we are talking about.

Over dinner the Air Boss says that we might be busy tonight as the Army plans to knock down a lot of doors.

Wednesday: TQ Day 113.

We learn from the Air Boss that there were 6 or 7 Iraqi KIAs in the convoy that was attacked yesterday, and about ten are missing. Today, eleven bodies were found piled up in an abandoned truck. Gotta love these people.

Go to bed fairly early (2300), thinking that we may get more work tonight, but we don't.

Thursday: TQ Day 114.

Another busy day, today. At 0910 the radio goes off, we have incoming "on the pad." Throw on shoes and head straight over. One Army soldier, frags through the leg. Joe, who is on duty today, plans to take him to the OR when we hear that we're getting four more. They arrive in a few minutes, four Iraqi contracted truck drivers whose convoy was hit. Joe changes the plan, he will take a guy with frags in his back to the OR, I will take a guy with frags in his side, and John will help whoever needs it.

I get into the OR first and get to work quickly. The patient has two pairs of wounds in his right side, looks like "in and out" wounds that are fairly superficial. The ultrasound done by the ER doc was negative for bleeding into his belly. More on that later. I get to work with the patient tilted up on his left side and rapidly discover that the wounds do not match up like we thought they did. When I get to the bottom of it all, I am looking

Zsolt has just stepped out of the OR to tell this U.S. Army Bradley crew that the casualty they brought in did not make it. The crew had shot the Iraqi as he was aiming a rocket-propelled grenade at them from an overpass. They then retrieved him, gave him what medical care they could, and brought him straight to the "hospital."

Casualties could arrive by any means of transportation, usually by Marine helo, but on occasion by Humvee, truck, Bradley (as shown here), or even on the back of an Abrams tank! Most casualties would arrive straight from combat with little or no medical treatment except for bandaging or tourniquets.

at a big hole in which I can see three organs in three separate body cavities at once: his lung in his chest, his liver in his abdomen, and his kidney in his retroperitoneum. The frags have opened up his side and detached his diaphragm from the wall of his torso — it's the diaphragm that keeps some of those spaces separate. Since Joe has yet to start on his case, John scrubs in with me and I repair the diaphragm (which would have been a bitch to do if he was lying on his back, his liver would have been in the way) and close up the hole in his side. Then I put him onto his back and open his belly and fix the liver. It was, as they say, a "sweet" case and the guy should do fine. Lots of blood in his belly, too, despite the "negative" ultrasound.

Joe's case is pretty straightforward; we finish at about the same time. In the meantime, another two Iraqi contractors have arrived, unannounced, and Bob works on one's hand GSW. One of them had come in a Bradley AFV (Armored Fighting Vehicle, essentially a tank), which Jeff and I get pictures of (we sit on top with the crew). Eventually it all settles down. John and Bob finish the hand, I do e-mail, and Joe goes to Lakeside to get a haircut. I am heckling John and Bob in the OR when we hear that there will be another one coming in, this time an EPW. I go outside to wait.

Very cool sight, another Bradley comes churning up the road PDQ, grinds to a halt, spins around 180 degrees, and backs up on the pad. Of course I get pics of this. That's why I carry a camera pouch on my belt. The back ramp drops and the soldiers start dragging the patient, an Iraqi kid, out like he's a sack of manure off the back of a pickup truck. There is no room in the back of a Bradley, he was on the floor in the back, naked, and so they grabbed any available body part and lifted. One soldier says he had just stopped breathing. I take one look at him — white as a sheet — and we go straight back to the OR. As I pass OR 2, Mike is coming out and I say "OR 1 now, apneic GSW." Away we go.

He is thrown on the OR table and we get to work. CPR, intubating, IV access. Negative abdominal ultrasound by Tom again. He has a little hole in his left outer thigh, another in his left groin. It looks like another in-and-out, so why does the guy look like he has bled out? There is no blood to be seen anywhere. In a couple of minutes, it's pretty obvious that he's dead, but we keep going anyway. No one dies on us without maximum effort on our part. We open his chest from side to side, his heart has stopped. Holes in

Patients would arrive at any time, and on any means of transportation. While most patients arrived on Marine Corps helicopters, they also arrived in Humvees straight off patrol, trucks, civilian vehicles, the occasional M1 Abrams tank, or in Bradley armored vehicles like the one here, parked directly outside the "hospital." The medical folks would always try to feed and water the crews, as the creature comforts were often not available off the big bases.

his right lung, hole in his diaphragm with blood pouring through it — did that bullet through his groin get all the way up here? Open his belly, the round has destroyed his liver, right kidney, vena cava. He is very dead.

I get the story from the Bradley crew. They were escorting a convoy when they saw this kid on an overpass aiming an RPG. Shot him with a machine gun, dropped like a rock. Definitely a bad guy. Definitely won't be shooting off any more RPGs. The crew themselves look a little shell-shocked. Not about the dead insurgent; their only regret is that he didn't live to give them useful intel. They have spent the last couple of days picking up Iraqi bodies off the streets in Habbaniyah. Nice job, glad I don't have it.

John, Joe, and I get together and briefly discuss the day. No major issues. Except that, to date, we have not had a single abdominal ultrasound performed that was useful. Two cases of BFOB (belly full of blood) today, saw nothing either time. Ultrasound doesn't seem useful to us in war.

Off to dinner. Come back and go check e-mail. I am sitting in the SSTP tent on the computer when we get another call, "Three patients on the pad now, gunshot wounds." I walk out and am almost the first one on the scene. A guy with glass in his face and a frag in his left shoulder, under a bandaid. A guy with a sore left elbow without any wounds. A guy with a small frag in his left forearm. All nothingburgers.

Eleven so far today, all by ground. We have had at least three sets of wounded in the past three days who arrived with absolutely no advance notice. Huge problem, since the gate is at least five minutes from where we are, and that five minutes will give us the chance to get up to the SSTP. In a few cases, five minutes could make all the difference. The ECPs are not calling us; we will have to get that sorted out.

Saturday: TQ Day 116.

Another busy day today. Started with incoming casualties at 0730, Iraqi truck drivers. A guy with a broken leg, that Joe and Bob take to the OR for an ex fix, and a kid with frags in his head, neck, chest and back. He's mine and John's. I think our usual Saturday meeting is going to get cancelled...

This kid, 17 years old, has problems. He was intubated at the Level I and sent to us. He has a frag in the back of his head. When he arrives, he is taken to the STP tent and we look him over: while he would need his neck explored, his big issue will be the hole in the back of his head, about a half inch in size. On x-ray, he has scattered small frags going deep into his brain. He needs a CT scan and a neurosurgeon, but we have a dust-storm and the helos can't fly. An added complication is that, as the Army switches its docs out in Baghdad, they have not replaced their neurosurgeons, so now Balad is the only place that has one. Not good in the duststorm season.

We wait for the kid to "come up" as the drugs used to intubate him wear off. The single most useful piece of information one needs on a head-injured patient, which we don't have yet, is his neurologic status — if he is severely comatose, then there is nothing for us to do, he will die in short order. The kid does come around a little, by that meaning that he moves his arms a bit. Not much, but better than nothing. To quote Miracle Max from *The Princess Bride*, there is a difference between dead, and mostly dead. However, his injury is in a place where I have never seen an operation done (it can be, I've just never seen it), and it's not the traditional place for drilling holes to relieve pressure on the brain. But since we can't ship him, we take him to the OR for his other injuries.

We fix the holes in his neck and back, no major injuries there. Bilateral chest tubes. After the case, Mike has him on a propofol (sedative) drip, which I tell him to turn off. While technically this is John's patient, he is taking my lead on this stuff as the guy with the critical care board certification. The helos can't fly, but the Air Boss will launch for us as soon as he can. Which is what I'm worried about. I don't want anyone taking unnecessary risks for a kid who, regrettably, will probably die anyway. The sedation wears off, the kid is motionless. Over the next couple of hours he loses his brainstem reflexes and his pupils are blown. While we cannot do formal brain-death testing here, he fails on the tests we can do. There's not much else to do at this point, so I go running. People say I'm nuts, but the dust storm wasn't too bad — I could see almost 300 meters sometimes!

When I get back, the Army has brought in the kid's dad, who had his son's dried blood and brains on his shirt — they were driving the truck together. We allow him to sit with the kid for a couple of hours as his son's body takes its time figuring out that his brain is dead. Eventually, John pronounces him dead at 1658. We all decide that we love Iraq: here is this poor kid, he has a real, honest job, and he gets killed for it.

Go to dinner. At 2030, we hear of three more coming in. One dies en route (a suspected EPW), the other two (U.S. Army) make it to us. One we take straight back to the OR; he has a big hole in his neck, behind his jaw, blood pouring out of it. Not a good place, extremely hard to get to surgically. John and I get on with it. During the case, at one point I had my finger in the guy's mouth pushing from the inside, and another on the hole pushing from the outside, to get the bleeding controlled enough for John to work around my fingers. Twelve units of blood total, including two from the walking blood bank. Ended up being jugular vein and internal carotid artery at the base of the skull, one of the hardest places in the body to get to. Earned our pay on that one. By this time, the helos are flying again and we ship him off to the CSH in Baghdad.

In the meantime, Joe has already sent off the other soldier to Baghdad for a chest CT. As we were finishing up our case, a small convoy had pulled up and disgorged three injured SEALs. They were driving in convoy when an IED went off under their vehicle. One has a broken leg (Joe and Bob are taking him to the OR), another has lots of frags to his right leg, and the third has an arm burn. John and I take the frag guy; it takes about 30 minutes in the OR. Pulled about a half pound of metal in bits out of his leg, but he'll be okay.

By the time we are done, a bevy of other SEALs has shown up, including their CO, a LCDR. I give them the rundown on the injuries; they talk to their guys post-op. The SEAL Team Seven CO asks if there is anything they can do to expedite getting their guys moved along to wherever they need to go next. I tell him that if he really wants to do something to get his folks out of here early, he should pray to the weather gods.

I get to bed around 0300.

Tuesday: TQ Day 119.

It's midnight as I write this; it's been another busy day. Started out getting up at 0830 or so, for no particular reason. Greg, Jeff, Eileen, and I went over to Lakeside in the new (but old) king cab pickup truck we have been assigned. We took the scenic route, down by the lake, and took our picture with the only palm tree around. How nice! Greg and Jeff got their hair cut, Eileen shopped, and I wandered around.

Then we went to my real objective, the coffee shop. The "Black Sheep" t-shirts they had ordered have arrived, so I bought one, of course. You'll like it. Headed back around noon-ish. I dropped them off at the chow hall, and then went over to the Texans for some officialish business, the Army awards...

I get back to the hootch right at 1400, having also picked up the big box you sent me. Birthday stuff, I assume. Go run, and then sit around. At 1615, just as I'm getting ready to go shower, we hear that we have incoming casualties. It turns out to be quite tragic.

An Iraqi family has been hit by a VBIED (vehicle-based improvised explosive device, i.e., a car bomb). What makes this worse is that they were then shot at, too. We are brought five girls, all siblings, ages 2 (twins), 11, 16 and 17. The oldest sister and her husband were killed in the blast. The 17-year-old has a hole in her scalp; she is intubated and sent on for a head CT. The 2-year-old twins arrive near-dead, and quickly expire. Looking at their wounds, it looks like they were shot in the back of the head.

While we are working on these four (the fifth was uninjured), we hear five booms in rapid succession. Lovely, incoming fire. We then hear that we will be getting two Marine casualties from CLR 25 (i.e., our parent Marine unit)—the rounds had hit in Lakeside. But they aren't serious and won't be coming for a bit until the EODs check for UXO on the road. Eventually they arrive around 1900, six total, two needing washouts of wounds in the OR, but none too serious. Four can go back to work, their Purple Hearts will be in the mail.

Finally get all of this taken care of by 2100. Dinner has passed but they brought us chicken and rice from the chow hall.

Wednesday: TQ Day 120.

The usual Wednesday morning biweekly intel brief. The natives have been very restless lately. Lots of insurgents killing Iraqis. The rockets yesterday were big ones, 122mm; they haven't used those in months. And other great news, classified of course (ooooo)...

Friday: TQ Day 122.

Went to sleep at midnight. Back up at 0105 for an incoming patient. We learn it is an Iraqi kid with a GSW to the finger. Okay, how does this meet criteria for "life and limb?" At about 0130, I go to the COC to answer a phone call, it's from some admin weenie at MSOC (Medical Something Ops Ctr), the guys who are supposed to handle our Medevac stuff. He asks me if I will approve bringing the kid onto the base. Huh? Shouldn't this call have come before they woke up 50 people? So I ask what exactly the kid's injuries are, he can't tell me. Well, can I talk to someone who can? Okay, they will have the ECP medic call me. I wait, and wait. No call. I call the Texans' HQ on the radio — it turns out that the ECPs do not have telephones; they only have radios, on a different net from ours. So I call MSOC back, which is manned 24/7, but they don't answer the phone. Back outside to wait.

Around 0200, two armored humvees pull up and they take the kid out. He's about 8 years old, shot through the side of his left index finger — devastating, not. I have a quick talk with the Army staff sergeant, whom it turns out I know. The kid shot himself in the finger handling his uncle's AK-47. They are from Karbani, same village I went to earlier, about as "good guy" as Iraqis get around here. The Muqtar (village headman) himself drove the kid and his uncle up to the ECP and flashed the lights, the signal that he had told Civil Affairs they would use if they needed help. Of course, the ECP did not know this and didn't know what to make of it. Eventually, the QRF (Quick Reaction Force) went out, and got the story. Civil Affairs told them to bring him through. The bottom line: the kid needed to be seen for political, if not medical, reasons.

Anyway, we have a large number of disgruntled, sleepy people at the SSTP. I sent most of them back to bed. Wash the kid's finger out in the OR, the bone is nicked but not broken, give the uncle instructions on what to do next, and they go back out on their merry way. Back to bed around 0400.

Friday: TQ Day 129.

Earlier day than planned. Up at 0130 for two U.S. casualties, fragged by IEDs. John has the point, he heads back to the OR with the first guy with Joe; I look at the 2nd guy, who ends up needing nothing surgical. I then go to the OR to see what is going on. The guy has lots of frag wounds, he's already asleep, they are shooting films, and John is planning to operate on him to clean him up. I look him over briefly and ask him about the head wound — a laceration, he tells me. So I put the "probing finger of death" in the wound, feel bone and something suspiciously like metal sticking out of it — open skull fracture with underlying brain injury until proven otherwise. That ends any thought of a case. He's shipped to Balad for an urgent head CT (no point washing his wounds if we miss a brain injury). We learn later that he had a small subdural haematoma there (blood on his brain), that did not get an operation. Still, the Old Trauma Surgeon was right, a brain injury. Sometimes I think that the inclination to jump straight in and operate on what we see is in pretty much every surgeon. Me, I like to play pessimist and worry about what we can't see and could be worse. Pessimists are never disappointed.

Back to bed at 0330. Up at 0500. It's going to be a long day; Greg has a road trip planned for us. He picks us up in the "bread truck," a big cargo van, and drives us to the other side of the base where we meet up with the MP convoy. Greg and his roomie, another Marine reserve LtCol, will have the first and last humvees as they know where we are going. The three of us, and a couple of other officers, will ride in the back of a 7-ton, the other enlisted shooters will be in another 7-ton. All vehicles have machine guns. Not much of a view from the back of an uparmored 7-ton with the canvas on it, but we don't want anyone to see what's in the vehicles (personnel vehicles are more likely to be targeted). Head out after 0600.

We get to Camp Habbaniyah after the 30 second ride of death again, and then tool around a while longer to get to the classroom. We pile out and go inside.

The guys teaching us are a specially selected group of Marines who are weapons experts. They spend most of their time teaching Iraqis, some of whom spent 10 years in the Iraqi Army but never learned to sight in or clean their weapons. No wonder we ran over them taking over Iraq. They are tickled to be teaching folks who speak English, and we will be getting a 6-day class in one day. Besides the lack of interpretation delays, almost everyone in the room already knows how to use an M16, knows the safety rules, knows how to sight weapons, and so on, so a lot of the basics we won't have to do. Except for the three medical folks, of course, but Greg has been drilling us with pistol stuff and the instructors know that we are "special." And while I'm no Marine, I'm also not a novice and know how to work an AK-47. Hobbies come in handy, sometimes.

I meet the senior instructor/unit CO, a CW05 (Chief Warrant Officer). This guy is a Vietnam vet, and the senior "gunner" in the Marine Corps. Warrant officers are former senior enlisteds who are technical experts and then commissioned as officers. I think they have to have at least 10 years' service, most have far more. By tradition (British Army, of course, up until the Cardwellian reforms of 1870–1872), officers used to purchase their commissions, so your rank was determined by what you could afford, and military retirement was to a large extent what you sold your commission for when you left the service. Of course, in this system, technical and military expertise was irrelevant, so a special group of technical experts was required to ensure the day-to-day functioning of the system (artillerymen, engineers, paymasters, and so on). Hence, some enlisted personnel were made officers by Royal Warrant; they did not purchase their commissions like everyone else. They were technically junior to all other officers and could only command in their own special areas. In the modern U.S. military (Army, Navy, Marine Corps and Coast Guard, not AF), warrant officers still exist. Unlike many senior enlisteds that I have met before, I have never met a CWO (there are, oddly enough, no "Warrant Officers," they are all Chief WO) who was not a good leader and soldier; they all know how to get the job done.

Now, part two of the history lesson. CWOs in the Navy and Marine Corps have traditionally been known as "gunners" (NOT "gunny"—that's a different Marine rank), because they were all originally experts in artillery and ordnance. If you think about the relative low-techness of the military until the end of the 19th century, this makes sense; there really was no technical branch to the services outside of engineering and artillery. And, unlike the infantry or cavalry arms, the engineers had always attracted the few technologically inclined officers, so they had never needed CWOs. Hence "gunner," denoting what they did. As technology improved, the need came for people who knew how to handle communications, mechanical maintenance, and so on, and eventually computers, electronics, logistics. But most people still called CWOs "gunner." HOWEVER, artillery/ordnance CWOs are really the only true "gunners" in the military, and they will never call another CWO "gunner" unless they are true gunners. So if I talk to more than one CWO at a time, I always make sure that I know if one is a true gunner or not — that way, the real one is called "gunner" and the other, "Chief Warrant." And in the Marines this is easy to figure out because the true gunners have a rank insignia on one collar and a "bursting bomb" (little round bomb with a flame coming out the top, representing the first medieval grenades) on the other.

As you know, I love this sort of stuff, and it's one of the things I like about the military — I can combine my love of trivia and work.

We spend two hours in the classroom learning how to strip and reassemble the AK-47 (assault rifle), RPK (light machine-gun version of AK-47), and PKC (medium machine gun). These things are, while crude compared to U.S. and Western European weapons, beautiful in their simplicity. The AK-47 has eight moving parts; the RPK is identical except that it has a longer, heavier barrel for accuracy, a bipod for stability, and a switch that allows for barrel change when it is too hot. So much simpler than what we use, and almost as good.

After this, back in the trucks and off to the range. This is way off to one end of the base, facing open desert. So no greenery or scenery for us today. The range is a 300 meter dirt lot surrounded by berms. We get out and practice all sorts of dry-fire drills. These guys are like Greg who will keep telling you that shooting is 99 percent mental; you need to do most of your training before you ever put ammo in the weapon. Then we break into two groups and take turns on the range.

First, we all zero our weapons from 25 meters. We fire groups of three aimed shots, then inspect the targets, then three more, and so on until the groups are tight and centered. I have never fired an AK-47 before and we are doing this prone, and of course my helmet keeps slipping over my eyes. So my first three shots are interesting. Two are an extremely tight pair, too high but centered; the third is way high, as I fired right when my helmet fell down. The second group is nice, still slightly high. But close enough for this. I'm done. I look around, and am surprised that I have one of the best groups out here. Greg, of course, is kicking ass.

By now, it's lunchtime, but we have options. Go to the chow hall, or shoot Russian automatic weapons. Hmmm, let me think about that one for a minute. So I spend another 90 minutes in the middle of a dust storm (authentic, huh?) with five others doing close-quarter drills on targets at 5 to 15 meters. We are not here to do marksmanship stuff, we are here to do rapid-fire stuff like you would have to do in an urban environment, and that is what we practice. Stand on a line, weapon down but ready. The instructor yells out what we are going to do and then blows a whistle, and we do it. "Controlled pair" — bring up weapon, sight rapidly (sight over center of mass, i.e., chest), fire two shots, bringing sight back over center of mass each time. "Hammered pair" — sight once, fire twice, good body position and weapon control should allow the second shot to be close to the first. "Failure to stop" — hammered pair to chest, one to head, the way to stop a guy who won't stop otherwise. So a lot of quick firing, practicing body position, rapid sighting, and so on. After the first 30 rounds, we go look at our targets. Gunner walks down the line looking at targets (full size silhouettes with a three-inch box in the head and a twelve-inch circle in the chest). "Good shooting, doc," and he walks on. Later, Greg tells me that, for Gunner, this is high praise indeed. I had one shot outside the circle in the chest, and the head was shredded.

Do this stuff a few more times, it was a hoot. Then everyone else gets back from lunch and we go back to alternating two groups. Lots more of what I had already been doing, and again, I seem to be doing very well compared to most others. Greg is still kicking ass, he's the only one on the line better than me, overall. I say this not to brag (too much), but because I was a little surprised that the Marines weren't better. They were good, but not great. Later, though, I am standing next to a Marine MP and, even though we are doing rapid shots at 15 meters (we should be able to raise the weapon, flip off the safety, and take two quick shots at the chest in less than a second), this kid puts all of his shots through the head, not the chest. Damn fine shooting, and he was funny to watch when I made a big deal of it and shook his hand. "Corporal, that's just showing off..."

After this, we get to play with the machine guns. I have fired the SAW (Squad Automatic Weapon) before, this is the light machine gun equivalent of the M16, it fires the same ammo, but the SAW is very different from the M16. The RPK, however, looks just like a longer AK-47, is a little heavier for stability, strips the same way, works exactly the same way. And fires the same way. I have to admit, overall, I like firing the AK-47 and the RPK more than

Zsolt the Birthday Boy, walking downrange with an AK-47 and a stuff-eating grin. My Marine buddy, Greg, had invited me for a day at the firing range on the Iraqi Army base, a rare but welcome escape from surgical duties. Greg only learned later that it was actually my birthday, which made it even cooler.

the M16 and SAW. They are simple, reliable, and easy to fix and unjam. Like trauma surgery, they may not be pretty but they get the job done. We fire prone at 50 and 100 meters, fully automatic, 4- to 8-round bursts, then go look at the targets. I do really well at 50 meters, about ¾ of the rounds are in the torso circle. Still pretty well at 100 meters, again, better than most of the Marines. Gunner comes by again and renders his opinion. Shannon, who had never fired a rifle before today, and a pistol only twice, has hit the target about 6 times with the first 90 rounds; Eileen, maybe 25. My target looks like Swiss cheese. "You ladies can provide suppressive fire (keeps the enemies' heads down); Doc, you can come on my missions." Cool, man.

We pack up and head out a little after 1700. I have spent 7 hours shooting, dunno how many hundreds or thousands of rounds, and it was a lot of fun. Happy Birthday to me!

We get back around 1820, having missed nothing at the SSTP. Eileen and I go to the COC to check back in, and Eileen gets some snide comment about where she has been. No one has the nerve to say this to me. Eileen had told me yesterday that the Chief had actually told her that she should not be going out and doing things like this, "Think of your husband and family," that sort of crap. Eileen is married to a retired SEAL so that did not sit well with her, as she had been on the other end of this for years while he was out on missions.

Eat dinner, call you, shower (I am positively filthy), and go over to Greg's for the celebratory near-beer. I thank him for my birthday present, thus making him the only one here who knows it was my birthday today. He thinks that is great, since he had really set this up for me; the girls were along because they have worked hard and shown an interest.

Get an e-mail from my Department Head back at Portsmouth, saying that because the GWOT is increasing the military divorce rate, he needs an assurance from me (or better, you) that I won't get divorced if I extend. I tell him that, after 22 years, 7 moves, medical school, residency, 9 deployments, fellowship, and now this, it'll take more that a few rockets to get us apart. Besides, we had planned on a year anyway. I volunteered for Iraq, and you figured out a long time ago that you married an idiot. We'll see if that reassures him enough.

Finally get to bed at 2300. Back out of bed at 2314, incoming casualty. An interesting case, actually. RPG frag that entered the middle of the neck, right below the Adam's apple, and ended up under the opposite collar bone. So we explore the neck, find that the top of the windpipe (crichoid cartilage) is lacerated, fix that and give the guy a tracheostomy. Back to bed at 0230.

Sunday: TQ Day 131.

Up at 0930, check e-mail. Discover that Moof (our aging Rhodesian Ridgeback) has gone, on my birthday. At least that will be easy to remember. I knew it would happen, he'd been sick and immunosuppressed for a while, but I had somehow hoped that he would last until I could get home to see him one more time. Maybe it's better this way, at least for me. I get to remember him when he was still healthy and all "Moofy." At least he didn't linger — you did the right thing with him when his leg became infected. Sudden is sometimes better, and you had been giving him lots of trips to run around in the field and plenty of attention. Still, I would have liked to be there for you, too. I hope Geena (our German Shepard) is okay.

I had reserved the SUV from 1030 to 1330 today, figuring I would get a few people and go to the coffee shop, sightseeing, that sort of thing. Well, I decided that I didn't really want company so I just headed out on my own. Drove all the way around the base, crawled into some old Iraqi dugouts. Went up into an Iraqi guard tower for a better view, and found a nest of pigeons, including babies, so that was nice. Drove around in the wadis down by the lake, poked around in the old bunkers and storage sheds. Drove by where the Bradley (tank) platoon is, chatted with them, and got to sit inside and get my picture taken. Then headed back. There are times when solitude is good.

After that, a long run. Dinner. Called you to talk about Moof. Then went to Greg's roof at 1930 for our weekly O call. A number of loud booms off in Habbaniyah, but no work for us. I left at 2100 to do some e-mail and work on another abstract to submit to the trauma surgery meeting, if I can get the data together in time. Having things to do is good.

Wish I was home with you and Geena.

Tuesday: TQ Day 133.

I'm awakened at the crack of 0830 by one of the base GMOs who comes knocking on the door; he wants my opinion on butt pus (perirectal abscess). I'm against it, of course, anything else? He says the patient will be back at his BAS at 1330, I'll see him then. Back to sleep until 1030.

The butt pus was a joy to behold, made my day. Another save. I exorcise the butt pus demons from my soul by running and doing weights. A little before dinner, around 1630, I get a call from the BAS at Camp Manhattan that they have a guy with appendicitis, I tell them to send him over, and then go eat because he will be there in "a few minutes." He arrives at 1845, a civilian contractor. Yup, it's a few minutes to drive over here, but first you have to get the armored convoy set up...

I had promised Carmen a while back that she could help me with my next appy (actually, this is the first one that I have done here). So the Czech South African has his appendix taken out by the Hungarian New Zealand American surgeon, assisted by his Cuban Spanish American nurse. Quite the war we have here.

Wednesday: TQ Day 134.

Long intel brief this morning, lots of things have been blowing up in the past week. We did not see much of it, though, as there were few U.S. casualties. Lots of Iraqi policemen targeted.

The usual 5-mile run. As we are sitting down for dinner, we hear that there are casualties coming in, two U.S. Thirty minutes, so we finish eating and head over. First guy has a lot of holes in his legs and goes straight to the OR with Joe and Bob, the second has a couple only and can wait. We then hear that two more are coming in, including an Iraqi with a GSW to the chest. That usually is very, very bad so we get ready to crack a chest. When they arrive, John takes the Iraqi straight back and I look at the soldier — turns out that he shot the Iraqi when he wouldn't stop running towards their outpost, and then he got hit himself by a ricochet. He has a few minor frag holes, nothing that needs an operation. I go see what John is up to, and it turns out to be a cool case. GSW into thigh, ends up in belly. Take out a few feet of small bowel (I get to show John a really fast way to do this), look at all the big blood vessels in the thigh and belly, a nice anatomy lesson. The guy should do okay.

Afterwards, it's about 2130. I check e-mail and get good and bad news at the same time. The Hospital looks like it will approve my extension. Yes, it's what I wanted, but I was also secretly hoping that they would say no, so I could come home to you, instead. I really do miss you so much, and the puppy (now singular, unfortunately). But it's what I asked for, and I feel that somehow I need to do this. I spent years saying this is what I want, now I feel like I need to do it for as long as I can, to either prove that it is what I want to do, or to get it out of my system and get over it. So good and bad news.

6. July 2005:
"The guy is full of holes..."

Friday, July 1, 2005: TQ Day 136.

Run for 5 miles, it's hot and windy and I'm kinda tired, but it's good for me. Stop by the Texans and drop off t-shirts (the new "TQ Surgical" t-shirts have arrived and I had bought some for our friends). And one for the medic who saved that kid with the frag through his subclavian, too. It turns out that he will be getting his CMB (Combat Medic Badge) at an awards ceremony on Monday (July 4th) and he wants me to pin it onto him. Cool! Guess someone out here appreciates me, even if the Navy doesn't (sniff, sniff, wipe tear away with corner of hankie).

Get back, sit around drinking Gatorade outside, reading. I am slowly metamorphosing into a lizard; I sit outside in the sun, basking on my rock. Well, on a chair in the gravel, which is lots of little rocks. At 1430, we hear a strange boom. Doesn't sound like the usual incoming, though, kinda flat like someone had dropped something really big. Still, a couple of minutes later the Big Voice goes off. Jeff and I go back into the hootch, put on our battle rattle, and go back to reading. I call us in on the radio for accountability and, as usual, they can't hear me. Three days they kept my radio to fix it and no change. I lie down and nap in the body armor. It briefly flashes through my mind that I look like a modern knight on his tomb, in effigy, lying on his back in his armor. Oooo, I hope not...

Monday: TQ Day 139.

Around 2000, on Greg's roof... We discuss a "brewing" situation. Combat Outpost in Ramadi had called us about a couple of people, a brother and sister (adults), who had been beaten up by some locals who supply insurgents. Rumor is that they had also killed their father. They do not appear to need additional medical care, but are afraid that, if the U.S. forces release them, they will be killed. When I had first heard about this from the boss, my reaction was that they need protective custody, not medical care. So if they are brought here, what do we do with them — same problem, but they are even further from home. In addition, if they are brought here under the pretext of medical care, then our counterintelligence guys are not allowed to talk to them to find out what is going on

(CENTCOM regulation). That makes it even harder to help them. Finally, my guess is that this is not the first time that "good" Iraqis have been beaten up by "bad" Iraqis; what was done the last 500 times this occurred? They need help, but pretending to do it as medical care may not be the best move. Greg agrees, this is a civil affairs/Intel issue and bringing them to medical will tie their hands somewhat. Greg actually found out about it right after I did and kicked it up to the head shed (the General's staff) pretty quickly.

We watch some fireworks over Habbaniyah, including a very big boom followed by a big red parachute flare, suggesting an IED and a distress call. About 15 minutes later, we hear of an incoming casualty. It turns out to be a 9-year-old Iraqi boy, shot in the chest. The secondhand story is that the Army shot him after he fired an RPG, but this is unclear. Anyway, he is intubated, has a chest tube which is putting out a slow but steady amount of blood, and the trajectory of the bullet comes mighty close to some really big vessels in his chest. But his vitals respond to the blood, and he is on the fence for an operation: will he slow down and stop, or will he continue to bleed and require an operation? Elsewhere, I would CT him and see if he has a major vascular injury, this could all be lung bleeding which typically stops on its own. With some misgivings, I decide to send him onwards to Baghdad; he seems stable enough for the ride. Hope he is lucky and needs no surgery. If he does, it may be a bloodbath. He is on the helo around 2200.

Happy Birthday, America.

Tuesday: TQ Day 140.

Another day in paradise. I am up at 10-ish, make coffee. Greg comes by to pick me up at 1100; I had promised to help him do some cleaning today. He has a number of conex boxes (shipping containers) that belong to Civil Affairs over on Lakeside that he needs to clean out. But first we eat lunch, a rare treat for me. Afterwards, we go over and get mighty dusty, sweeping and throwing trash in the back of his pickup. He then goes over to the warehouse to get some uniforms for folks in his unit who are in Fallujah. While I'm waiting, I wander over to a bombed-out building and find some old Iraqi training manuals, including a picture of soldiers showing how to wear chemical suits. Nice souvenir, just to remind me that there are no WMD in Iraq. While I'm rooting around, get a call that we have incoming. I get Greg and we head back.

It's an Army guy shot through the leg, or so we are told. He is completely stable. Has some odd wounds for GSWs, though, but maybe they were ricochets and so are not nice round holes. As third banana today, I don't get to operate. The guy will need his knee joint washed out, so John and Bob do it.

Wednesday: TQ Day 141.

Feel pretty good today, ran the full 5 miles at a good clip, plus the weights. I get back and check e-mail. My *JAMA* article on "Death and Life in Iraq" came out today, and when I check my e-mail, I have four from people who have read it already. One person said that she "bawled like a baby"; one retired Army colonel will read it at a poetry recital; all were unequivocally positive. That was pretty cool, to know that someone liked it. I forwarded them all to you so you could read them.

Thursday: TQ Day 142.

I run into Greg and ask for some help. Since he works in the Dark Tower, can he get us the scoop on what's really going on with the FMF ribbon. This is a cool, colorful ribbon that the Navy gives for being assigned to a Marine deploying unit for a year. In war, the 12 month rule is waived. You have to do various PQSs (Personnel Qualification Standards), i.e., get signatures much like I had to for the Surface Warfare thingy, and pass the Marine Physical Fitness Test (PFT). However, it was rubber-stamped and passed out to everyone who went with our predecessors and, by instruction, the regimental commander can waive the formal requirements for exemplary service. A shiny new FMF Warfare device is coming out which will make the FMF ribbon obsolete so it will no longer be available in 6 months. Everyone is spun up about getting the new warfare device, even though it is not yet officially available. The PQS for the device is the same as the ribbon, but no PFT is required. So I ask myself: "Gee. Didn't we know about the FMF ribbon six months ago, before we came out here? Couldn't we have been working on it for the last five months?

The obvious problem here is that we may not have time to do the device PQSs, which have to be taught to us by Marines, and then sit before a board, run by Marine officers. The CLR 25 guys are already in a dither over getting ready for the RIP (turnover), the last thing they want is to wet-nurse a bunch of Navy officers.

As we discuss this, a patient comes in. Iraqi contractor versus circular saw, sliced his thumb and across his hand. He may or may not lose the thumb, we'll see. I duck out to see a possible appendicitis patient (doesn't have it). When I stick my head back in the OR, John has already scrubbed with Bob and stolen the case from me. So I mock him royally as they wash it out and put wires through the bones to fix them in place. I then go do e-mail.

I finally manage to get the e-link for my *JAMA* article and save a copy, which I send to my old surgical mentor Norman and a few others. Also to my fellow surgeons, as a tribute to them. I suppose it will make the rounds, I wonder what people will say, if anything. I read it again, it's pretty good, but I would change a couple of things. Writers, never satisfied.

Saturday: TQ Day 144.

Started out as a usual Saturday. Out of bed in time for Grand Rounds at 0930. It is announced that Jeff has been selected for promotion, at last, three years late. Congrats. At 0940, we hear two casualties are en route, U.S. soldiers vs. IED, coming in from the field. End of Grand Rounds. Eventually they get to us, and are taken into the ER tents.

Joe is primary, I'm back-up. Since Joe has seen that they both appear to have head injuries and will therefore most likely have to fly right back out again, he decides not to take them to the OR. Me, I tend to take stuff to the OR anyway because, even if we don't operate, we have better equipment, better light, better access to emergency stuff that we may need. And I can chase people out more easily. But today, it's Joe's call.

Since Joe is looking at one guy out on the pad, I follow the other into the ER tent. He has lots of lacerations to his face, and the top of his head is wrapped up. The boss has this guy. He is awake, talking, answers questions, but prefers to lie on his side because it's easier for him to breathe. Bad sign, and on top of that, his face is swelling from blast burns. I tell the boss that he needs to be intubated. In the meantime, he's telling the corpsmen to take the bandages off his head. No sir, he needs to be intubated — airway before all else, just like we are taught in every course we ever take in medicine. If you unwrap his head, it may bleed all over the place, he may have more pain, why make things difficult? So I intubate him. I check out the rest of the patient quickly, nothing going on but his head, and then I take off the bandages. Big cut on his forehead, I see broken bone through it, but fortunately no brain sticking out. Still, it does not require the "probing finger of death" to figure this out. He needs a CT scan of his head and possibly a neuro-surgeon. We get to work packaging him. Of course, he gets his eyeballs ultrasounded...

I come back from checking his x-rays and ask what's going on with the second guy. He, too, has a head injury. Jeff has pointed out to Tom, who is running this one, that he needs to be intubated, too. He's tubed and a corpsman points out that his most recent blood pressure is 200/100, heart rate 55. Hmmm... Hypertension and bradycardia, signs of Cushing's reflex, which occurs with increased intracranial pressure (ICP). In other words, it suggests that he has a brain injury and has the potential to herniate (his brain squeezes out the bottom of his skull). Not much we can do for this but hyperventilate him and give him mannitol, a drug that sucks water out of the brain and temporarily reduces swelling — in other words, temporize until he can get to a CT and a neurosurgeon.

Sunday: TQ Day 145.

I'm up at 10-ish, make my coffee. Around 1100, we hear that there is a casualty coming in, one soldier from an IED blast...

What started out as one urgent patient, half an hour later has become two, less urgent, priority patients. I figure that they are dividing by fission like an amoeba, each new half-patient taking half the injuries and therefore becoming less urgent. I predict that more divisions may occur, and am not disappointed, when three patients actually arrive. One has a burst eardrum from the blast, otherwise nothing. The other two have holes in one arm each. The first one off the pad I look over while John looks at the second. John's guy has a bigger hole than mine, so his can go to the OR first, but they both sup-posedly have pulses (suggesting no arterial injury so they have blood flow).

Once the patient is actually moved to the OR, John discovers that the patient does not, in fact, have a pulse as reported in the ER. Which is why I always check for myself — I make surgical decisions based on my own findings, that way I can't blame anyone else for my mistakes. So we get to work. The frag has gone in below the elbow and ended up above it, on the other side of the arm. So the trajectory is right across the brachial artery, the only arterial supply to the forearm; it comes down from the shoulder and divides into two below the elbow, so it has to be fixed. We fillet his arm open from mid-forearm to mid-upper arm, get between all of the muscles, and dissect everything out. Amazingly, the frag has ripped through and essentially removed the brachial artery bifurcation. More amazingly, all three ends of severed arteries (the brachial, radial and ulnar, which meet in a Y) are not bleeding, the little muscles in their walls have spasmed off. It was so cool, we took pictures of it. We put in a temporary plastic shunt to connect the brachial and radial arteries and get blood flow restored (you only have to reattach the radial or the ulnar, not both, as they both go down to the forearm and hand). While I am finishing this, John is digging a vein for use as a graft from above the guy's ankle. But he is disappointed, it's way too small. I get him to open the vein, clamp it six inches up, and then inject saline under pressure into it. It balloons up nicely, and we have a graft. Yup, score another one for the old trauma surgeon... Actually, it was a trick I learned on my rotation at Arizona Heart; the cardiac surgeons there could use almost any size vein with this technique. So we get the graft out and sew it into place, and it is a thing of beauty. Clamps are off, he has a nice pulse in his wrist, and the arm is saved.

Thursday: TQ Day 149.

Happy Bastille Day. According to Norman, the party season in New Orleans officially ends on Bastille Day (it runs from Labor Day to Bastille Day, the summer is just too hot in 'Nawlins).

Up at 1000, make coffee. Stick my head outside and see that, well, I can't see. We are in the middle of a dust storm, visibility is about 50 meters, so no helos today. As I enjoy my second cup, the radio says that we are getting two EPWs from Combat Outpost, by ground. They had actually been there for over an hour but since the weather stayed bad and the helos weren't flying, they drove them instead, about thirty minutes. When they arrive, John immediately takes the first one to the OR with Joe; he's been shot high in the back and the bullet came out of his neck. I look at the second one, a nasty GSW to the right calf. The bullet hit bone, and the bone fragments blew a big hole out of his leg. Classic "secondary fragmentation" in action. I, of course, took some nice photos for lectures. I take him to the OR with Bob. Our psychiatrist happened to be around and asked if he could watch one of the cases. I had him scrub in with John; he had fun.

Neither has anything life-threatening and we are done around 1400. Jeff and I compare notes later and agree that people are getting very testy, especially when it is pointed out that they are doing things that they shouldn't be doing after being here this long (like putting IVs in an arm that has been shot).

After dinner, we had another pistol class with Greg at 1900. We practiced doing the USMC pistol qual by dry-fire. Have to whip out the pistol and fire, fire twice, fire, and change magazines and fire some more, all with various time limits and at varying distances. One more class and then the range next week; it should be fun.

Friday: TQ Day 150.

We're supposed to turn in our radios again this morning at 0800 to be re-encrypted (and mine is supposed to be entirely reprogrammed to send with more power). In a daring act of civil (well, military) disobedience, I barely hear it and go right back to sleep. Jeff takes it up for me, instead. I get out of bed at 1100, retrieve my radio which, surprisingly, works no better than before! Do assorted chores, put away laundry, clean my pistol until the scheduled test of the Big Voice at 1400, after which I run.

When I get back from running, I learn that today was a Black Flag day; i.e., due to the temperature and humidity (up to 42 percent today), "All unnecessary outdoor physical activity on the base will halt." Good thing I didn't know about it before I ran, I might have hurt myself. Or something.

Thursday: TQ Day 156.

Up at 0500; eat breakfast since it will be a busy day at the range. Everyone's ready (Eileen, Shannon, Jeff and Greg), so we pick up our stuff and head to Greg's to drive out in his king cab pickup.

We arrive at about 0620, the Marines are already there. We then start shooting. From 0630 to 1330, about 400 rounds total. Do a lot of practice drills, quick fires, and so on. Then we run through the USMC pistol qual as a practice run. At the 7 yard line, we do 5 single shots: raise the pistol, off safe, fire a double action shot (trigger pulls hammer back and releases it, i.e., not pre-cocked), put safe back on, and pistol down. Timed, the shot must be fired in less than 3 seconds. As you remember from our .22 pistol, double action is a lot harder to squeeze off than single action. I kicked ass on that. Then 4 pairs of shots: raise pistol, off safe, fire one double action (this recocks the pistol), then single action, on safety, back down. Timed, 4 seconds for the pair. Kicked ass again. Back to the 15 yard line. This time, we load two mags with three rounds each. Raise the weapon, fire double and then two single action shots, change mag, fire three more single action shots. Timed, 20 seconds. I really blew that one away. Then we move to the 25 yard line. This time, we have 10 minutes to fire 15 single action shots, pure accuracy. I take my time, relax, fire about one every thirty seconds. Feels good. Walk up to the target, since I can't see it well from 25 yards — where did all the bullets go? Really, really bad. I had shot mostly 9s and 10s on the 7 and 15 yard lines, but did absolutely dreadfully on the 25 yard line. Out of a total of 400 possible points (40 rounds, 10 points each), I would have scored 269. Enough to qualify as marksman, nowhere near the 345 required for expert. I was on track for the E before the 25 yard line.

Quite the conundrum, Greg and I spent some time trying to figure it out. It's something about the way I shoot; it's not the pistol or it would be consistently off at the shorter ranges too, just not as much. Do I need glasses? One difference, though, is that at the 7 and 15 I can see where I hit, at the 25 I can't, so I am blithely shooting away my 15 rounds (150 possible points), feeling pretty good, not adjusting anything I do like hand position or grip, because I don't know that I'm missing. When we go back again on Monday, Greg will bring binoculars. He had planned to but forgot.

After about 6 hours of shooting, with assorted breaks and training sessions, we are done with pistol for the day. Then, the surprise. The Marines have brought along a toy, the 240G — a medium machine gun. Guess who gets to shoot it? Yup, 200 rounds worth. I was lying on the ground, blazing away, right on it the Marines were telling me. They tell me that you should shoot in bursts of 8 to 10 rounds. This is timed by saying to yourself, "Die, motherfucker, die," as you fire. Whatever works.

I religiously clean my weapon and mags before dinner. At dinner, almost no one is there from the SSTP. Greg stops by to eat with us (he usually eats later but had missed lunch and, beanpole that he is, has a voracious appetite), and afterwards we (Jeff, John, Greg and I) go over to Greg's. We do some more pistol practice; I spend lots of time working on my grip. I think at the 25 I am squeezing with my whole hand instead of just my trigger finger so am shooting low and to the left. Greg gives John a half-hour pistol lesson, too. He still wants to teach the rest of the SSTP officers to shoot for their Marine Corps qualification. He's decided how he will do it: he will hold four one-hour pistol tutorials. Attendance of three will be required. When that is done, he will ask CLR25 to arrange for ammo and range time (it's their job, after all, to do this for us). Greg will then make the SSTP officers manufacture their own targets (cardboard silhouettes), and off to the range they will go. However many actually show up, that is.

Up at midnight for two U.S. casualties, their Humvee was run into by a tank. Some scrapes and cuts, nothing serious, although they were sent to us as "urgent surgical." Back to bed at 0100, read for an hour.

Saturday: TQ Day 158.

Up at 0400 for a casualty since I'm duty doc. It's a Marine driver of a 7-ton truck that fell on its side. The guy has a big bruise on his hip; he has, in fact, broken the left side of his pelvis. It's a nasty but stable fracture, and the accident actually occurred at 2100, 7 hours ago, on a convoy from Fallujah to here. They stopped to tip the truck back up again and continue on. But why must the simple things be complex?

I see the guy's x-ray and the broken pelvis, so I order a chest x-ray as well — I tell it directly to the HM2. He goes off to do it. I then hop over to the OR to tell them we won't be operating. While I'm gone, HM2 comes back in and tells the other x-ray techs that they are done and can go. What about the chest x-ray, they ask? "They [?] cancelled it," says he. Joe, who is standing there, tells him that "CDR Stockinger ordered the x-ray, if you are not going to do it, you'd better tell him." HM2 leaves. I get back to x-ray, where the boss is looking at the films. I ask if the chest is done yet, and he says that one wasn't done; the techs say that the HM2 said it wasn't needed. I send them back off to shoot the film and go and find out what's going on. I discover that he has gone back to bed, so I send someone to get his ass. Okay, now I'm a little pissed off. Mike has heard me send for him and asks me what the problem is. I don't think I need to explain it as it doesn't concern him and I'm pretty steamed, so I just tell him that it's about x-ray; it has nothing to do with him or supply issues. Mike says, "You know you can't kill him." "No Mike, I can't, but I can try to teach him the error of his ways. It's about time someone did."

Sunday: TQ Day 159.

At 0700, the call comes through that there are patients and vehicles on the pad. Roll out of bed, sneakers on, run up to the SSTP, I'm the first doc there. Two guys out of a Humvee, one with burns to his face. I take him to the ER tent and we start to work. He has a total of about 40 percent burns, on all areas (all four extremities, front, back, face.) It's the face that I'm the most worried about, he will need to be intubated. By now Jeff has arrived and I tell him what I need, while I keep looking him over. The guy is awake and doing well, but knowing big burns, he will get sick and unstable later, his lungs will get wet, and he'll need to be on the ventilator even if he did not have facial burns. I leave Jeff with him and look the other guy over.

More SSTP folks are arriving, and I go to look at the second guy. I finish making the rounds, it turns out we actually have five patients, all Marines. They are the guys who find and blow up IEDs; they were going to check one that an Army convoy had spotted. Apparently their Humvee ran over a landmine, was hit by an RPG also, and blew up. No deaths, but the burned patient was trapped for a few seconds before getting out. He is the worst off. One guy has a frag in his hand which will need a washout; another has a wire sticking out of the back of his leg, which I help a corpsman pull out; one has a piece of gravel behind the knee, also taken out in the tent, and the last seems okay but was knocked out and then acting goofy for a good half hour — he'll need a head CT. Bob takes the hand guy to the OR as the only case. I go back to see the burned guy.

Things calm down. We need to fly the burn patient out, but the helos can't fly, the viz is too low from the dust. So I set up the patient as our first "real ICU patient." I write proper ICU orders, we put various monitors on him, and I start monitoring urine output, play with the ventilator, and work out sedative drips. We then hear that we have a window to fly; he is put on a helo and away they go.

At about 0930, a Medical Corps Admiral comes by for an official visit. He specifically wants to meet with the surgeons, and we head into the new "conference room" that the Seabees had built for us on the back of the SSTP COC tent. (Yes, we build plywood shacks onto the backs of tents.) I am noticeably the only one in PT gear and not in uniform. John gives the usual quick slide show about what we've done, the Admiral spends a lot of time asking about the "en route care" thing, which as you know I think is highly overblown. I am then called out of the meeting by the Chief. The burn patient is back — the helo got a couple of miles, the dust closed in, they turned around. The Air Boss comes by. I tell him what's going on and that the guy will get a lot sicker in the next few hours. He says he'll work on getting us a C-130 cargo plane; they can fly in almost anything. I go back to the meeting, which is winding down. At one point I'm asked, as the trauma surgeon, whether I have any comments on whether we need anything or whether we should change anything.

Opposite, top: **The boys on Hesco Beach had box seats when the Arizona Cardinals cheerleaders came to town. The driving range was closed for the evening, but everyone got over it. The stage was a tractor-trailer, across the road in the background.** *Bottom*: **During a rocket attack there's not much to do besides put on your body armor, brew some coffee and work on a crossword puzzle while you wait for the "all clear"— or the call for incoming casualties.**

Everybody stares at me, I know that they're worried about what I might say. Things flash quickly through my mind — truth or consequences? Truth *and* consequences? Odds are that the O-7 will listen to the O-6s over me, and little will change. So I say two sentences: "We have pretty much all the equipment that we need if we are not going to be a Level III with a neurosurgeon and a CT scanner. Regarding personnel, we are pretty heavy all around, given our workload." And leave it at that. The Admiral has no additional questions or comments.

After dinner, another pistol class, just me and Jeff, the ladies do not appear. We then sit on Greg's roof, chatting after dark, when around 2100 we see a huge flash on the horizon, out towards Habbaniyah. Six seconds later, a very loud boom. At 300 meters/second, that's 1,800 meters, a little more than a mile. Probably someone attacking one of our OPs. Then several smaller, well-spaced flashes, 11 seconds (3,300 meters) away, which would be counterbattery fire from Habbaniyah at the bad guys. Then, out on our airfield, a big explosion with sparks flying a hundred feet into the air. That would be a rocket. We hit the deck — well, the roof — which is surrounded by a parapet, and about thirty seconds later the Big Voice goes off. Wow, I got to see my first rocket explosion. Sweet. We call the COC to let them know that we survived, and after about five minutes get back into our deckchairs to watch the fire engines zip by. And then zip back. There is no fire to put out, we assume. By 2200, no "all clear" but no more booms, so Jeff and I head back to the hootch. We need our sleep; it's up at 0500 tomorrow for another day on the pistol range.

Monday: TQ Day 160.

Up at 0500, breakfast, take our gear to Greg's. Off to the range. When we get there, the Marines are already there, setting up the targets, as planned. We start with some pistol drills. First, groups of three shots at 4 yards — should be able to put three rounds on paper that overlap each other, and I do pretty well at this. I'm happy. Back to the 25 yard line, where I'm not so happy. I am doing better than I was last week, but still not good enough to make me pleased, as I hit the black 10-ring only three out of 15 times. But almost everything else is close to it. A few more drills, then Greg has us "prequal," i.e., shoot the course without actually scoring. I know, however, that he is going to score us anyway, but it may take the pressure off the ladies, who were doing badly by the end of the day last week. We do the course. Perfect is 400, expert 350, sharpshooter 305, marksman (passing) is 245. Mike, who competes, gets a 350 out of 400. Jeff is disappointed at 303. Shannon gets a surprising 327, Eileen 313, and I pull 321. Oh well. Good thing I got "expert" on the Navy course; I still get to keep my medal. The Marines, some of whom have never fired a 9mm before, are all over the place, but they are not being officially scored.

We then do the course again, the Marines for real, us for fun. All of the Marines pass, one as expert. Mike, Shannon and Eileen's scores drop, Jeff's goes up to 351, mine goes up to 357. However, these were not official for us, as we had already qual'ed. Too bad. We then spend the next two hours doing various drills, the most entertaining being

Greg's "stress course," which we do one at a time. He demonstrates: from 50 yards back, you load your weapon with a 15 round mag with the safety on. Run to the 25 yard line, fire five shots, safety back on; run to the 15, another five rounds, safety back on; run to the 7 yard line, last 5, safety on and mag out. Time limit, one minute and 15 seconds. Greg does it in 55 seconds, scores 137 points out of 150 possible. Now the fun starts, because to "stress" us, as each of us runs along, he is yelling and screaming at us to distract us. I get to the 25, fire my shots and run. He is yelling "stop, stop" but I figure he is trying to distract me so I keep going. When I fire my next five at 15 yards, I see that he is still back at the 25. I only fired three rounds there. So I run back to the 25 (backwards, pointing my loaded weapon downrange at all times), do two more rounds, then up to the 7 yard line, and finish the mag off. Still did it in one minute five seconds, but only scored a lousy 64 points. Better than anyone else except Jeff, though, who got 101.

We learn from the Marines, who do the counterbattery radar and therefore track the incoming rockets, that the big flash we had seen last night was actually another rocket out by ECP 1. So we received two rounds of incoming yesterday.

We return to the hootch at around 1300, tired but happy. I stow my gear and weapon, get changed. At that moment, the call comes in, one incoming patient. I'm duty surgeon today. Run up to the SSTP. The report is an American soldier, shot in the neck, coming by helo. Twenty minutes later we hear that he is going to Balad instead, he needs a neurosurgeon. Okay. Ten minutes later, he is coming here again because he's unstable and can't make it to Balad, but he's now an Iraqi soldier. Eventually he arrives, completely stable. I take him straight back to the OR as is my habit and we look him over. He has a gunshot wound in one side of his neck and out the other, reported to be quadriplegic at the scene. So I know he's hosed. The bullet must have hit his spinal cord, nothing can be done about it. He needs a neck exploration, he probably has an esophageal injury also, but the neuro boys will probably want to repair or evaluate any sort of leaking spinal fluid he has, to minimize the risk of meningitis. I look at the guy's eyes, they are roaming around, but of course he is not moving anything—he is waking up from the intubation drugs he got at Ramadi Med, assuming that he's not awake already, so we sedate the hell out of him.

Since he is otherwise stable, we send him on his way again.

Am back in the hootch for another ten minutes when the radio goes off again, two more incoming, Iraqis with gunshot wounds. Back to the SSTP. We hear that one dies in transit, we wait for the second. The helo arrives and when the ambulance pulls up, they are both getting CPR. Litters off the ambulance, onto the pad. Make sure they are stripped and have no weapons, ordnance, or explosives on them. One guy has a big exit hole in his belly that I can see, but he also has a pulse I can feel. So he does not, in fact, need CPR—he's still alive. The second guy has blood pouring from the back of his chest, the fact that it is still coming out means that he's not empty yet, maybe some hope. I yell to Joe to take the belly guy to the ER tent and look him over; yell to John to get in the OR and get ready to open the chest. As soon as chest guy is searched, we go back to the OR.

When we get there, I do my thing, evaluating him rapidly. The guy is full of holes... He has a hole in the back of his left shoulder, pouring blood, into which I shove a pack and tell the medevac corpsman to put pressure on it. A hole in the left side of his neck, not bleeding but heading straight for the spine when I put my finger in it. An in-and-out hole in the front of his right thigh, also not bleeding. And he, too, has a pulse. So he is also alive.

Okay, everybody calm down now, he's not "almost dead." He will need surgery on his shoulder or chest (if I can figure out which blood vessel is bleeding in the chest), neck, and thigh. But we have a couple of minutes to plan. X-ray of his neck shows that the bullet went in fairly far back in his neck, and stayed on the back side of his spine, missing it. Lucky SOB. The odds are that the neck bullet hit nothing major. The thigh has no bleeding, I can stick my finger through the holes and the bullet path is superficial. He has a pulse in his foot, so no major vascular injury there, either. The chest x-ray is another issue, though. He was shot in the back of the left shoulder but the bullet, on x-ray, is lying over his heart. In his heart, for all I know. So it could have hit every major vascular structure in his chest on the way there. Great. And now the chest tube he came with is pouring out blood, too. John and I get to work, me as primary.

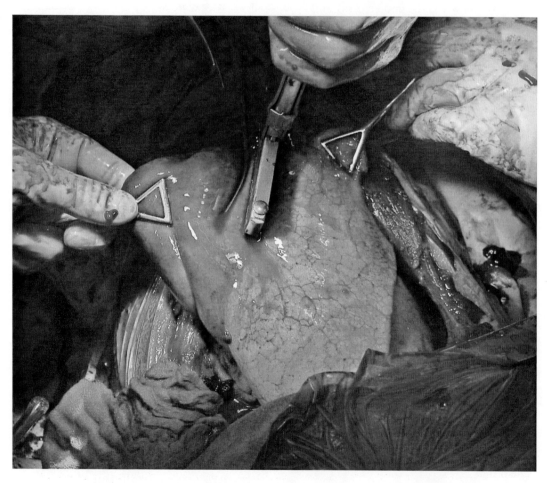

A portion of bleeding lung is rapidly removed with a surgical stapler. In trauma surgery, haste makes speed.

I split his sternum lengthwise to expose the heart and get control of the vessels going to the arm. When the sternum is retracted apart and I open the pericardial sac, what do I see but a bullet, bouncing up and down with each right atrial contraction. Again, lucky SOB, the bullet stopped in his heart muscle without making a hole in it. I remove it, and we move on. The pulmonary vessels are fine. Open the pleura (the membrane separating the heart cavity from the lung cavity) and find lots of blood. Suck out about 2 liters (half the blood volume of the average person) and find blood gushing from the hole in the back of his chest where the bullet came out of his shoulder. I stick my finger in the hole to control it and feel the corpsman's finger on the other side. Okay, the bleeding is slowed down but it's going to be a little tough for me to operate with only one hand. John suggests getting someone else to scrub, but I have a better idea. I get a urinary (bladder) catheter, which has an inflatable balloon on the end to stop it coming out. Wrap a lap pad around it, shove it in the hole, inflate the balloon and, voila! No more bleeding. So that problem is temporarily under control.

Take a few seconds to stop and consider what to do next. Quickly remove a chunk of lung the bullet went through that is leaking air, making it harder for Tim (my anesthesiologist) to ventilate the patient. Note that we are about twenty units of blood into the case so far. I had activated the walking blood bank earlier; this Iraqi contractor is now full of American blood. Looking at the bullet path, I decide that most of his bleeding is coming from the subclavian vessels, which run from the aorta in the middle of the chest, along the upper back inside of the chest wall, and into the arm. I start to dissect out the subclavian artery where it comes off the aorta, to clamp it and get the bleeding to slow down further (you can't sew a vessel while it is bleeding, you must get control of its blood supply first). As I dissect along, I find and explore a large haematoma, which turns out to be from the innominate vein, one of the biggest and most fragile veins in the body, which drains blood from the left arm and left side of the head back to the heart. It, too, has been lacerated, and as I expose it, it also bleeds like stink. Slap a clamp on it, sew up the hole. Bleeding stops.

Now I can actually get to where I can deal with the bleeding shoulder. I have isolated the presumed holes in the subclavian vessels by getting control of the artery that supplies blood to it from the aorta, and putting an incredibly tight blood pressure cuff on his arm. Sort of like standing on two ends of a hose with a hole in it, the water stops leaking out. The cuff also stops most of the venous blood going through the subclavian vein, which sits next to the artery, by preventing the blood draining back out of the arm into the heart. I make a long incision from his upper arm, across his chest to just below his collar bone, and dissect down to the subclavian vessels. The nerves surrounding it seem okay. The vein is completely destroyed, so I just tied the ends off (you do not take time to repair veins in people who are trying to die). I find the artery, which seems okay, take the clamp off and the pulse comes back into it. Artery is okay.

At this point, I happen to look up and notice that the Commanding General and his 2nd in Command are standing over by Tim at the head of the bed. Tim is just telling them that "the heart and lungs are under that blue towel" (I had covered it up to minimize heat loss). I say "howdy" and ask if they want the guided tour. They seem a little taken aback, and say that they don't want to interrupt. "Oh, no problem sirs, we're at the point where bleeding is down to a dull roar and Tim needs a little time to catch up with the transfusions." So I point out the vessels in the shoulder; then have them come up behind me as I remove the towel so they can look down into the chest while I move the heart and lung out of the way; and finally I show them where the bullet came through. We so totally rock, dude.

Time to reassess. Subclavian fixed. Innominate fixed. Heart fixed. Lung fixed. He is oozing all over, due to the massive blood transfusions he has received. In fact, he holds our record: 24 units of packed (stored) blood, 24 units of whole blood from our walking blood bank, 2 litres (4 units) of retransfused blood from the chest tubes, 18 liters of other fluids — 36 liters of blood and fluids in total, and the average person has 5 liters of blood. But he has no surgical bleeding, meaning bleeding that sutures or clamps will fix. We put in chest tubes to drain the inevitable blood that will collect in his chest, and I close the sternum. As I do so, he becomes harder to ventilate and, as expected, his belly is pretty big too, swelling from the fluid resuscitation. He has developed an abdominal compartment syndrome, where the bowels swell and fluid oozes into his belly, from the huge amount of fluid required to keep him alive. This pressure then pushes up in his diaphragm, giving his lungs less room to work. John and I quickly open the belly to relieve the pressure and sew a plastic IV bag over the hole in the abdomen, to keep the chitterlings in. We spend a little more time making sure that he's stable enough to transport — he is, of course, SAS (sick as ... snot) and will not be stable for a while, assuming that he lives.

Then off he goes on the helo to Baghdad. I hope he makes it.

Joe's guy, meanwhile, had a gunshot to the chest that went through the lung, into the belly, across the liver, and through the colon. Fairly straightforward, actually, and Joe was done in a couple of hours. But his guy had had trouble ventilating post-op, so in addition to handling my own bloodbath, I was doing consults for Joe's guy whenever he came into the room to ask for advice. As I was finishing up my guy, Joe took his patient to the OR to reopen his belly and look for anything else. He found two small bullet frag holes in the guy's diaphragm, which were blowing air into the belly. When they were closed up, the guy did better. He goes off to Baghdad after my guy.

In the meantime, as I had been finishing up the paperwork on my patient, another Iraqi GSW comes in, this time a stupid guy who tried to pass a convoy and was shot. He ignored the flares they threw at him, ignored the warning shots, and was shot. One through the leg, no major injury but a nasty wound. Bob and Phil, our PA, take him to the OR while I heckle and do the paperwork. A quick case.

I love days like today. Fun military stuff, fun surgical stuff. Bad for patients, good for me, but still...

Get back to the hootch around 2300, take off my nasty PT gear (the OR gowns are not, unfortunately, waterproof), and shower. The water is red, initially, and my sneakers have achieved a new height (or depth) in disgustingness. I decide to do one quick crossword puzzle before I retire for the night, to unwind. Ten minutes later, the radio: "There is a casualty on the flightline." I sprint up to the SSTP. It's a guy with heat cramps. We got 54 people out of bed for this...

Back to the hootch. Ten minutes after that, another call. Incoming U.S. casualty from Ramadi, no details. We all get back to the SSTP, and learn: heart attack. And they are bringing him here? Word of my cardiothoracic surgical skills seems to have gotten around; they are sending me a patient for a bypass already. Back to bed at 0230.

Wednesday: TQ Day 162.

Up for the usual 0800 Wednesday AOM, now mercifully down to once a week. I get to the SSTP a little early and check my e-mail, I discover from the trauma coordinator (nurse) at Baghdad that my "great case" from a couple of nights ago "was declared dead in the EMT [ER] at 2358," which would be about 25 minutes after he had arrived. I send off a reply asking if she could let me know who the surgeon was that saw him so I could "get a few more details." I don't want to ruin the good relationship we have with the Baghdad guys over a patient who would probably not have made it anyway, but I'd like to know what happened.

I stop off at the S-2 shop (Intel) and give their guy some, um, flak, about not showing up to do the Intel brief at our meeting. He overslept, they've been busy the last few nights. I tell him it's because he's been there, done that, and now that I gave him the official SSTP t-shirt there is no longer any incentive to come over. I con him out of an Iraqi Police poster that details their "rules of engagement," i.e., when they are allowed to shoot people. Which I am certain they will follow. They have a few spare posters since the last time they went to the local police stations they couldn't find any of the policemen. Hmmm...

Friday: TQ Day 164.

Jeff and I had planned to get up early, meet Greg, Shannon and Eileen, and do a Marine pre–PFT. I awaken at 0505, 5 minutes before the alarm goes off, and decide that Jeff needs to sleep in as a nice birthday present. So I turn off the alarm and go back to sleep. At 0540, the radio goes off, one incoming. It turns out that Jeff had done the same thing with his alarm clock.

The sun is barely up when the Army patient arrives, frags in his arm and leg from an IED. But since the sun is up, it's a new day, I am no longer duty doc and John steals the case. Doesn't really matter, as all four surgeons scrub on it and it's done in less than an hour.

After that, I run. It's about 0900, pretty damn early for me, and man! is it easy to run when it's only 90 degrees. I am done with PT by 1000. So now what do I do with the rest of my day? When I sleep until 1030, I PT at 1200, finish around 1400, cool off and read, shower and dinner at 1600, then patients roll in and I go to sleep again at 0200. But it's only 1000, what to do for the next six hours?

Jeff PTs and then opens his assorted birthday presents. He has received a "Party in a Box" from one of his gal pals. He's been e-mailing her for about six months, exchanged phone calls, they seem to get along very well. She's sent him all sorts of books to read, which he's been enjoying. So today she sends him this thing, and it's hysterical when he opens it. Confetti, a couple of books, jelly beans. But the really funny parts are: a horn to toot, a birthday balloon to blow up, and a snake that jumps out of a can on a spring. So, to summarize, this woman sent him a hooter, a latex product, and something that pops up when you play with it. Jeff could be in for quite the time when he gets home.

At 2000, go over to Greg's with Jeff for a rooftop birthday party. As we get there, the radios go off, an incoming EPW by ground, shot in the chest. Back we go.

A Humvee gun truck pull up on the pad; we drag a dead-looking EPW out of the back. There is blood all over the floor of the vehicle. John, who is primary, takes him straight back to the OR. As John gets ready to open the left chest to clamp the aorta and look at the heart, I put in a right chest tube. Chest is open, the left side is full of blood. The guy's heart is empty (he has no blood left). John works on clamping the aorta while Joe does manual cardiac massage. For exposure, I open the chest the rest of the way from left to right, so now we have the guy's chest propped up like the hood of a car, we can see everything. John gets some clamps on the bleeding lung. I get some suture and large bore IV tubing, and show John how to put in a right atrial line—to pump fluid directly into the heart. IV access doesn't get any better than that. But he's still dead. While John does the paperwork, I help the corpsmen sew up the chest to make it pretty. Then back to the rooftop.

Sunday: TQ Day 166.

I learn from the ER doc in Baghdad that my patient from last week was, in fact, seen by a surgeon but died in the ED. I'll see what info I can get from the surgeon.

Not much else happens for the rest of the day, until about 1900. I am called to the ACE (the helo squadron medical unit, right next door to us) to see a patient. Some U.S. EOD (bomb disposal) contractors on Camp Palladin, about 5 miles away, have brought in one of their Iraqi contractors with belly pain. While they have brought their Jordanian translator with them, it's still like practicing veterinary medicine: I can't talk to the patient, he can't talk to me, and the questions I ask are not answered. Example: "Is the pain worse now than it was yesterday?" Three minutes of back-and-forth between the patient and the interpreter. "He has to pee." However, I decide that he has appendicitis, based on the way he jumps when I push on where his appendix is. The contractors then tell me that they need to leave in the next twenty minutes; they have to get back to Palladin before dark. I try to get the interpreter to tell the patient that he needs an operation. Another several minutes of back-and-forth: "He says he feels better now and wants to leave." "Does he know he can die from this?" "Oh yes, but he is better now, and we must leave." I tell his boss that appendicitis does not get better by itself, and I expect that he will be back by tomorrow morning. They leave, I shake my head. Unfortunately, our own interpreter never showed up.

7. August 2005: The Probing Finger of Death

Monday, August 1: TQ Day 167.

We are supposed to be up at 0930 to turn in radios prior to our "5 month anniversary" scheduled for 1000; but at about 0800 I get a radio call. The PA from the ACE tells me that the appendicitis patient I saw last night, who left with his boss, is on his way back from Palladin. There's a surprise. At 0845, I am there seeing him and yes, he still has appendicitis, probably perforated by now. Now their Jordanian interpreter tells me that he does, in fact, want an operation. Oh goody.

Normally when I am on duty, the primary gas-passer is Tim, the nurse anesthetist. It's a new day, though. I am doing the case because it's my patient; but Jeff is the duty guy today. I get Jeff, especially since we live in the same hootch, and he's happy to do the case. In fact, he'd like to do it without having everyone else around, for a change. I feel pretty much the same way on my end; let's just do this with the minimum of fuss. We get into the OR around 0930 and get started. Oh, damn, we are operating during our monthly "attaboy" meeting, and we had *so* wanted to be there. I wonder how many sand-bags we filled in July?

As we do the case, Angel, one of the scrub techs, mentions that she doesn't like appies because we always get traumas coming in during the case. Today is no different. We hear of an Iraqi Special Forces guy, shot in the arm, coming from Combat Outpost. The appy is done just before he arrives, and John takes him straight back to the OR. A straightforward GSW, nothing spectacular, without a pulse in his hand. John and Joe get to work as I'm third banana today; but when they find the injury and John decides he needs to repair it with saphenous vein graft (yay!), I scrub to harvest the vein for him. It's a beautiful piece of vein, and I show Joe how to blow it up to make it nice and big. I hand it to John as we hear that two more patients are incoming, from Camp Manhattan across the street, from an IED blast. I scrub back out and take a look at them...

Not much goes on in the afternoon except that the power, which went out at 0800, did not come back on until 1700. A box of Thin Mint Girl Scout cookies Jeff had left out is now one large cookie-glob in the box.

At 1900, Greg has pistol class for all of those who now want to do pistol quals (i.e., have to do it for the Marine warfare pin). I wonder how many showed up?

Tuesday: TQ Day 168.

I'm up before 0800, for my 0830 "Warrior Transition Brief." Everyone returning to the States (going back for 2 weeks) must go through one of these — it's where the chaplain tells you that you shouldn't ax-murder the family when you get home. I'm sure that was on everyone's list. The great part is that he spends thirty minutes talking about "combat stress." Our shrinks tell us that the publicity about "combat stress" is half the problem: you tell people they are going to get it, they will. Most people will have some short-term adjustment issues, get over it, and move on. At the start, he asks, "Who here has been in combat." No one raises a hand; we're all REMFs (Rear Echelon Mother F...s). "Okay, who here has been outside of the wire?" I am the only one to raise my hand, since I have done it three times, twice being the 30 second ride of death to Camp Manhattan. "Okay, who here has seen someone seriously injured or killed?" Again, I am the only one to raise my hand. So now people who have not been in combat are given a thirty-minute lecture on how to deal with the combat stress that they have no reason to develop. Lots of people have issues when they get home from deployments, but that is NOT the same thing as "combat stress." If you fought with your wife or argued with your kids before you deployed, that won't have changed when you get back home. But they will all go home now, thinking that anytime they want to kick the dog, it's "combat stress-related," and if they turn dysfunctional later in life for any reason, it will be blamed on PTSD (post-traumatic stress disorder). Combat stress and PTSD are real, but not everything is combat stress.

At 1000, the SSTP officers have a mandatory "safety stand-down." First, we get a lecture on tactical vehicle safety, aimed at vehicle drivers. Great, except that officers are not allowed to drive tactical vehicles in the Marine Corp. Then we get a lecture on fire and electrical safety. Never, ever, daisy-chain electrical outlets together. Interesting, given that every hootch on base has a Hadji 220V power strip plugged into the wall outlet for the 220V fridge and AC, into which is then plugged a 220-to-110V transformer, into which is then plugged a 110V powerstrip so we can run our American appliances. Finally, a lecture on prevention of heat casualties. After which, I go run at noon in the "black flag" heat condition.

Did quite well with the PT today. I have 33:00 minutes to run 3 miles; I did it in 24:03, in black flag. I think I should be able to pass the Marine PRT on Thursday.

Wednesday: TQ Day 169.

Shortly after we are done with another FMF class around 1100, we hear of an incoming casualty, a GSW to the butt that came out the groin, with no pulse in the leg. As I walk up to the SSTP, I am already thinking about how I will approach this one: me and John will open the belly to control the iliac vessels from above, while Joe can open the groin to control the femoral vessels below, thus obtaining vascular control in half the time. However, shortly after arrival I learn that the patient is, in fact, going to the CSH in Baghdad over us. Stand down.

I spent about an hour chatting with a Marine Staff Sgt who had come looking for me earlier. Have never met this guy, but a surgical colleague, Karen (from Okinawa), had told him to look me up. They had been stationed in Rota together. We talked about various things. He is a reservist, a Marine recon, and he knew the six snipers who were killed a few days ago in Haditha, near Ramadi. We chat for a bit about that but I can't put it down here. "Top Secret" and all that. The fact that they were killed is not, though, since Jeff had read about it on "Yahoo! News" today. The SSgt is on his way home now, to Baton Rouge of all places, so of course he knows of the fabled Charity Hospital where I did my trauma surgery fellowship.

We then get another call, another inbound helo. Then we stand down again, it has no patient on board. Then yet another inbound helo, from Combat Outpost, a guy with frags to the face. When the ambulance pulls up on the pad, I take one look at his extremely messy face and take him straight back to the OR, over Tom's protests. The guy will need to be intubated to protect his airway, and that alone is reason enough to go to the OR in my book. While intubation can be done in the ER tent, if there is a problem there's more gear in the OR. On top of that, with his facial trauma, if he needs a surgical airway, the OR again is the place to do it.

So we bring the guy back. He's awake and lucid. As we come in, I announce that no one is dying, there is no emergency: we can talk to this guy, I will explain to him what is going on, we will intubate him, and then we will do the rest of his evaluation. Airway first. So Tim and Jeff get his history, and start an IV to push drugs. I talk to him, tell him what we're going to do, that he will be okay but we will have him go to sleep, and that he will wake up later in a different place. I check his vision, see that he has a hole in his right eye, and wave the OIC and his ultrasound away — later, sir (if at all). While they get ready to tube him, Tom is yanking at the guy's wedding ring, which is annoying the hell out of the patient. I tell him to stop — we can do that later, it's not important. This is why I try to get these patients into the OR; the ER people get into a frenzy about doing everything at once. There are times when that needs to be done; this is not one of them.

The guy goes off to sleep; the boss does the eyeball ultrasound and is happy. His face is badly cut up, and there are frag holes peppering most of the left side of his head. His left arm hurts. But the most serious things are the eye and the possible brain injury; so he will need an ophthalmologist, a head CT, and (hopefully not) a neurosurgeon. He is packaged and goes off.

Saturday: TQ Day 172.

Stop by the Texans, as is my habit, chat with Habeeb a bit since he's back from leave. He gives me an official Texas Army cigar; it has the unit logo on it and everything. Finish up the run, read a bit. As I am getting ready to shower, we hear of two incoming Army casualties, so off we go to the SSTP.

The word is that they were flying to Baghdad when one became unstable and they diverted here instead. As they come off the ambulance, I see that one has a GSW to his hand — he can wait — and the other is reported to have a bad blood pressure, so I take him straight back to the OR. He has a GSW below his ribs on the right. He has a chest tube in, and his chest x-ray from Ramadi shows bullet frags close to the hole. John helps me open him up and we find that, as far as getting shot goes, he's pretty lucky. The bullet actually came in under his diaphragm, so he did not in retrospect need the chest tube, but they can't be faulted for doing one based on the location of the hole. I would have done the same thing. The bullet has fragmented in his liver and stopped there. No other injuries except that his liver is shattered. But it's not bleeding too much; I'm pretty surprised given how cracked it is. Pack the hell out of it to stop the bleeding, wrap him up, and send him on to Baghdad. He will need the packs taken out in a day or two but should do okay in the long run.

Meanwhile, Bob and Joe have washed out the other guy's hand, and while they finish that up, I go shower. It's about 1715; the liver case took less than an hour all told, pretty good. Jeff and I head over to dinner. As we're getting up to leave (and I'm toying with going over to the Texas weekly BBQ), we hear of more casualties coming in. Back to the hootch, change back into PT gear, and off to work.

This time, the patients take almost an hour to get to us, by ground. We get two from a VBIED blast, and one from a different convoy also hit by an IED, with a frag in the groin. They all arrive about the same time so I triage them on the pad. The guy with the frag in his groin will need to go to the OR but is not bleeding. The two others have facial and head trauma and need to be intubated; one has a lot of facial lacs and burns so I take him back to the OR, in case we have an airway problem that requires my criching him. The guy is awake and talking, and Jeff intubates him quite handily. I then unwrap the field dressing from his head and see that he has a big divot out of his forehead with a readily palpable skull fracture. I could probably put my finger in his brain if I pushed hard enough, but the Probing Finger of Death has done enough. So he and the other head injury get packaged to go to Balad. In the meantime, John has come in to tell me that he is taking the groin guy to the OR; he has cut loose with bleeding.

I walk into the OR and see that the Phil clamp is in place. By that, I mean that Phil, our PA, is leaning with both hands over the wound, stopping the blood from squirting out. We get him prepped and go to work. Phil steps back, a big squirt of blood shoots out, and then my fat finger goes into the hole and stops it again. The Stockinger clamp replaces the Phil clamp. We get the femoral artery and vein controlled above and below where my finger is, and then look at the injuries, themselves. He has had a good length of his femoral artery and vein completely destroyed. In addition, the frag has passed on into his thigh, broken his femur, and torn lots of small arteries and veins deep in his thigh. John and I spend a fair amount of time getting all of this under control. Eventually, he has a temporary shunt in his artery, the vein is tied off, an ex fix is on the femur, and we have done fasciotomies (long incisions on his calf) to release the pressure from the swelling that occurs with return of blood. I toy with doing a primary repair of the artery but we have already used 24 units of blood (12 stored and 12 from the "walking blood bank"). This guy needs an ICU, and I need to send him while he's still transportable. So, to my regret, I do the right thing and send him to the CSH in Baghdad. Ah well. But I can say with pride that it's the only shunt I have done since I've been here; everything else I have repaired.

As I sit here, around midnight, e-mailing Baghdad about the latest case they are getting from us, my radio decides to unencrypt itself and start beeping. For whatever reason, the radios sometimes lose their encryption and become useless. Good thing I am in the hootch with two other radios.

Sunday: TQ Day 173.

Up at the crack of 1100. When I check e-mail, I discover that one of the Army surgeons has sent me a CT scan of my liver guy. It's the worst CT of a liver injury that he (or I, for that matter), have ever seen. Good thing the guy had the sense to not bleed too much from it. The femoral artery bloke did okay, too. I pick up my radio, which has been reencrypted, to discover that someone has stolen the belt clip off it. Nice.

I hear an interesting story about some of our casualties yesterday. Along with the guy shot in the liver, there was a guy shot in the hand. I had not seen him, being a little busy at the time. As the story goes, he's an Army Guardsman who had spent eight years on active duty with the Marines. He was in a patrol in Ramadi, and the sergeant leading the patrol was lost. Again. (Apparently he has a history of getting lost and denying it.) So the patrol stops in the middle of Ramadi and he gets out and starts walking around the Humvee, looking at a map. Another guy gets out with him. After a couple of minutes, some local finally realizes that they WANT to be shot at, and obliges. The other guy is shot in the liver, and the sergeant freaks. The former Marine jumps out, runs over to the injured man, starts yelling for a medic — they have at least two medics in an ambulance. The medics do not get out of the armored ambulance. He bangs his rifle butt against their door, they still refuse to get out. He yells at them to drive their ambulance over to where the wounded man is, about thirty yards away, and they move it about ten yards. The former Marine runs back to the guy, starts dragging him to the ambulance, when he, too, is shot. The bullet goes through his hand, through the butt of his rifle, and hits his SAPI plate (body armor), giving him a huge bruise. They put the liver guy into the back of the ambulance, the medics still not getting out of the vehicle, and finally head out. It took them as long as it did to get to us (no helos due to dust), because they really were lost and it took them a while to find their way back.

Monday: TQ Day 174.

Up at the ungodly hour of 0900. Drink coffee. Run. As I'm making the two-mile loop, the radio goes off: we need "100 percent accountability." Of course, when I call in, they don't hear me. So I call back in every couple of hundred meters until I get back to the SSTP. And as usual, the Chief acts like it's my fault that they can't hear me. "Sir, we fixed your radio last time." "Chief, you've fixed my radio six times already." "Sir, we replaced your radio last time." I show him the radio; it still has on it the old "Firestriker" call-sign sticker from our predecessors. "No, you didn't. S-6 (Marine comms) reencrypted it and reprogrammed the power output, and it still has the same problem. It has never been fixed successfully, and you have never replaced it. As long as I can hear base, I don't care, but YOU need to stop acting like the radio's malfunction is my fault. And I am NOT going to have this conversation with you again." I leave them my radio and walk off: "I expect you to find me and give it back to me when you are done with it." One of our ERC nurses who is supposedly our "Comms Officer" comes by the hootch later to talk about my radio problem. I tell him there is not much to talk about: fix it, replace it, or quit whining to me about it; this has been going on for six months. He tells me that they will get me a new one. Yeah, last time they took my radio for three days with that excuse, and still gave me back the same POS. I don't mind that the radio has problems; I mind that they act like it's my fault.

There's a rumor going around that, in addition to the pistol qual and the Marine PRT, we also have to do a 6-mile "hump" with backpacks, etc. Our Team is supposed to be gone in a month, CLR 25 still has no answers for how the FMF board will happen, but we have to do a 6-mile hump?

Tuesday: TQ Day 175.

Around 1600, a casualty comes in by ground from Camp Smitty, a new Marine base somewhere between here and Fallujah. Guy with frags in his neck from an IED. He comes off the Humvee talking and looks pretty good, but his neck is wrapped up, and the corpsman tells me that he has a hole in the very back of his neck. So, since this may very well be nonoperative, I let him go to the ER tent. Mistake.

After a quick look at him, I see that he does, in fact, have two largish holes and a haematoma on the left side of his neck. He will need a neck exploration. He is also complaining of left shoulder pain. Knowing how frantic they get in the ER, I stand close and watch everything. I tell them that after he has two IVs in and they shoot neck and chest x-rays, he will go to the OR. We can shoot shoulder films after he's asleep, since moving that shoulder causes him a lot of pain. I pop over to the OR to tell them the plan, and then come back in. They are finishing the last film; I walk over to Phil (the PA) and ask if his neck has been examined. Very important, since I will have to move his neck around to get it into position to operate on. Phil says he doesn't know. The patient answers, "No one has looked at my neck so far." So I palpate the back of the guy's neck, starting at the bottom, and he complains of excruciating pain in the midportion of his neck. Not good, and I stop. That answers that; he may not get operated on after all, at least, not here. If he has a broken neck, I don't want to be turning it for an operation and possibly giving him a spinal cord injury. I put a spine collar on him and we go to the OR.

Get into the OR and Mike wants to know what's going on, the guy has a collar on. "Is his neck clear?" "Definitely not." "But they said it was clear." "I uncleared it." I look at the films and see that he has a big fragment, I can't tell if it's a frag from the IED or broken bone, in the middle of his neck; but I am suspicious that we're looking at a fracture. This is most certainly not a "cleared" cervical spine. The safest thing to do is CT his neck before operating on him, so if he's stable he will need to fly. I go back and look him over; he has two big, and a couple of small, holes in the left side of his neck, a fair-sized haematoma, but no active bleeding. I tell the patient what is going on. He is intubated with full spine immobilization (normally the neck is extended for intubation). And away he goes.

In the hootch, Jeff asks me what happened, and then asks how I explained to the ER guys why I moved the patient to the OR to intubate him. I told him that I do not need to explain to anyone why I move my patient to the OR. But if they had wanted an explanation, it would have been easy: you just screwed up the neck exam on this patient, clearing him of a spine injury he may very well have, and now I should trust you to maintain spine precautions while you intubate the patient? I don't think so.

We get word two days later that the patient did, in fact, have a broken neck.

Wednesday: TQ Day 176.

A busy day today. At the AOM this morning, there is an issue. Our ERC nurse brings up what he perceived to be a problem yesterday. When my urgent patient with the hole in his neck was sent out, we sent out two other patients who had sat here for a couple of days due to bad weather (i.e., dust). The helos would fly for us for urgent cases, but we did not want to make them fly for post-ops who, while they should be going, can wait. In the OR, as we were packaging the guy, HM1 had come in and said that we could fly out all of our other patients on the same bird. Great, no problem, thinks I as the duty surgeon with the urgent patient. So they are packed up and chucked on the same ambulance, no more than a five minute delay. Well, our ERC nurse had issues with this. Why wasn't the ERC nurse consulted? What if something had happened? He already had one sick patient, what if another one had gotten sick? And so on, and so forth. Jeff pointed out that the patients added to the flight would not have gone with a nurse anyway, so the medevac corpsmen should be taking care of them.

Bob rolled another issue into this problem about the availability of "milk run" helos to fly patients out at night. Some nights the milk run is cancelled due to weather, because those patients are, by definition, routine (can wait 24 hours), and so they will only fly if the patient is urgent. But sometimes the milk run is cancelled because the squadron doesn't want to fly; they are busy or whatever (which is odd, coming from an Army helo squadron whose entire job is to do nothing but medevacs and, since they are unarmed, they usually fly at night anyway). So there are times when we might have to upgrade the status of patients we want to get out, from routine to priority or urgent, to make the helos fly. We always have to remember that for urgent patients, the birds fly lower, faster, and straighter, so the mission is more dangerous.

The discussion lasted for over half an hour; I tried really hard to stay out of it, but in the end I couldn't. So this was my take: we have two issues with helos. In the first, the issue is helo nonavailability, and we can force that issue by changing the patients' status. In that case, there is not a huge reason to add nonurgent patients to an urgent medevac. In the second, the issue is inability to fly due to weather, in which case the helo is a "lift of opportunity" and we should take advantage of it, if possible. That is the call of the physician whose patient is being urgently medevaced — if he thinks we can wait the extra minutes to load more people on the bird, do it. I was the surgeon of record yesterday, and I had no problem with it. The bottom line is that we will do what we can with the resources that we have.

After this, FMF class on radios. As we are ending the class, we hear that there are 5 Iraqi Special Forces (aren't they all?) patients coming in, at least three with GSWs to the abdomen. Sounds like a busy day ahead. We head over to the STP. Eventually they arrive. There are two straightforward GSWs to the belly, looking bad; one GSW to the butt that exited the penis (that was ugly); and one GSW to the flank, both stable. No fifth patient yet, but we hear that there is another on the way, shot in the back. We had three ORs ready to go; John and Joe have headed to the OR with the first two, leaving our suboptimal back-up OR left. Decision time. Both the remaining guys need operations, but have good vital signs. One more serious-sounding patient is on the way. If I take either of these two back and the last guy is crashing, he's SOL. If I wait until he gets here, one of the others may get worse. I decide to give each of them two units of blood and send them out. They are both over an hour out from their injuries and look like they can get by with an additional 30 minute flight. I turn to the nurses and the corpsmen and say, "Stop everything. I want both of these patients packaged and ready to get on the ambulance in three minutes, with two units apiece. Just do it." No arguments, it's done, and off they go, blood hanging. We'll see if I guessed right. (I did, they arrived fine.)

I go to the OR since I can scrub out when the 5th patient arrives. John has Bob with him on the first guy; Joe is closer to starting so I scrub with him. The bullet has traversed the liver (not as bad as my guy last week but bad enough). The bullet then completely transected the duodenum, the most difficult bowel injury to manage, and barely missed the kidney, nicking the ureter. We fix the various holes and pack the liver. The fifth patient is still not here yet, supposedly about ten minutes away. I suggest to Joe that he do the paperwork while I close (sew a plastic bag over his wound as he will need at least one more operation), and take a quick look around as I do so. He has a hole in his gallbladder, too. The hole was really small and tucked up under his liver so we hadn't noticed it. Out comes the gallbladder.

The fifth patient has arrived. An EPW with assorted bullet holes in his back, leg and arm. None seems to have hit anything major, though. So, in retrospect, I could have kept one of the other patients and sent the other. But better safe than sorry.

John's patient also had a hole in his liver but, otherwise, not much else. Interestingly enough, he has *situs inversus totalis*, meaning that all of his organs are reversed: heart, liver, everything is backwards. No big deal, except that being shot on the left side of his chest means that the bullet did not go through his heart as it normally would have, but did end up in his liver when it entered his abdomen. Pretty cool, hope he got some photos.

The two liver guys then get on the same helo and fly off. Twenty minutes later, we hear that one of them is "crashing" and they're coming back. (In reality, the helo had a mechanical problem and was coming back; but one of the patients was, in fact, doing badly.) The helo lands, one patient is transferred to another helo and leaves again, and the other is brought in straight back to the OR. A quick look at him, he has a pneumothorax (collapsed lung) on the right. Slap a chest tube into him, he instantly gets better, is repackaged, and shipped off again.

Around 2100, hear about an incoming patient. I get to the SSTP first, and field a call from Ramadi. Marine, hit by mortar, hole in the front of his belly with an exit in the back. Looks bad, coming our way. When they get here, there are actually two patients. John and Joe go straight back with the first, while I honcho the second. My guy is holding up his own IV bag, a good sign. I spend a few minutes quickly looking him over, and tell Tom what films to shoot. He will need wounds washed out but is okay, so I go back to the OR.

John has his chest open and is putting a clamp on the aorta. His heart is motionless. No bleeding from his chest. I suggest that he and Joe open the belly and pack it, while I do cardiac massage. I tell Mike to hit him with vasopressin, my favorite wonder drug — he does, and the heart starts to beat again. John packs the belly. I show him the heart. But his heart is empty, that is, there is no blood in it. I tell John to drop a line into his heart, which he does, and now, when I assist the heart with compressions, we have a blood pressure of 150 in his arm. Could it be...? I know it won't work, but we keep at it. But not for long, the heart poops out again. We are 12 units of blood into this, have not even identified all of his injuries yet, and his heart has stopped again. John asks me, I concur, and we call it. But we will always save the next one...

As they close and clean up, I go out to the ER to the other patient, a soldier from the Utah Army National Guard, and explain to him what we will do. He goes to the OR, John comes in to help. Wash out holes in his butt, thigh, and wrist, take a frag out. He wakes up just fine. Talking with him afterwards, he's a nice kid. A Mormon Indian kid from the rez in Utah. He cried when he finds out that the other guy did not make it — he did not know him, but he cries. "It's just not fair," he repeats over and over. They are both twenty-two. But he also wants to know when he will be better, so he can go back to his unit. That is what I love about the Military, people like this.

Friday: TQ Day 178.

Despite my best efforts, I am out of bed by 1000. Drink coffee and get ready for the gym, when we hear some booms and the Big Voice goes off. Two rockets, they hit on the airfield, fortunately hurting no one and damaging nothing. After the inevitable delays and accountability drills, we go back to what we were doing. By now it is Black Flag; I run the 2-mile loop and stop off at the Texans. I walk in the door to discover that the ops guys have just taken off for ECP 1; apparently there is a vehicle coming in with three wounded from an IED, no other details. Their SOP is to check out what is going on (unless they have clear info that the wounded need to come to us) and either send it away (if it is minor and Iraqi), treat it at their BAS, or bring it to us. So I run back to the STP at a leisurely pace and wait. We never hear anything, so presumably nothing major.

Jeff and I are ready for dinner. I go down to the DFAC (chow hall) at 1700 — closed, will open at 1800 today. I assume this is because they had extended lunch hours to take into account the Code Red from the rocket attack at lunchtime. I buy Kleenex at the PX and come back. At 1745, Jeff and I hear a couple of really loud booms, the building shakes, and we put our body armor on and sit on the ground. After a couple of minutes,

I run outside to see if I can figure out where it is. It felt close enough to be somewhere in "tent city," in which case there will be casualties. Can't see any flames, smoke, yelling, or panic anywhere. We change into PT gear and go to the SSTP (still in body armor), in case there are casualties. One of our corpsmen says that he heard the boom and saw the flash behind the DFAC. He ran over to see if there were injuries, but there weren't any. One rocket left a nice hole in the dirt, the other put a hole in the road — right where I run every day. How nice. I'll have to get pictures tomorrow.

Saturday: TQ Day 179.

Up in time for Grand Rounds at 0930. Good thing too, since I was the one giving it. Talked about "ER thoracotomies," with plenty of "Separated at birth" mock slides thrown in, at least one for every officer. At the end of the talk, I get two predictable questions. First, what is the role of ultrasound in this? Answer: none. Second, what are my thoughts on this procedure being done by non-surgeons (all ER docs want to "crack chests," but most can't do it and, even if they get in there, they can't fix anything that they find). I answer that the answer to this is contentious, but that all surgical groups agree that nonsurgeons should not be doing surgical procedures. Thoracotomy is a surgical procedure. He pushes the point — "What if a guy comes in with a single stab wound to the heart?" Then he should get a pericardiocentesis (put a needle in to draw the blood off from around the heart; this is a well-known but non-surgical way to temporize). "Oh. Er..." Wasn't expecting that answer, was he? But he keeps pushing it. "It's not about opening a chest. It's about opening a chest and treating the injuries that are found. Repairing the heart, resecting lung, fixing the aorta are all complex surgical procedures that many surgeons are not comfortable with, but you are saying that non-surgeons can do this?" "Well, no..." It's the usual ER thing, they want to do what they consider to be a fun procedure, but they don't want to deal with the consequences.

Sunday: TQ Day 180.

At 1400, the hottest part of the day, Black Flag of course, I go running. I find the hole in the road made by the rocket; it's not nearly as impressive as I had been led to believe. Still, glad I wasn't there when it hit, bet that would have impressed all sorts of things out of me. Finish the run, read outside for a while. I get a radio call that I have a message in the COC, which I return. One of the Army National Guard docs in Baghdad, whose medics have been rotating up here, had called to clear up the status of the program — he had been told it was cancelled. I explained to him that it will be on hold at the end of the month, so they won't be here during our turnover with the new crew. The Army guys, quite frankly, will just be in the way during a turnover; and the new Navy folks will need to learn their way around before they get comfortable letting someone else have a crack at it. What we don't want to have happen is for the Navy to become immediately resentful of the Army personnel — "It is OUR unit, after all..." So to head that off,

I had told them to stop sending folks after the 22nd — that way, nothing can get screwed up while I am gone, and I can try to get it going again after I get back.

As I chatted a bit more with the guy, I discover that he is a Colorado Army National Guard doc, assigned to the Texas Guard as a GMO. He is actually a trauma anaesthesiologist at Denver General, which is one of the more famous trauma hospitals in America, right up there with Charity. He is bored out of his gourd — do we need any help? I take his details and drop an e-mail to our acting Group Surgeon. Why doesn't Group ask to borrow this guy for a week and send him to cover Fallujah? (They had asked if we could cover Fallujah.) That way our anaesthesiologists don't have to go, the new guys don't have to arrive early, and everyone is happy. Probably too simple.

Monday: TQ Day 181.

Up around 1100. The usual morning routine. Around noon I go to the STP to do e-mail before I run, and we hear of incoming: 5 Iraqi policemen from a VBIED (Vehicle-borne Improvised Explosive Device, i.e., a suicide driver). Then it becomes seven patients. I make sure that we are ready for whatever rolls in, as I'm the duty surgeon. I tell Barb to get everything open for a case, with a tech scrubbed in — we are sure to get something to operate on, even if it's not a dire emergency. I then find Tommy and tell him to get the other room ready too, with the instrument sets and the techs in the room, but not open. And the third room should be ready if necessary. Tommy, for some reason, is opening boxes of exam gloves and dumping them on the OR table, but he says okay. Five minutes later, Tommy is still opening boxes and has done nothing.

Eventually the helo comes in with five patients. None is intubated, none is dying, so I have time to give them all the once-over out on the pad. One has lots of holes in his face and neck; I take him back to the OR. Since we have four other patients, for once the ER guys and hangers-on do not follow us there, so it is fairly calm and collected in the OR. Once he is intubated, I finish examining him. He needs a neck exploration for all the holes in his neck, but he also has a hole above his left eye that tracks behind the eyeball — he'll need a CT scan and an ophthalmologist. So he's going out. Get him intubated (with me standing by ready to trach him if necessary), packaged, and ready to go.

Back out to the ER tent. John tells me that one other guy has a hole high up in his neck, in what is called zone III — you prefer not to operate in these, they can be pretty ugly, so he needs a CT scan, too. Finally, there is another guy who has burst eardrums and no other apparent injuries, but for some reason Tom has intubated him — "he was acting goofy." He can't really explain why — the guy was awake and talking, the interpreter had not yet arrived, he was speaking Arabic, but Tom knew that he was goofy? Too late now, he too will have to go for a CT. So three of the five will need to go to Balad, the only place with both a scanner and a neurosurgeon.

We receive confirmation that we will not get the other two. Since one OR has my eye guy in it (sans eyeball ultrasound, of course), I tell Barb to get the other room going with one of the other two patients who are not going out: one has a frag through his thigh; the other has frags to his left knee and right foot. I need to call Balad to tell them about the three we are sending.

John heads to the OR with the thigh guy. I go to call Balad. Get the OR there: "Please hold." After a few minutes, <click> I am disconnected. I call back. "Please hold..." <click>. I call the ER. Same thing, twice. Finally, I get "This is the Ramstein switchboard, the number you have dialed is not assigned or not in service." I have wasted over twenty minutes trying to call them, to no avail, the patients are already halfway there. I drop them an e-mail, saying that I hope someone reads it before the patients arrive. What I would like to say is that if they want info on what is coming in, they'd better find a better way to get it. Maybe they could set up something like the "e-mail watch" that the Army guys have in Baghdad. Often, phoning doesn't work. Of course, if they had an e-mail watch, then whoever is there would be unable to surf the web while on duty...

I go back out to discover that Bob has taken the other patient to the OR already and is half-done with the case. Joe has scrubbed with John. So there I am, the duty surgeon, five patients, and I'm the only one who doesn't get to operate. The gods are cruel.

Note to self: new rule, after five minutes of phone tag to Balad, screw 'em.

Tuesday: TQ Day 182.

Out of bed, check e-mail. The Chief has sent me an e-mail to the effect that I have to fill out my "leave program checklist." Hmmm, let me look at it: weapon to armory (a week before I leave; don't think so); personal gear secured (I'm still using it); must wear flak and Kevlar to plane (how do I get this checked off before I get on the plane?); one duffel no more than 50 lbs (okay); pack sleeping bag (but I'm sleeping in it); 5 copies of orders and leave papers (CLR 25 doesn't have them, so how can I?); Warrior Brief (done August 2nd, no thanks to Chief, who didn't know when it was); depart in cammies (again, how do I get this checked off now?).

After my noon run, we have FMF class. Pure excitement. Picked up mail, received the fake internship certificates that you printed out for me for the departing team. I'm sure that they will be appreciated. We receive one patient at 1630, a 50-something Iraqi woman in a vehicle that was fired on when it failed to stop for a checkpoint. One bullet through the flank. John and Joe operate as I am "post-call." I stand around and mock. Miraculously (or is it the Will of Allah?) the bullet has hit nothing at all. Nada. Zero. John manages to make her liver bleed a little when he puts traction on it, teaching him a valuable lesson in taking down the falciform ligament properly. Told ya' so.

After dinner, I spend the evening working on various slideshows. One week to go before I get leave...

Thursday: TQ Day 184.

Not much else happens for the day — PT as usual — until about 1545, when the radio says that we are getting nine Iraqi civilians coming by ground, from a car wreck. I get to the STP (I'm duty surgeon) to discover that this is not even an official medevac call: one of the comms NCOs from CLR 25 had overheard a radio call from an Army convoy, telling their parent Army unit that they were heading in with Iraqi casualties. No one ever notified the medical system at all. I call the Texans to tell them what's coming, since it is their job to see civilians at the ECPs to decide who gets in (we are supposed to treat only life-threatening injuries here, the Iraqi Ministry of Health wants everything else to go to Iraqi hospitals). A few minutes later, MSOC (the medical people in the Dark Tower) call to say that they are already at the gate and will be here in a few minutes. A few minutes after that, a civilian pickup rolls up with three Iraqis and some Army medics in it. All three have head injuries, one is combative, and all need to be intubated. We scurry off and get to work. When I'm done with mine, we find that there have been three more delivered, most with scalp lacerations, assorted bumps and bruises. And finally, we end up with all nine. The first three are flown off for head CTs; we treat the rest and put them on the ward.

The story, as told by an Army medic with the convoy: they were on patrol when a vehicle rolled over down the street, and another vehicle hit the first one. They go down to investigate. The Army medics want to notify higher authority and have the Iraqi Police come and take the patients to Ramadi General Hospital. Their battalion commander countermands this and says that they have to pick up all of the patients and bring them

Day or night, rain or shine, patients were always triaged and searched before being brought into the unit. Triaged to decide which patient area to be sent to, searched to keep out any weapons or explosives. Even friendly forces coming in from the field could be carrying all sorts of deadly cargo.

to us. Completely contrary to the CENTCOM Rules of Engagement for civilian personnel. They drive through our ECP, without stopping, and deliver all of the patients to the Texas BAS. The BAS looks them over and send them to us in batches.

There are a couple of problems here. First, if I was an insurgent, I would think, "Hmm. The Americans all come running when there is a car wreck. What a great way to kill them all with some IEDs or a suicide bomber with a vest." Second, this sort of thing has a potentially serious impact on our ability to look after our own. CENTCOM, the State Deptartment and the Iraqi provisional government all say the same thing; that the Iraqi people must be cared for by the Iraqi healthcare system. In essence: if we don't shoot 'em, we don't treat 'em. What do we do if we have nine Iraqis filling our tents and then wounded Marines or soldiers show up? The Geneva Convention and the Law of Armed Conflict both state that patients are treated based upon injury severity, not nationality or status. I wouldn't want to have to make that sort of call. If we are here to treat our own, that is what we should do. If we are here to treat everyone, then give us the resources to do so — which requires State Deptartment approval for humanitarian aid, more money, better facilities and equipment, resources for proper follow-up care, and so on. This is classic "mission creep" — having units doing things outside of their mission, without adequate resources. There is also a third problem. In addition to sucking up our medical resources, any patients we see who have serious problems get medevaced to Baghdad or elsewhere. Those are the same helos used for military missions, so the patients adversely impact our military capability, too.

Of course, now we have a problem. We have six wounded Iraqis — Kurds, it turns out — sitting on our ward, none of them more than sixteen. What are we supposed to do with them? They will need follow-up medical care, but their initial care has been taken care of. Anyone have a plan for that? MSOC — it's not their problem since the patients don't need to be medevaced. So what do we do? Drive them to the gate and set them free? I call Greg, and he intervenes and somehow makes contacts using the Intel guys; eventually he works it out that some relative will pick them up at ECP 2 at 0800 tomorrow morning.

Don't get me wrong. I don't mind looking after civilians — in fact, it would be interesting to look after more of them (with appropriate security in place, of course). What I mind is having the same issues regarding their care come up every single time, yet no one has a coherent plan for how these situations should be handled. Every time, it's as if it has never happened before. And the medical planners are the least helpful people of all.

Saturday: TQ Day 186.

Am up at 1000. Do the usual run. At 1400, we have our last FMF class. There, I learn that our 6-mile hump will be next Friday, and that CLR 25 has finally figured out that they, not Group (the Dark Tower), will be giving our oral boards. Something that I suspected would happen by default (meaning that Group wouldn't want to deal with it) weeks ago, from Greg among others. And of course all of this will occur after I leave, and they will most likely all be gone before I get back. So I will get to start over from scratch with the new guys.

Before dinner, Greg drops by. I have him sign the "Sensei Greg School of Zen Marks-manship" posters, so we all have copies signed by everyone. He thinks this is very cool, but I wish I'd been able to make him a proper ghetto plaque out of an ammo can. Just couldn't find the right materials, unfortunately.

At 1800 I go over to the Texans, where they are having their weekly BBQ. I talk with Geoff (their PA). Our trip for tomorrow to Camp Manhattan is on, we leave at 1500. Cool, Hajji food for dinner. We also talk a bit about the Iraqi civilian incident from Thursday. Turns out that there were actually twenty patients that arrived at their BAS, they sent us nine and sent the other eleven back out the gate. So we only got half of them. "Texas Mike," their newest doc, said it was quite bizarre and rather comical. Hajji pickup truck with about twenty people in the back pulls up. He walks over; they are all staring at him, not moving. He tells them to get out of the truck, which they do — and then they start wandering all over the place. He had to get more guards to form a perimeter; the Army guys who brought them in were just standing there, doing nothing. But they finally got it figured out.

After that, over to Greg's roof to watch the sunset, and we chat until almost 2200. Three days until I'm supposed to be on a plane, and still no orders or arrangements for storing my weapon or gear.

Sunday: TQ Day 187.

A little before 1500, I gird my loins for battle and head over to the Texas HQ — road trip! We have their CO's Personal Security Detachment to take us there. "Texas Mike" and I are going, along with six of their medics who have never been over to Hab-baniyah. We get over there and go straight to the Army BAS. They are the 1/110 (1st Battalion, 110th Infantry Regiment), National Guardsmen from Pennsylvania and Kentucky for the most part. Their doc is an FP, a Major, 8 years in the Guard and doing his first deployment (three month stay; the rest of them are here for a year). He seems to be a nice guy, appears competent, and he and his PA (who works for a cardiothoracic surgeon) have a good division of labor going — the PA does the procedures, and the doc does the intubations and other medical stuff. Most of their problems are comm-related: their phones don't work and they have no internet access. I give him some pointers on how to get this taken care of (including telling his boss that people will die if they can't pick up the phone to make a call), the Texans will help them out with the internet stuff, and they are very interested in getting training, they will even provide transportation if needed. So, when I get back, if I can convince my new bosses (Marine and Navy) that this would be a good idea, I can go over every couple of weeks to do my trauma lectures.

As we are getting ready to leave, we hear that TQ is in condition red, a couple of incoming mortar rounds. So rather than sit around at TQ in battle rattle, we sit around in the shade at Manhattan until it is over, and then head back. An entertaining time was had by all.

After dinner, Jeff and I go to Greg's roof to watch the moonrise, it is fairly predictably around 2030. Because of the dust, it rises as a giant orange ball, and gradually turns to the usual color as it gains altitude. Possibly my last rooftop get-together, as I have my obligatory going-away party tomorrow.

Monday: TQ Day 188.

Up at 1000. I chose to not PT as I do not want to generate any additional laundry that will stink the place up for a few weeks. I finish the last of my packing, throwing stuff into my seabags and footlocker. I can leave in ten minutes if I have to. As I do this, we hear three or four "booms" and the building shakes. The Big Voice goes off. I continue packing. Whoever was shooting, they missed me, and if there are casualties, someone will let me know.

Around 1200, while we are still in Condition Red, we hear of an incoming casualty — Iraqi Army, supposedly had his leg blown off by an RPG. A few minutes later I field the call from Combat Outpost — leg blown off by a landmine at the hip, he will probably be dead before he gets to us. When he arrives, he is. No cardiac activity, DOA. We look the parts over — they sent the leg with him — and see that the middle of his thigh is missing. His lower leg, however, is completely intact, boot, trouser leg, and all. Couldn't be a landmine, or else his foot would be shredded; the RPG story makes the most sense. He is bodybagged and sent to MA (Mortuary Affairs) and we go back to our usual routine. After six months of this, no one is particularly fazed by it any more.

I eat lunch with Greg afterwards ... really good cheese and chicken quesadillas, well worth coming back to Iraq for. Afterwards, I check in with CLR 25. No, still no orders. "So tell me Staff Sergeant, when should I start getting worried...?" "1800 sir."

At 1800, still no word on when I leave. But they claim to have my orders, which I can pick up tonight or tomorrow morning, and I should be able to leave tomorrow, they are waiting for the passenger manifest from the air boys tonight. "What about my weapon?" "You'll need to check that into the Armory." "Whose?" "You don't have one?" "No, that's why I have been asking you about this stuff for the last two weeks. And how about storing my personal gear?" "You can leave that with your unit." "My unit will have left by the time I get back." "Oh." And people wonder why I have dents in my head...

My "going away" party is at 1930. We all sit around on HESCO Beach. A very low-key affair. John gives me a season pass to Six Flags TQ, which entitles me to ride in or on all rides, vehicles, aircraft, armor, tactical and nontactical vehicles, play with expended or live ordnance, shoot all weapons, and so on. THAT was cool.

Tomorrow is supposed to be the big day...

Tuesday: TQ Day 189.

I learn by e-mail at 1000 that I'm leaving tonight, I have to be checked into JACOT (where planes leave from) at 1400. Nice of them to call and tell me. So I race over to CLR

An Iraqi MiG 25 fighter serves well as a slip-and-slide. The base had dozens of derelict aircraft and vehicles, some destroyed as far back as Desert Storm in 1991 and never cleared away.

25 in the SUV, get my orders, find my way to the Armory and check in my pistol. Get back, say goodbye to John and Joe, take a shower, and leave. Jeff is running, so I don't get the chance to say goodbye to him, but he is stationed at Portsmouth so I will no doubt be seeing him again. I commandeer the SUV again and Greg drives me to JACOT.

I meet up with the Texas Intel officer, who is also going home on leave. We board the C-130 at around 1645, sit in it for over half-an-hour before it takes off. Sixty people, all in body armor, 120 degrees outside and climbing (no A/C when we are not flying), but eventually we leave. We arrive in Kuwait in about 90 minutes. Bus to a gravel lot, then another bus to Camp Somethingorother.

We then get to spend a couple of hours on various lines. Check our flak and Kevlar into a huge warehouse. Go through video debriefings. Sort out destinations (Atlanta or Dallas and beyond). And finally, assignment to a nice, clean, air-conditioned tent with bunkbeds. Surprisingly efficient. Guess they've done this with a few people before.

Next morning, breakfast, and then at noon, those of us going to Atlanta go into "lockdown." We are herded into a barbed wire enclosure, and all of our gear is unpacked and inspected for U.S. Customs, which is handled by the Navy here. We then sit around in deck chairs for about six hours, and finally head to the airport and get on the charter plane for the States. Officers get first-class seats, can't complain.

Wednesday: On the Way Home.

Stop to refuel in Ramstein, Germany. Hang out in the air terminal made famous by the Berlin Airlift and which they say will be closed in a few weeks. I pick up a copy of *Jaws* in the USO freebie box to read on the plane.

Long flight home. Once we get to Atlanta, more customs (a formality), then to the Delta counter for plane tickets. I get to leave about thirty minutes later, at around 1000. On the flight, a Marine and I are the only ones in uniform, so the stewardesses move us to First Class, how nice. I know that there are other enlisted Marines on board, but because they have changed into civvies, the stewardesses can't get away with upgrading them (I asked). Lucky me! And so ends my first tour of duty.

8. September 2005: Breaking in the New Team

Saturday: Heading Back from Leave.

Everything up to Wednesday will be brief, as it is from memory. Up at 0400 to get the cab, what joy. Not really looking forward to going back: besides leaving home, everything is once again up in the air since New Orleans flooded. Oh well, I get six months to come up with Plan B.

Sunday: Kuwait.

The stopover in Ramstein, Germany, is brief, about a half an hour. Then away we go again. Arrive in Kuwait around 1800, so it's still light and I can see things as we fly in. Not that there is much to see. Flat, ugly sand or dirt, with little square buildings along the coast.

Off the plane, onto buses and a 45-minute drive to Ali Al Saleh Air Base. Dark by now, so not much of a view. Inprocessing is fairly quick — scan our IDs in, get our destinations recorded, pick up our body armor and tent assignments. The folks headed to TQ muster at 1030 tomorrow morning, about 50 of us. I shower, decide not to stay up for midrats (midnight rations, i.e., food between 0000 and 0200), and go to bed.

Monday: TQ Day 190.

Eat breakfast, do some crosswords, and muster at 1030. The 50-plus expected people do not materialize, there are about ten of us. Where did everyone else go? The Army clerks can't tell me, but I suspect that there was an earlier flight and they came and found some people to put on it. Fine with me, I got some sleep and the plane will be less crowded. We get on the bus with about a dozen other folks waiting for "hops" around theater and drive out to the flightline. Sit around for about two hours, another bus, and then out to the C-130. Twenty-two passengers in a plane with 68 seats, so I get to lie down and go to sleep after we take off.

Wheels up at 1630, arrive around 1810. Grab my gear, call the SSTP to tell the duty

131

driver to come and get me, which they do. The new Marines with us have no idea where anything is, so I show them the scenic route back to the SSTP (past the lake and the one and only palm tree), which they appreciate. Stop at CLR 25 on the way, to drop off my leave papers. The duty NCO is confused about what to do with them; I suggest making a copy and giving it to the S-1 (Personnel Officer) in the morning.

Walk into the COC; ask if they have a radio for me. Our Marine Sergeant is there. A pleasant surprise, since I thought he'd left with everyone else. Guess not; he was involuntarily extended and is now officially assigned to us and in charge of our drivers. Chat a bit. No radio for me, we are "short" and not everyone gets one. I experience déjà vu — visions of the Chief telling me that only "key personnel" get them flash through my head. I really hope not.

Walk over to the hootch. No one is there, so I quickly look around to see what's missing. Nothing of mine, fortunately. I unpack important stuff and lock it up, then go to eat dinner.

Finally meet some people. My new OIC, a colorectal surgeon that I know from the Hospital, is in my hootch; he says we need to talk tomorrow. Great. The hootch also has the unit psychiatrist, a chaplain (currently at Al Asad I hear), and the most senior nurse. I also meet John, the surgeon from Pensacola who had e-mailed me before coming out. He seems like a good guy. Hmm, I extend in Iraq for six months and they move the chaplain and the shrink in with me...

Tuesday: TQ Day 191.

I stay up reading, finally go to sleep around 0300. Greg gets me up at 1000 to ask if I want to go for a run. What, without coffee first? But I'm supposed to track down the OIC today; I have to get my weapon from the CLR 25 Armory, and so on. So I'm up, and get the SUV to go to Lakeside. Picked up the weapon — no problem. I then find the boss, and we have our "little talk."

He warns me that people have already started to form their cliques, so I will be an outsider. On top of that, I am from the "old group," so they will be suspicious since, of course, the new group will want to do things their own way, some of which will be different. I tell him that I'm used to being an outsider, that is not a problem — my clique is the "anticlique." Also, that it's a mistake to assume that I agreed with everything that the previous Team did. Yes, I think we did a lot of things better than the Team before us which I'm sure that they would disagree with, but there is more than one way to skin a cat. I plan to be a fly on the wall; I will make suggestions when asked, or if I feel that there is something that really needs to be different. He seems happy with that.

Then he gives me even more good news. There has been an "incident" with the narcotics lockers, and an investigation is required. He has convinced the CLR 25 CO that I should be the investigating officer — I am medical and so understand the system, but not one of the new crew, so will be unbiased. Great, I get to interrogate people I don't know but will have to work with for six months...

After this, I walk over to DFAC with him to watch him eat lunch; I don't normally

Posing with Paul (right), the OIC, in front of the unit's sign. At the request of the sign painter, the sign was taken to the rifle range and ceremonially shot to kindling just before we went home.

eat lunch, but I figure I should try to be sociable. As we sit there, we hear of an incoming casualty. I tell him I'll head over, he can finish lunch (he's duty surgeon), then I go change and off to the STP. Everyone is in uniform except me — they'll learn.

Eventually the patient comes in, a Pakistani contractor who speaks no English, with both legs injured by an IED. Their PA looks at him on the pad, and takes him into the STP tent. I do the fly thing. The boss and I chat for a while; he does not go in the tent. Hmm. After about twenty minutes, we finally go check it out. The guy has his right heel blown off, and holes in his left leg, obviously a case. They seem to be letting the ortho guy, Mike, run this for some reason. I ask what's going on, no one seems to be doing anything — the ER doc says that they are waiting for a translator to find out if he is allergic to penicillin and to test his peroneal nerve function (whether he can move his foot up and down). I point out that the interpreter may take hours to arrive, or not show up at all. This guy is Pakistani and so probably does not speak Arabic, anyway, so the interpreter most likely won't be of any use. His odds of a pen allergy are minimal, and you can always give him another antibiotic. You can test his foot function using sign language. But the ER doc says that the ortho guy won't go back to the OR without the interpreter first. Uh huh.

Meanwhile, a prior patient is getting ready to be flown out somewhere. The litter bearers carry the guy out onto the pad, they are walking towards the ambulance as it pulls out of its parking spot, backs up while doing a 90-degree turn, and drives straight backwards towards the group, without the required assistant driver directing it from outside the vehicle. It screeches to a halt a couple of feet from the group, which the driver could not possibly have seen at that point. The litter has to back up so they can open the door. I mention to a couple of people who have been watching this that they might want to have the ambulance pull up and stop before bringing the patient out. That was an accident waiting to happen, and later in the year when it gets cold and windy, patient hypothermia can be a problem. Point taken.

The Pakistani is pretty stable, no one seems terribly interested in my being there and I am trying (unsuccessfully?) to be unobtrusive, so I find something else to do for a bit, come back to the OR in about an hour, ask what's going on. Patient is still not in there. I get the same answer directly from Mike. "What's the big deal? Only one patient and he's stable." Yeah, only one patient right now. If you get five more thirty minutes from now, you'd wished you'd started this an hour ago since you'd be done by now. Whatever. A minute later, the patient arrives in the room, which ticks ortho off even more. Tim, the anaesthesiologist from Portsmouth whom Jeff knows and recommends, has finally brought him back anyway. The interpreter was useless, the sign language thing was done, and he has no peroneal nerve function. So the case starts.

I have looked at the x-rays. His heel is trashed, and he has a fragment close to the knee on one x-ray. Ortho says it's in the joint and it needs to be washed out. Hmm. How do you know on one view? The frag could be way behind the knee, in which case it is more likely to be a vascular injury then a joint injury. Oh... More x-rays are done once the patient is asleep, the frag is way posterior. I would argue for exploring the wound locally and injecting the joint to see if it leaks, rather than just open it up. But he is the orthopod so I say nothing. I amaze myself with my own restraint (hahaha).

Who is to scrub? It's Mike's case so he will scrub with the PA, who is an ortho (hand) PA. So I suggest that John and I scrub to do the other leg; in that way we can double-team it and be done in half the time, and everyone gets to play. And away we go. As I scrub, I quietly ask the OR nurse (rhetorically) how many techs are scrubbed — one. Okay, so we have four surgeons doing what are essentially two operations simultaneously — how about a second tech? (What I'm thinking is gee, these guys must be really jaded, after 13 days here, if their techs don't want to scrub on cases.) A second tech scrubs in.

I walk John through the debridement of the heel. In the States, he would get his foot amputated and a prosthesis. However, I opt for not doing this — this guy is Pakistani, what sort of care will he get? If he is the typical contractor, his company will find a way to send him home, give him a check, and tell him to have a nice life. So he's unlikely to get a prosthesis or rehab. In the 1940s, he would have gotten six months in what is called a Trueta cast, changed weekly, and eventually the mashed bones would fuse into a solid glob that, while providing no flexibility, may give him enough function to walk on. Barring that, a Syme amputation through the ankle joint would give him legs that are of different lengths but leave him still able to walk, albeit with an impressive limp. So I hope that whoever we send him to doesn't just lop it off later (unless, of course, the foot turns bad).

While we do this, Mike does a fasciotomy. I suggest that John watch the other procedure while I finish the foot, which I do quickly with a wash out. The knee joint didn't have a frag in it after all.

After this, I run. Only one loop, a little over two miles, I don't want to overdo it since I haven't run in three weeks. I then get a call from CLR 25, from the S-1, telling me that I need to come over to meet the XO or CO so I can get appointed as the "narc." I set that up for 1000 tomorrow. Then dinner, and I spend the evening finishing my unpacking. I unpack the stuff I brought with me, repack my "go bag" that I can just grab and live out of if I have to go somewhere in a hurry, and unpack all the stuff I had crammed into seabags and footlockers so it didn't get lost or misplaced in my absence. At the end of an hour, I am more unpacked than my roommates who have been here for 13 days. Practice, I suppose, and the need for less crap.

Spend a little quality time on Greg's roof in the evening.

Wednesday: TQ Day 192.

The new group — the Green Team (my recommendation instead of "Puce," I might add) — has kept the Wednesday meeting/patient conference format for 0800. They go over the three or four traumas they have seen since taking the helm. Nothing big or bad, which is good. Every time someone said something, it seemed like they looked at me to see what I would add, which was usually nothing. At one point, as they discussed how things in general could go better, they got into the discussion of how triage should work, who should do it, etc. The same arguments we had had in the previous team. These guys have only one ER doc (a LCDR) and two FP docs in ER billets, but the same arguments — the triage PA should look them over, ask the surgeon if he has questions, and so on. When I am asked, I flatly disagree. "Trauma is a surgical disease. The only person to decide who goes to the OR and in what order should be a surgeon." I suggest that the PA and the surgeon, with one litter team, meet each patient: the patients are stripped and searched, and the surgeon calls the shots. Besides the ER doc, one FP doc and the orthopod disagree with me. I tell them again that I flatly disagree. When I'm the duty doc, I will meet the patients and call the shots on them, operative or nonoperative. "You don't have to be a surgeon to run a resuscitation." No, but it's the surgeon who should decide where the resuscitation will be, and who should be doing it. Bottom line: for trauma, I can do what they can do (probably better), but they cannot do what I can do. And this is a trauma unit.

We also get into a discussion about using the OR to resuscitate patients — the orthopod even suggests that the nonsurgeons can use the OR to do this, but it's pretty clear that both the surgeons and the gas passers have a big problem with this (after all, if the OR is not in use, the surgeon can do the resuscitation, so they have no reason to be there in any case). The boss makes some noncommittal comments about this. He does, however, happen to mention my comment about the ambulance yesterday and says it will be our policy — I suspect this was a move on his part to point out that I do, in fact, have good ideas from time to time.

I meet with the CLR 25's XO, who seems like a very nice guy. He gives me the scoop on what he wants me to investigate. I get the JAG Manual from the S-1. I also ask the S-1 what the deal is on the FMF qual, the FMF ribbon, and the Iraq Campaign medal, since it was all up in the air when I left. She tells me that I have the ribbon and medal already taken care of. The Chief handled it and should have the paperwork — uh, he's gone. Oh. So she'll check on that for me. She also has me meet the Marine Captain who has been handed the FMF pin stuff.

This Captain has been in Iraq for less than two weeks, and has one guy working in his shop. He's a little overwhelmed, and I tell him that I am not offended that this is not a priority. However, I would like to know the status of things. Turns out that, while everyone was crammed through the last exams and the board in a couple of days, no one has their paperwork done. His turnover for that job was a box of papers in the corner of the room and word that the FMF lectures are on the "x" drive on the server. I look through the box, find mine, and find a list of who had done what and who was deficient in what. I need to take three written tests, the oral board, and do the six mile hump. I also note that none of my previous Team has had any of their official paperwork done to be sent to the General for signature, i.e., the official authorization for the pin. The Captain has no time or people to do this.

Time to make a deal. I tell him that, if we do not have a designated liaison for the FMF program, I will find him one. If I find him a guy to do the scheduling and help him work this from our end, AND get his typing done so he can close out the old Team's box and get it off his desk, will he look into the written exams and find out when I can take them? It's a deal. In the back of my mind I think that Father Tim, our Catholic chaplain, and I are the only "rollovers" not quite finished. I'll see if I can work it out so that we both can do the three requirements together and be done with it.

On the way back to the STP, I stop at the Black Sheep Coffee House to drink way too much coffee. As part of the action taken for the narc issue, the boss has mandated a unit urinalysis today, so I need to generate some. Of course, a urine drug test can't pick up the drug we have a problem with, but it demonstrates that we take this seriously. I am fairly certain that the whole thing is actually merely sloppy bookkeeping, but we'll see.

When I get back, I start my investigation in earnest. Can't really get into it here, but it's somewhat comical. Those who found the problem did the right thing by reporting it — but then didn't document it and discarded the evidence. So they are eligible for a pat on the back, followed by a slap on the hand. Since I am meeting one-on-one with six or seven people, I take the opportunity to chat with them about other stuff, too. But it was funny to see how nervous people are, even when they have done nothing wrong. I just needed to talk to anyone with access to the narcs, even if they were not involved, to document it. But as with everything, the more info I get, the more convoluted it becomes. Add to this the problem that I have three days (by the JAG Manual) to do this, and none of the previous Team is available as they are no longer in Iraq.

In the COC, one of the female corpsmen asks me how things are going, I tell her fine. "You don't remember me, do you sir?" "Yes, but you have a nice tan now, and I thought you'd said your orders had been changed because you didn't pass the PFT." "Wow, you do remember!" She was one of the Hospital corpsmen who had actually seemed interested in working. I tell her she needs to set a goal: you have six months, and your goal is to pass the Marine PFT. Not the Navy one, the Marine one. Every day, do the Marine PFT. Do the sit-ups, the pull-ups, and the run. You won't do well for a while, it'll be hard, you'll have to walk part of it, but you have six months. Just do it every day. And just to make sure, I will run it with you three months from now. "<Gulp.> Yes, sir." Needs some motivating, but she seems like a good kid. Besides, how can you be nineteen years old and not be able to run 3 miles in 33 minutes?

Thursday: TQ Day 193.

We get casualties fairly early, around 0900. Three ISF (Iraqi Security Forces) soldiers, hit by an IED. The boss and I are there when they arrive. First one in is pretty much dead; he and I open his chest in the ER and quit. The second one has a frag in his back, looks stable. The third one has frags to his chest and leg; I go over to the other ER tent to see how he's doing. Then the fun starts.

At some point, I knew this would happen. I walk in, I see the guy awake, lying there, with bandages on his chest. The Family Practice doc is saying "He needs a chest tube, get ready to intubate him." Not sure who he is saying this to as the room is quite chaotic, but he does. I ask him why he is intubating the patient. "He needs a chest tube." Okay, but that's not a reason to intubate him. "Well, the last time we tried to put a chest tube in an awake patient, he was jumping around all over the place, so I want him intubated." Okay, so sedate him and give him lots of local anaesthetic, that's still not a reason to intubate him. "Doctor, are you taking over management of this patient?" To his surprise I say "Yes," and take him to the OR, where the boss joins me. After I take the bandages off (which hasn't been done and therefore no one had seen the wounds yet), I see that he has a hole in the middle of his chest, another below his armpit, and one in his leg. All right, the hole in the middle of his chest IS a reason to intubate him, because it is very suspicious for a tracheal injury, but that is best done here in the OR in case he needs it done surgically. Once he's asleep, the chest tube is placed by the OIC; he gets no blood out. I examine the chest wound. It turns out it tracks under the skin and does not go into the chest itself. However, he has blood coming out of his endotracheal tube and his chest x-ray shows a huge lung bruise. OIC says he will operate on this guy to wash the wounds out; I should go see the last guy. Okay, I think this guy may not be so simple, but, hey, the OIC is the duty surgeon after all.

Actually, it turns out that he's the back-up, but John had not picked up the radio from me yet, and so didn't hear about the casualties. By now he's here, looking at the third patient, who has a small hole in the middle of his back. We take him to the OR as well and wash out the wounds.

When we are done, we check in with the boss's patient. Chest wound has been washed out and they are working on the leg. When they are done, there is some concern because he still has blood coming out of the ET tube, from his lung. He will need an urgent medevac for a chest CT, before he gets too unstable to send. No one is excited about operating on him for that as it would mean taking the lung out, never a good option for this. The two are packaged and leave. I end up coordinating this so both can go on the same helo, since I know how to do it. The OIC decides that we need to "hot wash" this event, since there had seemed to be a fair amount of mayhem — we'll do it at 1300.

Check e-mail, and then hear that the helo is coming back. They had barely gotten off the ground when the guy started "pouring" blood out of the tube, so they turned around to drop the one patient back off. I get him into the OR and we right mainstem him, i.e., shove the tube down far enough that it goes past the split in the trachea to just the right lung, isolating the injured left one. The left one will keep bleeding, but the tube will be ventilating the good right one and blood will not spill into it. A couple of units of blood, and he is ready to go again. I have some misgivings, I think that he might need an operation, but it's damned if you do and damned if you don't. And this is not a good place to watch him.

Meanwhile, we have also received a seven-year-old boy with a GSW to the head, diverted here for instability. This kid is intubated and sent on the same bird with the other guy to see a neurosurgeon.

After all of the excitement, the boss changes the "hot wash" time to 1700, so I go run a couple of miles. At 1600, I go to MedLog to check their records for my little investigation, and then up onto HESCO Beach at 1700 for the meeting...

Friday: TQ Day 194.

Head over to CLR 25 in the morning around 1000, to drop off my "Preliminary Inquiry." The 1st Lt in their Personnel Section, who is supposed to provide me with admin support, spends time reformatting the thing in various ways. "Oh, no, sir, there have to be TWO spaces after the number, not one." Whatever, I have my suspicions that he is making some of this stuff up. I had planned to "pop in" if the XO or CO was available to give them a verbal report as well, but they were out so I just left it there. If they have questions, they will ask. The report basically says it's a clerical error and there is nothing to do.

Afterwards, I head back and do some e-mail. Since I have no radio (yes, we are going through THAT again!), I notice that the boss walks in wearing his OR hat. We have incoming casualties. As I walk over to the hootch to change, I run into the General. He's here for the year, like me. "What's up, doc?" "Gotta change for the big game, sir." "What do you mean?" "We have casualties coming in." "Oh. I'll go up and have a look." So I go change and the General walks up to the SSTP in his PT gear.

When I get up there, we hear that there are at least two Iraqi soldiers coming in with gunshot wounds. The General and I stand there, leaning on HESCOs, chatting. People rush around, seemingly oblivious to us. "Sir, I know you've been there — you're the 'old guy' in a new unit, and you have to restrain yourself from jumping in and interfering all the time." "Yeah doc, I know what you mean. Just as long as the cat gets skinned."

Folks seem a lot calmer in the ER tent today. John and I take one patient back with a big hole in his groin that's not bleeding but needs to be explored. He has a funny-looking pelvis x-ray, so we suspect that the frag is in his belly, but we can't be sure. Explore the groin, the hole keeps going. I suggest opening his belly; we do. The frag did not make it all the way in, but the blast effect bruised his colon. He will need another operation tomorrow to make sure that the colon is not dead, so we "Bogota bag" him (sew a plastic IV bag to the skin to cover the hole, easy to remove for a second operation). Goes well, and this Team has its first ex lap (open abdomen).

We finish up, while the boss and Mike, the orthopod, wash out some minor wounds on another guy. We had four Iraqis total, two operative cases. Afterwards, the boss and I are sitting around outside, talking. He tells me that people were asking whom I'd been hanging out with at the HESCOs; he'd "looked familiar." They were floored when they found out it was the General. Maybe my stock is going up a little bit... While we chat, the Texas Intel guy walks up and I make the introductions. We re-seal the deal for the bi-weekly Intel briefs as he had done with the previous team. He was on the plane with me to Kuwait, after which he went on to Dallas while I did Atlanta. He had a great leave, even went to see J.J. of the broken leg/Jessica Simpson fame in San Antonio.

At 1900, I go to Greg's roof for his farewell party. Ultimately, there are about forty people up there, all having a good time. Lots of picture-taking.

Back to the hootch, at which time another casualty arrives. An EPW, "shot in the back." The boss is the duty surgeon; he lets the ER guys handle the triage again. After a while, we go in to look at the guy. They are shooting x-rays. They assess that he has buckshot in his back, no big deal. "Buckshot? That's a first. I know there are a few Remington 1200s around, but I've never seen a patient here with that." He has one little puncture wound on the right side of his back, and a bunch of what they think are superficial pellet wounds in his left flank. "Hmm, let's look at the chest x-ray, looks like blood in his right chest to me." They don't believe it and they want to shoot another x-ray with him sitting up. Okay, but it won't negate the first x-ray. He needs a chest tube. Go ahead and sit him up, but he still needs a chest tube. "But it's such a small wound." "Yeah, about the size that a 12 inch icepick would make but that doesn't mean anything." I talk them into placing a chest tube and 500cc of blood comes out. Score one for the ol' trauma surgeon. Now, how about the other side. Huh? Put in a bladder catheter, if for no other reason than he is an EPW and he'll be strapped down and won't be able to get up to pee. Catheter goes in and lots of blood comes out in his urine. Kidney injury. Score two for the ol' trauma surgeon. This was not a shotgun, it was multiple small frags from a bullet that ricocheted and broke apart, probably a machine gun bullet. So the guy goes from a "nothing" injury to needing a medevac for a CT to assess his belly (since on my assessment he did not immediately need an ex lap).

A little more street credit gained?

Saturday: TQ Day 195.

Up around 0800, in order to be well caffeinated for my Grand Rounds at 0930.

They go over well; I learn later that the primary care types really appreciated it — which was the whole point of doing it early in the deployment, of course. I had started it with the Kosovo music video, just to set the correct tone, which is a hit. Then straight into the lecture on the basics for initial assessment of trauma patients. Done around 1030, and back to the hootch.

As I change into PT gear, Greg comes in and invites me to run. Sure. So we run over to the Spring Lake pool, about three miles, chatting as we go, and take a nice twenty minute swim. Get a few pics, float in the inner tubes, that sort of thing. Then run back. He then heads out for lunch while I go read Tacitus' *The Annals of Imperial Rome* on the "Beach." As I get ready to shower before dinner, the boss tells me that the specter of sending surgeons to Ramadi has raised its ugly head again. Every time a new Marine infantry division commander comes in, it's the same thing: "I want a surgical unit where my guys are." My previous Team fought this, the Team before that fought it, now it's the new Team's turn. I had gathered a list from the docs at Ramadi of the patients that had arrived alive to them but who had subsequently died, and in the nine months I could obtain data for, there were at most two patients who would not certainly have died even if a surgical unit had been there. This is not to say that they would have lived, either. Whereas pulling surgeons from here cuts our capability by 50 percent.

Monday: TQ Day 197.

I get up at 1000 and start to work on the trauma database. At 1130, I get a radio call that I have a message at the COC. It turns out that it was a message from CLR 25 from yesterday that someone found and finally gave to me. I need to call the 1st Lt, the guy in Personnel who is "assisting" me with the Preliminary Inquiry that I turned in. Of course there's a problem. He has spoken with the XO and CO, and they want names named throughout. Okay, easy enough, not what the JAG manual says for this type of inquiry, but whatever. Now for the best part: he, the 1st LT, who knows nothing about medicine and little about law, has recommended to the CO that this go to a Command Investigation and be referred to NCIS (Navy Criminal Investigative Service). Great — then why was I appointed the Investigating Officer if he does not know all of the facts but will horn in on it anyway? The write-up is a summary of what I found out, not all of the details, and he has no clue. Best to go straight over and "nip it, nip it in the bud."

I go to the COC, run into the boss, and tell him where I'm headed, and why. Yup, he agrees that it's getting out of control. When I get there, the 1st LT shows me some medical info he downloaded off the internet to "brief" the XO and CO. Wonderful. He recommends a Command Investigation because, well, just because. He also says that my recommendation, "consult a JAG," is not an option; I have to choose "investigate further" or "no further action." So I show him in the JAG Manual where it says "consult a JAG" is an option. I also point out to him that, by the JAG Manual, CLR 25 cannot do a Command Investigation because they do not have the ability to do so — they can't go back to Lejeune, Cherry Point, Portsmouth, Jacksonville and who knows where else to interview people. This would have to go way outside of the command to be investigated. This is pointless, because it's basically a clerical issue. The only reason that I had not recommended "no further action" was because of the topic of the inquiry, narcotics; hence, I had suggested that the CO consult the JAG.

I go talk to the XO and make my case. The evidence is gone, there is little likelihood of criminal intent, and half the people involved are no longer in theater, so the odds of any investigation being productive are small — after all, you can't prove anything without evidence. But because of the issue, narcs, if I were the CO I would talk to the JAG for an opinion before dropping it. I would have spoken to the JAG, myself, but he had left already and, when I checked, the new one is not in-country yet. The XO gets it, says I should add this to my report, which is already longer than it's supposed to be. I go to their S-1 office to borrow a computer and do it right up, get it done.

As I sit there typing, a couple of Marines come in. Lo! And behold! It's the new Staff JAG, just coming by all of the units to say "hi." He finally made it to TQ — couldn't have timed it better. I ask if he has a few minutes, we go off to an empty room and I tell him what the deal is. He concurs that it should be dropped, says I can put into my PI that I discussed it with him. He suggests that I document that I tried to call a couple of people in the States from the previous Team, but that's about all.

As I'm already well-caffeinated for the day, I don't drop by the Coffee Shop. I stop by Greg's hootch to see if he's flying out today — nope, maybe tomorrow. We decide to go running, so I drive back and change. We run to the pool again. Then, after a refreshing dip, he takes me on the Taqaddum Death March. He asks if I want to go the "long way" back, which I take to mean that we will not cut across the dirt like we have been, but run on the road, adding about a mile. Sure, I'm game. Well, we run the road. Then down a back road, across a berm, up and down some ravines, up a hill, more ravines, and eventually back onto a road. Adds about three miles and lots of dirt. Wish we'd done it first, the pool would have been GREAT after that!

At 2300 I get into my rack, drop the curtains, and start to work on the diary. About thirty minutes later, I hear, "Psst! Zsolt!" It's Greg. He is officially leaving tomorrow. He has to be at JACOT at 0830 to start Customs, which means laying out all of his gear on blankets for inspection. That'll take hours, since there are about thirty people in his unit, plus whoever else is on the flight. So this is the "Big Goodbye." Some firm handshakes and he's off.

Greg has been a good friend and confidant, I will really miss him. I have been fortunate in my time here, first with J.J., and then with Greg. It's odd that I hook up with people not from my own unit, and usually people who are much more "military" than the Navy medical types. Wonder what the next six months will bring...

Tuesday: TQ Day 198.

Up at 1000, and I start work on the weekly patient conference for tomorrow. Not surprisingly, the performance improvement database does not work quite as advertised, meaning that the solutions to the problems do not jump straight out and hit a non-computer geek like me between the eyes. Good thing that I have John's e-mail address as he is the one who used to do this.

After a few hours of this, I go run about four miles, plus the gym. Gotta get back into the old groove. On the way back, I stop by the Army "CSM Store," a large shipping container full of stuff from care packages. Since the PX is out of paper towels, I pick up a dozen rolls, plus some pads, toothpaste, and nice TP. My roomies are a little startled when I run in carrying a trash bag but then, it's all a part of the mystique, isn't it?

Wednesday: TQ Day 199.

You can listen to other people's alarm clocks for only so long before you have to get out of bed. I had planned to get up at 0700 for the 0800 AOM. Our nurse roommate had set his alarm for 0530. It went on and on and on. Finally, he turns it off but doesn't get up. It goes off again at 0600, and 0630. It's nothing personal, but I will have to kill him now.

The Intel guy comes over for the first Intel brief for the new Team. Lots of gloom and doom, but then, good news is no news. Then I do the case conference. I emphasize all of the missing info — missing names, ages, injuries, operative reports, and medevac destinations, to point out that we will have no useful data this time around unless they start doing it better. The point is made. We need data if we are to improve how we look after patients.

I had planned to go over to CLR 25 afterwards to drop off the final draft of my Preliminary Investigation, but the car is gone so I run instead. The thermometer outside reads 140 degrees, which is probably because it's in an enclosed plastic housing that would heat up like a car in the sun, but what the hell, I get bragging rights. The weather report says only 104 today, which I don't believe either — maybe 104 on the third floor of the crack house, in the shade, with a breeze. Anyway, about three miles, shower, and I get the SUV at 1300.

I've invited anyone who is interested to tag along so I can give them a bit of a tour. We drive by the lake, photo op at THE palm tree; I tell them where the bat cave is, and so on. I then drop them off at the Hajji store on Lakeside while I go to CLR 25 to do the deed. Meet for a few minutes with the XO, who seems very happy that the JAG agrees on no further investigation. We shake, chat for a few, and when he gets a call, I head out. Pick up the guys and we head back.

Stop by Spring Lake, where they see the murals, Bunker PX, Coffee Shop, and pool. I point out to them that the rest of their stay will be all downhill from here. Lots of photos again. We sit around in the library of the coffee shop for about 45 minutes, chatting; they seem like pretty reasonable guys. Mike, the orthopod, seems like he's mellowing out a little bit.

I drop them and their battle rattle off in front of the hootches and, as I'm backing out of the gravel lot to return the vehicle, Mike (the Texas FP doc) knocks on the window. He's showing around a soon-to-be new guy, the PA for the incoming Illinois National Guard. He'd come out with their advance party to scope things out. Mike was walking him over to the SSTP to show him around, so I drive the 150 yards over and then give them the tour. He seems very interested in maintaining the same sort of relationship with us as the Texans did — in fact, he is a PA who works for a general surgeon and his doc here at TQ will be an ER doc, I believe. Sounds promising.

Thursday: TQ Day 200.

The nurse's alarm clock goes off at 0500 again. I will need to talk with him about this. I finally get up at 1000, make coffee, and eventually head over to the SSTP to check e-mail. I also discover that the boss has redistributed radios; I am now lucky number 7. Then off to run — it's red flag, and about time, too. Can't crow about green or yellow, only red or black.

Then, at about 2130, the radio says that we have two patients coming in. It takes six separate radio messages to tell us that there is a guy on a stretcher and a guy with a head injury. No time to arrival, no classification of urgency, no nationality, no mechanism, and so on. Have we never done this before?

The two guys show up, and there seems to be a remarkable lack of urgency shown by almost everyone. Eventually the guy is brought into the ER tent. He has a frag right between the eyes, is awake but looks pretty shocky, and he has a big hole in his ass. He'll need an operation for that, but the head could be a problem. What's his blood pressure? Oh, you don't have one? Maybe the machine's not broken — maybe it's because the pressure's so damned low that the machine won't pick it up. The boss decides to go and see if the OR is ready. After a couple of minutes, no word, so I go. Yup, they're ready. Back in the ER, I tell them to get moving — but they don't want to, they are still trying to get a blood pressure. Damn it, move!

Into the OR, there is a lot of foofurraw. I tell Tim, our senior anaesthesia guy, that I can drop in a central line for IV access if they need it. Since he has only one IV, is not yet intubated, and they are running around grabbing gear, he agrees. The boss and John start to scrub; I tell the OR tech to spray betadine over everything from the neck to the knees, and, as soon as the guy is intubated, I throw a central line under his collarbone. Takes me about thirty seconds and then we start pumping blood through it. The boss and John start on the belly. I rapidly scrub, and mention to the OR nurse that they might want more than one tech scrubbed in. As they enter the belly, Tim says he can't feel a pulse any more. There is a moment of silence. I tell the OR tech, "get the chest retractor," which is the hint to get the chest open for cardiac massage and whatever else. John and the boss do that while I stuff the belly full of lap pads to put pressure on whatever is bleeding in there. I happen to notice that the General is in the back of the room, but now is not a good time to say "hi."

They are trying to work through too small a hole, so I open the chest all the way. John has trouble with clamping the aorta, so I do that for him. But despite putting blood in as fast as they can, we're losing. I tell them how to put a line straight into the heart, we do that, pour blood through it, and the heart finally starts to work properly. In MY heart, I know that we're probably beyond the point of no return, but we're still going to do it all, this could be the one that beats the odds.

Get back to the belly. Big hole in the pelvis, dark blood shooting out — probably iliac vein — some papers claim this is the most lethal vascular injury there is. The boss is feeling the liver, "It's irregular." "If it's not bleeding, it's irrelevant." He also starts chasing holes in the bowel, putting clamps on things. Again, irrelevant for the moment. Gotta get the bleeding stopped. I suggest getting aortic control closer to the injury, then work on getting venous control. We do this. We have found the major bleeding, and are finally getting it under control. Then Tim tells us that we have no pulse again. John is closest so I tell him to look at the heart. It's over. About an hour and twenty minutes total.

Helluva case. We'll save the next one. It's not this Team's first death, but it is the first messy one. The guy shot in the head while I was on leave didn't count, as there's not much you can do for that. This guy was talking to us when he arrived so it's different. Several people ask me, aside, what we could have done differently. What do I say? Take it more seriously, don't act like these injuries are probably nothing. Evaluate the patients on the pad, move straight back to the OR. Don't waste time. Make the OR techs pay attention. Think ahead. Wouldn't have made a difference on this one, but maybe on the next.

Friday: TQ Day 201.

I spend the evening looking at some FMF stuff. I need to get my remaining exams over and done with so I can put this puppy to bed. Three exams, a 6-mile hump with flak, Kevlar and pack, and then an oral board.

Saturday: TQ Day 202.

Busy day today. At around 0800 I wake up when I hear a "thump," so I roll out of bed and put on my flak and Kevlar. The boss and Brian, the psychiatrist, ask what I'm doing. "Rocket." Oh. A couple of minutes later, the Big Voice goes off. May as well make some coffee and get the day going. Eventually we get the "All Clear."

A little after 0930, the radio goes off, incoming patients, and thirty minutes later, they arrive. Three Iraqis, injured by an IED. John is in the bathroom, I have just got back from there, and the boss is nowhere to be found. As I walk up to the pad, a panicky "Any surgeon to the SSTP" comes across the radio. I walk over and find there are three guys. One has a few scratches and punctures in his arm. "In the tent, he's okay." One has some lacerations to his face. "STP tent, check that eye." One has a big hole in his neck and his face is covered with blood. "OR, now." "But..." "OR. Now."

I take him back to the OR. He will need a neck exploration, but first things first. As Anaesthesia works on intubating him, I ask if they want more IV access. Okay, and since John comes in, I tell him to do it. X-rays. Belly ultrasound. Roll the patient — put a blanket under him now, he's easier to move later if he's on one, remember? The work-up proceeds quickly. I pull a big chunk of metal out of what remains of his left eye. He will need a head CT to look for a brain injury, his skull is obviously broken, and the neck will have to wait if it's not actively bleeding. I leave John to orchestrate his packaging, and go back to the ER tent to see what is going on.

There has been another radio call, telling us to expect sixteen more patients. What's the plan, I ask Ronny, our only real ER doc. He's informed the ACE and the dental guys, to form more stretcher-bearer parties. Nope, I have a better plan. Triage from the pad becomes critical for mass casualties: the ACE will get the minimally injured and we will handle the rest. Call the Texans, they will send over litter bearers and also their doc, PA, and a bunch of medics. They might even meet them at the gate and handle some of the minimally injured at their BAS.

I go to the ER tent. They have decided that this guy has an eye injury, so he will need to go, too. Mike is all excited about the guy's leg, which is badly broken, but it will have to wait as the eye is more important right now. Package him, too, so we can send him on the same bird. Have him ready in ten minutes. If we are getting more, then get these out of here now, while we can, to make room for more people.

Eventually they are packaged. Okay, where's the ambulance? I tell one of the Marine drivers to pull it up. Has anyone sent the "9-line (the message that requests the medevac)?" No. Why not? Oh, the ERC nurse is supposed to do that — we had decided on that at our last officers' meeting. Right, that would be the guy I've watched walking in circles for the last five minutes? So I ask him, and he says, "It's ready, I just have to say the word." "So say it." "What?" "Say the word. What are you waiting for?" Finally they leave.

The expected sixteen become two patients, both Iraqi soldiers with minimal injuries. It turns out that their hootch on Camp Habbaniyah (the Iraqi side of Camp Manhattan) was hit by a mortar. Glad I live here and not there. They get patched up.

Once it's all over, the boss tells me that there are other things going on. First, the Navy doc assigned to the detention facility in Ramadi needs to be replaced. "She" should be a "he." Someone has decided that a female doctor should not be treating male insurgents, don't ask me why. So they will send a "he." Also, there's talk about moving an FRSS (a surgical team) to Ramadi. Again, just like they talked about at the RIP when I got here in February. I have already written a memo documenting that the stats do not support this, all it would do is decrease the surgical capability here without adding anything there (I could find no one who died during 9 months at Ramadi who would likely have been saved by having a surgical team there, based on the info given me by the guys there and the info that we gathered when the patients got here). Over half of them were head injuries, which we could do nothing for, anyway. I have volunteered for pretty much every oddball thing to come along, and even I think this is a bad idea. The boss concurs, and he has told the "Powers that be" that, for all intents and purposes, the FRSS does not really exist here. All of the gear is mixed up with all of the other gear and there is no way to unmix it without having the unit fall apart.

Run a few miles, lift weights, read. Try to eat dinner at 1700, only to discover that the DFAC is closed. And when I walk to the new one, even further away, it is not yet open, but "might" be by 1900. So I walked about a mile for nothing. I end up eating my first MRE in Iraq. Thai chicken. Yum. This stuff really isn't too bad, although I'd probably get sick of it if I had to eat it all of the time.

I receive an e-mail from the Marine liaison to the local Iraqi division; he is trying to track down what happened to one of their soldiers. He has been working at it for 17 days, gotten nowhere, and someone gave him my e-mail. I send e-mails to contacts at both Balad and Baghdad, and a short while later learn that the guy died of a severe head injury 8 days ago. I pass it along, and tell him to e-mail me again if he needs info on anyone who might have come through TQ. I know what it's like to try to get follow-up patient info.

Tuesday: TQ Day 205.

I discover that we get to count bullets today. On order of the Marine Logistics Officer, we all have to show up at 1300 and have our bullets counted. This is a joke, right? First, find me a piece of paper with my name on it that shows that I signed for 30 rounds — they simply handed around an ammo can in Kuwait and we grabbed some. So at 1300, still in PT gear, I throw on my pistol harness and walk over. I am the only one in PT gear, but no one says anything. I really don't care. I got the message by word of mouth, so no uniform was specified; I was still all sweaty from running. They don't want me to take a shower and show up late, do they? 'Sides, PT gear is my work uniform — I work in the OR and this is what I operate in. The "garrison mentality" is getting worse...

Wednesday: TQ Day 206.

At 0730 there is a loud boom and the Big Voice goes off. Call in for accountability and go back to sleep. I learn later from Intel that it was a very large, truck-based, VBIED several miles away on MSR Michigan, not a rocket on base at all. The Big Voice went off because someone in the Crack House (allegedly the Air Boss) swears that he saw a rocket fly past the window...

Hang out at HESCO Beach in the evening, chatting with the boys. The two hot topics are Christmas decorations, and slogans for a unit t-shirt. We didn't really have one but fixed the "We fight for life" thing that 2nd Med had buggered up; the "damage controllin', death cheatin'" thing was a nonstarter, thank heavens. Suggestions included: "Shi'ite happens in the Sunni love triangle"; "TriQare Middle East (no paperwork, just people)"; "TQ Surgical — your first and only choice for trauma care." The latter two were mine from the last round.

Friday, September 30: TQ Day 208.

Am getting dressed to go to dinner when we hear of an Iraqi soldier coming in from Camp Habbaniyah who's apparently in a bad way. Actually, it will be three patients total. A mortar round. The first guy shows up already intubated, looking bad. For once, he goes from the pad straight back to the OR. He has a badly depressed skull fracture, and half of his back is blown off— his left shoulder is essentially hanging off. But he has no holes in his chest or belly despite the massive blast, and the injury to worry about the most is his head. John (duty surgeon) and I confer and decide that if we can get his blood pressure back up, he will be sent to Baghdad for the neurosurgeon. If we can't, he's history with that head injury. Within a few minutes we do manage to get the pressure up with four units of blood, and away he goes. I tell the ERC nurse going with him to expect him to die en route and, if he starts going south on the way, do NOT turn the helo around and come back as there's nothing else we can do for him here. I suspect that he did not survive to go to CT there; we'll see.

Of the two others, one Iraqi has a big haematoma on his chest; the boss has put a chest tube into him in the ER. He will need some surgery on his arm, at the least. The other has chest pain and a funny-looking chest x-ray, he needs a chest CT. As I leave the tent, I hear a huge explosion quite close by. Look around and see black smoke rising over tent city. Oh, excrement. People are running out onto the pad to look. I yell at them to get back under cover, as the Big Voice goes off. I go into the COC and call the direct line to the Air Boss, to tell him that whenever the helos start flying again after the "All Clear," let us know because we have a couple to go out. I am told that the helos are not grounded despite the rocket attack, so I go back to the ER tent and tell them to pack and ship these two, in case we get casualties of our own. We have no idea where the rocket has hit, it's not our job to find out, but we should make room while we can in case it's bad. With a little stimulation, both of these two patients are gone in a few minutes.

We wait. The Air Boss comes down. He tells us that the Chapel has been hit. Since it is now a little after 1700, i.e., dinner time, hopefully there was no one in there. The padres were up with us, so they're okay. But they are worried for their RPs (Religious Program specialists, the Navy does have such a thing). After about ten more minutes, we get the word. One casualty, neck pain. That's it. We're lucky. A young lady, very freaked out, hyperventilating. A little later, one of the RPs shows up, very distraught. He sits by himself on the benches outside the tents, looking dazed. Apparently he was in a cubbyhole on the other side of the chapel and is uninjured but scared to death. I start to rub his head. "What are you doing, sir?" "Rubbing some of your luck off onto me." He looks at me for a few seconds, then it clicks and he starts to grin. Father Tim rubs him, too.

9. October 2005: A Helluva Save

Saturday: TQ Day 209.

As I put down my book (Rudyard Kipling's *Kim*) to go to sleep around midnight, the radio goes off—one casualty with a head injury coming in. This "one" eventually becomes five SEALs who rolled their SUV out on MSR Michigan. We get it all sorted out eventually, no one has anything serious, and back to bed around 0300. I crawl out of bed at 0700 because half the unit does not seem to realize that the clocks were turned back at 0200 with the end of daylight savings time, and there is lots of radio chatter an hour early for the morning radio muster. Of course, we had all been up at 0300, so why do we need to muster four hours later?

Doesn't matter because a hand injury comes in around 0730 anyway. An idiot. A shell casing had been stuck in his machine gun and he had used another live round as a hammer to knock it out. Knocking the base of the .50 cal round (which is as long as a dollar bill and fatter than my thumb) sets it off, of course, just like the firing pin would, and it blows a hole through the guy's hand. He will only be able to count to nine from now on.

After that, I go over to the Chapel to take some pictures, because Base Ops is always quite quick at cleaning up the mess when a rocket hits. Wreckage is bad for morale, don't you know. The Protestant chaplain is there and he shows me a pair of heavy brass cymbals that have been warped and perforated. Wow. There's a fair-sized hole in the roof and wall, but most of the building is intact.

On the way back, hear that three U.S. patients are coming in by air. I go change. Of the three, five are now Iraqi "friendlies" and one is a civilian (?). Eventually, three come in, not looking good. The boss is the duty surgeon and heads out to the pad. He directs John into the first tent with one guy, I go with the next. Mine has a hole in his side, don't know how deep, and his big belly hurts. I ultrasound him, his largeness doesn't help, can't really get a good look for blood in there. The boss says that of the three, this guy is the worst, so he sends me to the OR to ex lap him. Okay, away we go. I'm plus-minus on the ex lap but it's a reasonable thing to do. I move him into the OR and, as we carry him in, I tell the anaesthesia guys what the plan is — shoot a chest x-ray to decide on a chest tube, then intubation, then possible chest tube, then into his belly. Efficiently but not madly, as the guy is not crashing. About two minutes later, after the x-ray is done

148

and the IVs are set, anaesthesia is about to push drugs to have him go to sleep when the boss comes in and says that this guy needs to move out to the PACU (the "recovery room" tent between the two ORs) because three more have shown up, one is already in the other OR, and another needs this one. Pick him up, move him out.

I go back into the OR as the new patient is brought in. His face and neck are covered in blood; he has a big hole in his cheek. He's built like a bull. Stretcher is dropped onto the OR stand (the stretcher serves as the tabletop), anaesthesia starts giving him oxygen and anesthetic drugs through the mask. He has no IVs at all; they are struggling to give him one but he is fighting and trying to sit up, and they can't "sleep" him without IV access. Okay, great, here's the plan: Ronnie (an ER guy), you try to put a central line (big IV) in his groin; Tim, mask him with gas as well as you can, it will sedate him somewhat; I will put a central line in his chest. Ronnie is already at work as I get my kit. My line is done in less than a minute, despite his trying to sit up twice during the procedure, and the drugs and fluids are flowing through it. Ronnie's line doesn't work (aren't I "The Man"?), that's okay, he goes off to sleep. Since he's pouring blood through the hole in his face and there is blood in his mouth, I stand ready to cut a hole in his neck ("crich" him) if needed. Tim is a good anaesthesiologist; the tube goes in through a special device called an intubating LMA that will need to be removed later. The chest x-ray is shot as I put the "probing finger of death" through the hole in his cheek, pull out bone fragments that I do not want to fall into his airway, and put my finger through his shattered mandible. Don't know how far this frag goes in, but it's heading straight back towards his brain. Head CT needed. I tell Tim he needs to get the fancy LMA out of the patient's mouth now or it's going on the helo with him, because once I put the packing in, it's not moving. He starts to work on that as I ultrasound his belly and see no blood anywhere. His blood pressure is okay right now. I tell them to start packing him to ship out. I look up — oh, hi, General, didn't see you there. This has taken about five minutes; I stick my head out to see what else is going on. The boss runs up, I give him the 30-second synopsis. He says, go in the other OR and help John, he has a clamp on the aorta and the orthopedic surgeon is helping him. The boss has a third OR to start up for another guy with a hole in his belly. Fine, my guy needs wrapping but someone else can do it.

I walk into OR 2, gown and glove myself without scrubbing, and dive in. This guy took a frag through the left flank and came into the OR with no pulse. John had taken my comments on the last such case to heart and immediately opened the chest and clamped the aorta to keep as much blood flowing to the brain as possible, and then opened the belly. He asks me to check the crossclamp, but it's good. Nice pulse above, none below, just like it should be.

In the belly, there's lots of blood gushing up from deep in the pelvis. I shove packs into where it's coming from, it slows down a lot. I show John how to expose the aorta in the abdomen. I get the clamp on the abdominal aorta and we take it off the chest; now he can get blood flow to more of his body but still purposefully not down to where the bleeding is. We work on exposing the aorta and vena cava further down; I suspect another iliac vein injury like last time. But that does not appear to be the case as the vessels look good down there. On the way, we take out a hunk of bowel with a big hole in it, about a minute's worth of work. John lets me lead a lot of this, since he's new to this and I'm in my element; but I have him do a lot of it under my prompting and direction. I show him how to do things fast, and then get him to do it. Lots of dissection with fingers, less with instruments. "Haste makes speed" is the trauma surgeon's motto. Or, "We may be lost, but we're moving." Once we're happy that the vessels are intact, the clamp comes off the aorta.

The frag has gone through the side of his abdomen and blown a hole through the muscles in his back, into the large venous plexus in the pelvis. This is a large g'mish of veins that you can't really get to and tie off, there are so many and they are so interconnected. You have to rely on pressure to make them clot. We are about 25 units of blood into this — we aren't winning but we are staying even. Time to cut and run. Pack the hell out of the pelvis to put pressure on things, start closing the belly from both ends at once. We are about half done when Gerry, our other anaesthesiologist, says, "I can't feel a pulse."

I look in the chest, moving the lung out of the way. The pericardium, the sack around the heart, has not been opened, but I feel it and his heart is not moving. Crap. Open the pericardium, start manual chest compressions. His heart is full of blood, so they have managed to keep up with the blood loss, but it's not pumping. I show them all how to put a hand under the heart and compress the heart up against the sternum from below, this is the most effective way to pump it manually — twice as good as using both hands, in fact. As I do manual massage I ask about how much blood he's been given, whole blood, calcium, and various other things. I ask about vasopressin — nope, not given. It's my favorite trauma drug in the world, the only drug ever to be shown to improve survival in hemorrhagic shock. Give it. I predict that, in two or three minutes, we will get a return of heart function, although it may not last long. Been down this road a few times in the last few months.

I keep squeezing the flaccid and otherwise motionless heart. Right now, he's dead, but in my book he's not dead until I say he is. My compressions are giving him a pulse, he is exchanging CO_2 (carbon monoxide for oxygen) in his lungs (we have a monitor to check this) so we know the lungs are getting a fair amount of blood flow. After two minutes, the heart starts to fibrillate. Not a good rhythm, but any activity is better than none. I tell John to finish closing the belly while I keep compressing. A few more minutes and his heart is actually beating every few seconds. Not enough, I keep at it. After about twenty minutes of manual compressions, his heart starts to beat again, properly, on its own.

Ever the skeptic, I say we wait. Seen this happen before, but no one like this had ever lived to get out of the OR. Still, I tell the OR nurse to track down the flight nurse, get all the gear (ventilators, monitors, oxygen and so forth) together now, in case he makes it. After a few minutes, he's still beating, he has a decent blood pressure. Damn! Close the chest, get him out of here. He's on a bird in ten minutes, and we hear that he arrives in Baghdad with a blood pressure.

We were in the OR for about two hours, all told. The boss had done a quick ex lap on a guy with a frag to the belly, packed it, and closed it — he'd been flown out already, as had the face guy. A couple of guys with frags in their legs are on the ward, a guy with a chest tube is getting ready to fly out, and there is a Turk in the ACE with a heart attack. But things have calmed down a lot. Stand around talking with the General, he seemed happy with how things went. Yup, we earned our pay today. Talked about the biggest case — if he lives, he'll be our greatest save I know of out here to date.

The Texas PA has wandered by to invite me to a BBQ tonight, around 1800. It's 1700 now, so no problem. At 1800, I head over there. Damn fine steak, juicy fat hot dogs, Texas-style beans. Good stuff.

Sunday: TQ Day 210.

I'm drooling on my pillow when I wake up, certain that I heard, "Attention all Ridgeways." I lie there, but hear nothing further for a few minutes. Must be a dream, and I drift back off again. Then I wake up again — "He may need intubation." Okay, I'm certain that I heard that. Roll out of bed, run up to the SSTP. Two Iraqis soldiers were unceremoniously dumped off on the pad by I don't know whom, their ride is gone by now. This was quite a few minutes ago. Somehow the call had not gone out properly, almost no one is there except for the duty doc, our most inexperienced family practice physician. We get to work and more people are showing up.

One guy has pain in his ass and can't walk; his x-rays are of poor quality; he may have a pelvic fracture but he's stable. The second guy has a badly broken shoulder and most likely a pulmonary contusion. He's having trouble breathing, which is not improved by a chest tube to drain the blood out. He ends up intubated, and they both go off to Baghdad.

Back to sleep, but I'm again awakened by the radio at 0700, this time for the morning muster. Great... I finally get out of bed at 0730 and make coffee. Unfortunately, we have decided to revive a tradition from my last Team which I had rarely partaken of, never being up that early: Sunday morning coffee at 0800, on the Beach. Fireman Joe, a former Marine, has planned to come, along with a few others. So I'm there at 0800, coffee in hand.

Joe shows up, the boss, John, a few others. We sit around chatting and eating biscotti. At 0830, the radio announces a casualty.

It's an Iraqi, with a tangential GSW to the back. Happened over an hour ago. He's very stable. He keeps saying, "Thank you, my friend," and says he's an accountant for the Ministry of Education. Apparently he ignored some warning shots as he drove up to a convoy, so his vehicle was shot at. Chest x-ray is okay, so no chest tube for him. I see that he has frags in his back, though. He needs a CT — after an hour, with no belly pain, I doubt if he has a significant injury that needs an operation, but we should be safe. Off he goes. I go back to bed until noon.

The boss tells me that our miracle patient from yesterday, the guy whose heart we restarted, died, along with the guy whose liver he'd operated on. Not good, but what can you do? This team has had more deaths early on in the rotation, but right now I assume that it's luck of the draw.

There's a CLR 25 officers' PME (Professional Military Education) lecture tonight at 2000 on the other side of the base. I tell the boss that I'll call them back if I need any help, as I'm staying behind as Duty Surgeon. About half an hour after they all head out, the radio says we have one incoming casualty, with a "near-total amputation" from stepping on a landmine. I walk over and we get the OR set up. A few minutes later I see the boss — the meeting was changed to yesterday, they forgot to tell us. Oh well. A few minutes after that, we hear that the casevac corpsman diverted the helo to Fallujah, even though it is farther away — someone's head will probably roll over that one, it's been an issue before. The Air Boss himself had called us with this info and he was pretty pissed off. What makes it even worse is that it's one of our Marines — an MP from CLR 25. The CLR 25 CO had driven over when he heard about the incoming casualty and is quite (understandably) unhappy about this. He heads over to the Crack House to find out what's what. I wouldn't want to be that corpsman...

We've had a busy few days, so I go to bed early at 2230.

Monday: TQ Day 211.

Only to be woken at 0200. The boss gets a radio call, there are 14 "urgent surgical" casualties somewhere, how many can we take? He says all of them, if we have to. What else can he say? They know who we are and what capacity we have. The person on the other end says okay and they'll send 6, but it may be all of them if necessary. Huh? Why ask? We roll out of bed and go up to the tent. Much confusion, but eventually we figure out that it's a group of Iraqi Army soldiers, coming from Combat Outpost. No idea of injuries. I get things ready, tell the OR techs to scrub, have the second x-ray unit brought over from the ACE, make sure we have warm fluids. Then we wait.

Around 0300, they arrive. I am out on the pad and, as the door opens, I see two Iraqis on stretchers, trying to sit up and look around. We get them onto the pad and I look at them. The blanket is lifted, and my first thought is, "Where is the injury?" This guy doesn't have a mark on him, and he's trying to sit up. Push on the belly, no pain, he can go to the ACE (where we send the minimally wounded during mass casualties). Next guy, a bandage over his ear, is also trying to sit up and look around. Pull the bandage off and find he has a small cut on his ear. "Minimal, take him to the ACE." Two more ambulances pull up and six more patients are disgorged. One is intubated but I see no overt injuries, so he goes to the STP tent. Start looking over the other five when I'm told that this is all we will be getting. The boss had started at the other end and tells me there's a guy with a possible broken leg, but he will put him on the ward for now. "Put him in the ER tent, so far he's our #2 casualty." The boss looks surprised.

When all is done, we just have the intubated guy, whom the ER guys have paralyzed because he was fighting the ET tube. The guy doesn't have a mark on him so maybe he didn't need to be intubated. No paperwork from Combat Outpost, so no idea why he was tubed. Me, I might have considered extubating him to see what happens, i.e., he could wake up and be fine. Another guy has neck pain, he will need a neck CT, and so these are the two to fly to Baghdad. For the other six casualties, their combined injuries amount to a little cut on the chest, a cut finger, a nicked ear, a bruised shin, dust in the eye, and a case of "severe belly pain," which was magically cured when we let the "patient" stand up to empty his melon-sized bladder. We go back to bed at 0500. It is made very clear to the admin weenies that we have mustered for the morning.

Unfortunately, we are still woken up at 0730, to be told that we have to have our radios at the COC by 0830 to be reencrypted. Didn't we do this two days ago? In an act of consummate civil/military disobedience, I go back to sleep. At 0815, the radio lists all of the radios (i.e., most of them) that still need to go up; Brian offers to take mine up there. Back to sleep.

Not for long. Urgent banging on the door at 0900, one of the Marines from the COC. None of the radios work now, so he's looking for any docs — we have a GSW to the head arriving in 5 minutes. Roll out, shoes on, away I go. As I get to the pad I hear someone yelling, "He's going straight back to the OR." Hold your horses, who decided that? Only a surgeon makes that call, and I am the only surgeon here. I get to the pad simultaneously with the ambulance and, as the door opens, we see the Medic is doing CPR. We pull the stretcher out and put it down on the pad. The top of his head is wide open and there is brain everywhere. It looks like the classic "swallowed a bullet" suicide. "Into the ER tent." "But the OR—" "Into the ER tent, now." It's already over.

The stretcher is dropped on the stands, CPR is ongoing. Stop CPR. I check for pulses — nothing. Continue CPR. I tell them to hook up the EKG leads, first priority. Check two leads, no significant cardiac activity. I call it — time of death, 0914. Not even time for an IV. I will do every possible thing, no matter how unlikely to succeed, for our guys, but this is futile. Let him die with as much dignity as we can give him. I turn around, tell everyone coming in to please leave, and drop the flap to the tent. I then tell everyone in the tent to please not discuss this outside of the unit. No idle chatter at the chow hall, nothing. We don't need to feed the rumor mill. He is cleaned up and I have a good look at his wounds, since I will be pronouncing him dead.

The top of his head is open. I feel around in his mouth but feel no broken palate, so where is the entrance wound? Wipe some blood off his face and see a hole to the right side of his mouth. Very odd for a suicide; they usually put the barrel under the chin or in the mouth.

At this point, the soldier's CO, just back from leave, and some of his officers come in. He looks pretty shaken. I wonder if he has ever seen anything like this before, probably not. He's not exactly a combat veteran. We talk for a couple of minutes; their chaplain says a prayer for him. I go out to do the paperwork. Won't be the first death certificate I've filled out here, or the last. So far, this is the closest to home, though. I did not know this guy, but I know many people in his unit. Even if I didn't know him, he was one of "my guys." It will be worse for his unit: most of these soldiers are from the same area, some of them may be seeing his family around town for years to come.

I learn later that it was witnessed and it was an accident. He mishandled his own loaded pistol. He was one of the best soldiers in the entire unit, too, I hear. His unit has had two deaths since they arrived ten months ago — one guy electrocuted while washing his Humvee, and now this, both within a month of each other. The Iraqis can't kill them, but they can accidentally kill themselves. They are less than two months from going home; too close to have stupid things like this happen.

As I am standing outside, leaning on some packing crates and filling out the death paperwork, the IDC from the ACE comes over to consult on a guy with tonsillitis; he thinks it needs to be drained. I caught myself just before I snapped at him, don't you realize that I have something more important to do? But he doesn't know and, in reality, I don't — the living before the dead, and paperwork last of all. I admit the guy for IV antibiotics, no surgical drainage. He should be okay in a day or two, but later the boss tells me that he wants the guy flown out on the milk run as the nurses and corpsmen are "beat" from all the activity of the last few days. This way they shouldn't have to staff the ward tonight.

Later, after running, I stop by the dead soldier's BAS and talk to their guys a bit. Their docs are pretty shaken. They had criched the guy (cut a hole in his neck to put in a breathing tube), on their hands and knees in the dirt. Neither had ever done one before. Talk with them a little, too; they should be okay.

At this rate, it is going to be a long war. But, upon introspection, I am not too gloomy or depressed about it. It is a challenge and there are obstacles to overcome, but somehow I know that all of us will. And it's what I came out here for, I suppose.

Thursday: TQ Day 214.

I happen across one of the Civil Affairs officers, we talk for an hour about various things. He tells me that two of the soldiers who saw that guy shoot himself a few days back are now having trouble sleeping, having flashbacks, and generally not doing well. They need to see psych, of course. Unfortunately, they left on a convoy to Al Asad for 5 to 10 days. I'm sure we haven't heard the last of this.

After dinner, I am buffing my Saturday talk when we hear of casualties again. Three U.S., one priority, and two routine, in 15 to 30 minutes. I get my coffee cup (I have just brewed some) and wander over. We wait. And wait. And wait. After an hour, we are told it will be another hour, so everyone disperses. Twenty minutes later, I hear a helo land at Post 1 (only medevac helos land there) and go back up to the SSTP. The ambulance pulls up and three Iraqis step out.

The most recently injured hurt his back three days ago in an IED blast. Another one scratched his eye two weeks ago. The third was shot in the leg 5 weeks ago and has some drainage from his wound. He comes complete with a hospital discharge summary from an Army hospital and several outpatient clinic notes, and a note from an Army medic dated two days ago that says, "Should make his way to Baghdad somehow for further medical care." All three of these patients are supposed to be going to Baghdad, anyway, as routine follow-ups, and should have been "milk run" patients. Five weeks post-injury? Needless to say, when the Air Boss found out, he had a cow.

Drink a near-beer on the beach with some of the boys and then head off to bed.

Friday: TQ Day 215.

Awakened at 0200 for a "KBR contractor dropped off on the pad." So we all get up and race over there. Well, "dropped off" isn't quite accurate. "Walked up" is more like it. A middle-aged Pakistani gentleman with sciatica. I think we need to revise the SOP for this. We shouldn't be activating the enter trauma unit for non-trauma patients. In fact, we shouldn't be seeing them at all unless they have been prescreened by one of the BASs.

Some people wanted to yell at the Marine in the COC, but he was just following the procedure he's been given—in writing no less.

Back to bed. Awakened at 0715 for the usual mustering radio traffic, then back to sleep until 1000. I get up, work on my Grand Rounds for tomorrow, then around 1215 I go to the SSTP to check e-mail before running. It's fortunate that I had gone to check e-mail, because it turns out that I had forgotten about our latest bullet count. It was a little scary, actually: people walk up and show their weapons to the clipboard guys to check serial numbers—without clearing their weapons. While we're not supposed to carry our weapons loaded while on base, you can never be too careful. We just had someone shot in the head this week, and no one is paying attention, especially not the people who are unfamiliar with weapons to begin with. I clear my weapon, lock the slide back, and try to show the empty chamber to the corpsman recording numbers, and he doesn't want to see it. I corrected his attitude a little bit on that account. Then the fabled bullet count again. I learn later that this exercise was, in part, stimulated by a Captain who had gone to the gym and left a pistol there. If the Captain wasn't medical and an O-6, they would have been standing before the General and quite possibly court-martialed.

Run, gym, read. At 1600 we get a radio call that, from 1600 to 2000, everyone has to be in their flak and Kevlar. Rumor is that during Ramadan last year, it was prime time for rockets. I eat at 1700, absolutely no one on line for chow. About an hour later, we hear of a patient coming in with a possible concussion. As I walk up to the SSTP, a panicky "Any physician to the SSTP now!" goes out. I am about fifty feet away.

An ambulance from the Army Guard Unit at Camp Manhattan has pulled up, disgorging an intubated Iraqi. As I walk up, I notice something quite unusual about him: he is wide awake and making motions to have us take the tube out. A quick search and I rush him into the ER tent. I ask the Army guys why he's intubated—he fell off a ladder. Okay, that makes no sense. So, as he quite calmly gesticulates to have the tube pulled out, I untape it and do so. He is very happy. We shake hands. I look at the medical record (one page) that came with him. If I believe it, it shows that he was paralyzed for intubation but not anaesthetized or sedated—boy, that would suck! Maybe they just forgot to write it down. The back of the sheet says, "Lost consciousness for about 15 seconds—resuscitated with CPR." All I can find wrong with him is wrist pain and ankle pain. Another save by the Team, thank you very much.

While this is going on, the patient we had actually been called for shows up. A young Marine, a truck driver, whose 7-ton was pulling a "water bull" (a large, 2-wheeled water trailer) when an IED went off. It trashed the water bull, did nothing to her 7-ton, and she was uninjured. This was 2½ hours ago. She is brought in with a "concussion" and a "bruise on her head." She didn't hit her head, I can't find a bruise, and it doesn't hurt anywhere. A little anxiety, that's about it. Lucky girl, RTD (Return To Duty).

Saturday, October 8: TQ Day 216.

Changing into PT gear, when I hear of incoming casualties. When they arrive, there are three Army guys from Combat Outpost, hit by a mortar. I take one to the OR with

Mike to put an ex fix on his femur and wash out various wounds. The boss takes another guy to open his foot up. The third guy will wait to get his wounds cleaned up. My case takes a lot longer, being both legs and the back, but the boss doesn't start the third case because we hear another one is coming in.

This one is a doozy. An EPW who charged his car at a checkpoint, shot by the same unit we took all the casualties from. He has an M16 round through his pelvis and looks pretty bad. I stick a big IV line in his chest (this is getting to be my "specialty," getting massive IV access in 30 to 60 seconds at the start of big ugly cases) while I tell the boss to scrub. We open the belly, but there's no blood in it. What he has is a massive retroperitoneal haematoma, the biggest that I have ever seen. It appears that he is bleeding into the tissues behind his abdominal cavity, around his aorta and vena cava, into his pelvis. Very, very bad. We open the haematoma and get to work, exposing these vessels, while he bleeds like stink — unfortunately we have to release the bleeding to find the source. After about 90 minutes of work, we still are unable to get it controlled — most of the bleeding is from his shattered pelvis, which the bullet has destroyed. He eventually bleeds to death despite our best efforts. During the case, both the boss and I have had to step out and hydrate, we've sweated so much.

When this case is done, I have one more to do, another ex fix on a broken humerus, again a frag from a mortar, again from the unit at Combat Outpost. These guys have a liaison officer whom we have been seeing far too much of lately. He has been hanging with us all day, seeing how his guys do. The two we lost on the same day last week were also his. They have been getting hit very hard lately.

Finally got done around 2230 — over ten hours of surgery today. I'm not so much hungry as tired and thirsty. And there are no post-call days here.

Sunday: TQ Day 217.

Got up at 0800 to drink coffee. At 0930, right as Mass was starting, a call for an incoming casualty. An Army sergeant, a tank commander, had been in the turret looking through binoculars. He saw the sniper just as the guy shot at him, hitting him in the left forearm. Nothing broken, no injured nerves, but he was developing a compartment syndrome, where increased pressure from bleeding and swelling will numb nerves and decrease blood flow. So off he went to the OR to get the wound opened up and cleaned out.

After that, I try to check e-mail, only to discover that I can't. For some inexplicable reason, I can't log onto the computer system at all, it won't accept my user name or password. That's not good. I walk over to the "Help Desk" behind the Dark Tower and lodge my complaint and they say that they will work on it. We'll see how long that takes. Then off to PT and the gym.

After dinner, the e-mail is still down so I go back to comms to check. I happen across a nice Marine lieutenant, who looks Chinese and about 14 years old and, who wears glasses — yup, computer geek. He hooks me up, and in about ten minutes my problem is fixed. For whatever reason, my access to the Marine net was erased and had to be reset; all my stored e-mails are still there, fortunately.

We have received word that we are to wear flak and Kevlar daily from 1600 to 2000, the "prime time" for rocket attacks, until further notice. Right after 2000, I go over to the AT&T Phone Center — unfortunately, everyone else has had the same idea, there are thirty people on line. So much for calling home for your birthday. Wish I could have been home for it.

Monday: TQ Day 218.

Around 0200, another five "routine" patients turn up, all dropped off by the milk run. Not sure why since they're all stable and supposed to be going to the Echelon IIIs. Is this going to become a habit? Fortunately, only the duty ER doc was notified, so we all rolled over and went back to sleep.

At 0715, roll out of bed for a report of three or four casualties, I can't remember exactly how many. The rest of today was a bit of a blur. Head up there, the boss is primary. All Iraqis, hit by an IED: one guy with a badly smashed humerus and some holes in the other arm; one guy with a broken ankle; one guy with a frag through his head who will die. Mike and I take the humerus guy back. It takes a while for Mike to get all the x-rays he wants when he finally does arrive at the tent (about half an hour late, he was out running). The boss starts on the foot guy. As I get ready to scrub, I hear yelling from the pad and I run out. Another ambulance has disgorged three more Iraqis; we received no warning on this load. One guy, with a hole in his arm, can wait. One middle-aged woman with a frag hole in her belly; she'll need an operation but she is sitting up and looking around. And a twelve-year-old kid, looking bad. I lift the dressing on his belly and see quite a large hole in his lower chest, the size of my fist, with his lung and liver sticking out of it. But he is alive and moving. I tell the stretcher bearers to go straight back to our third OR and tell the ER doc to send the other two off to a Level III as they are stable enough to go. I go back to the OR, stick my head in, and tell the boss what's going on. I tell Mike he's "on his own" and go off to work.

I spend the next three hours with this kid. I hear that we have more casualties, but am busy. Brian, our young family practice doc, has scrubbed in to help me, but he felt faint and had to leave in less than an hour, poor kid. About an hour into the case, the boss pops in and asks how it's going. "I'm fine, I've got this." "What do you have?" "Grade V (really bad) liver injury with a one pound frag in the retrohepatic cava" (the inferior vena cava, a.k.a. "Big Blue," the vein you never want to mess with, especially not behind the liver). Complete silence for a moment. "You need help?" "Why, is there nothing else going on?" "Yeah, we have plenty to do." "Don't worry, I've got this." He looks at me a little oddly but says okay and leaves.

I spend a good part of the case stopping myself from doing the one thing I really want to do, which is yank the fragment out. If I do, he'll bleed to death in seconds. Instead, I open his belly wide and connect it to the hole in his chest. That way I can see his liver from above and below, and get access to every blood vessel going into the liver, in case I need to clamp it all off. Every move I make, I let the anaesthesia boys catch up with blood and fluids. No hurry, a few jokes here and there. Finally, I'm ready: I get a

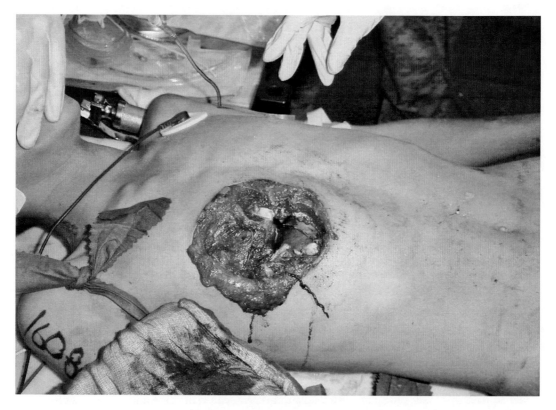

My most memorable case, a young Iraqi boy who had been fragged and came in alive and talking. He had a huge hole in his chest, with the lung and liver clearly visible. I pulled a frag the size of my hand out of the liver and vena cava, thanked God that there was no explosion of blood, and stitched the kid's chest back together again. He was spotted by a patrol 3 months later, playing soccer. They said it was the ugliest scar they had ever seen, but he was doing fine.

BFC (Big Damned Clamp) and yank the fragment out through the liver, accompanied by a fountain of blood, then pack the hole with a huge wad of gelfoam and put pressure on it. For ten minutes, I stand there with my hand on his liver, while more blood goes into the kid. Then I take a look.

A little oozing, but no major bleeding. Damn! Am I lucky or what? I repair his cava and his diaphragm — it's shredded but somehow I quilt it together. The repaired diaphragm also helps put some additional pressure on the gelfoam packs. I then close his belly, which will allow some additional pressure to build up and also help stop the oozing. Then I get to try to put his chest back together. With some fairly creative macramé, I get it mostly closed; he still has a hole through the muscle and ribs about 2 x 3 inches in size, but I manage to get the skin closed over everything. At the end of the case, he has a nice blood pressure, heart rate, and he's not bleeding much out of his chest tube. If this kid makes it, he will be a helluva save. Unfortunately, I have said that before...

I get out of the OR around 1330, drink a couple of quarts of something, and then go into the next case, helping Mike with a foot that has had the heel blown off. Afterwards, the boss and I walk around to make sure we haven't missed anything. Total patients: nineteen in two hours, eighteen Iraqis (military and civilian), and one U.S. Army soldier

with a small frag in the back of his neck. One dies outright (the frag to the head); operations on my liver kid, another guy with a couple of holes in his belly (the boss), an ankle
fracture (boss, again), the broken arm (Mike), and the heel guy (me and Mike.) A few
more needed surgery but were stable so they had been sent on because the ORs were full.
By the way, the worst we had with the Blue Team was nineteen in one hour, but we also
had one more surgeon, and never had to run three rooms. So we can feel pretty good
about today, if you ignore the human carnage part of it.

I get the story about today's events: a VBIED was driven into the town market in
Habbaniyah. No idea how many were killed outright, but we got all the wounded. Other
things have been going on elsewhere, at least nine to Fallujah, two Bradleys were blown
up in Ramadi with at least 2 KIAs. Who knows what else went on today. In addition to
the upcoming elections, we hear that apparently you get extra martyr points for blowing
yourself up during Ramadan.

At dinner, people are pretty chatty and pumped up, everyone feels good about the
job we did. I'd learned that my kid made it to Baghdad okay. He's in the ICU looking
pretty good. Keep my fingers crossed on that. The boss makes some pretty wicked comments to the FP doc about almost passing out in my OR, but I come to his defense: "Hey,
lay off, I really appreciated the help — for as long as it lasted!"

Called you at home tonight, wish I could have been there to give you a big squeeze.
Miss you a lot.

Tuesday: TQ Day 219.

Up at the crack of 10 today. Started work on entering the data from the last week's
casualties. Despite my constant reminders, the inability of these people to fill out simple
forms correctly remains astonishing. We received 19 patients from the same VBIED
incident in Habbaniyah yesterday. They all arrived by Army ambulance. Our diligent
corpsmen listed them variously as coming by USMC casevac helo; ground ambulance;
walking; being carried (I suppose these last two are correct if you figure that they walked
or were carried from the ambulance to the tent). Dates and times are incorrect, many
forms are missing, dead people have vital signs, live people don't, and medevac destinations
are missing or incorrect. That said, patients before paperwork.

Had planned to run in the early afternoon, but patients arrived. First, a TCN contractor fell off scaffolding near the DFAC and broke his arm; then a Jordanian truck driver
arrives with frags through his foot from an IED. I hold the guy's passport so the corpsman
can copy the patient's name and birthday; five minutes later, his paperwork has "unknown
Iraqi" written on it. How am I going to get follow-up? Why do I even bother?

Wednesday: TQ Day 220.

Worked on the case conference some more. As I had mentioned, the data quality
from this week is abysmal. Around 1630, three U.S. casualties come in, IED again. One

has facial burns and needs to be intubated, but should be fine. The second has his scalp singed and a frag in his scalp, he goes for head CT with the intubated guy to look for a brain injury. The third has a frag through his arm, no broken bones though, and Mike (orthopod) and Phil (ortho PA) take him to the OR to wash it out. The boss and I stand around and talk, and after about thirty minutes one of the OR nurses comes out and says that Mike wants one of us in there. "Okay, what did you make bleed?" "Why do you say that?" "Why else would you call us?" "Yeah, well..." The boss, as duty surgeon today, scrubs in to tie off a deep branch off the brachial artery that the frag cut on its way through the arm. I head off to dinner.

Thursday: TQ Day 221.

Happy 230th Birthday to the United States Navy. It's also Yom Kippur today, so two excellent reasons for the locals to drop rockets on us.

Friday: TQ Day 222.

I finally get out of bed at 1000, due to all of the banging. Phil, our PA, moved in yesterday, and he is quite the amateur carpenter. He has built various shelves, rearranged everything, and was hammering I don't know what this morning. Eventually he will finish, I suppose. Phil is a good guy though, a former IDC and chief petty officer who then went to PA school. So he does not fit the typical Navy hospital chief mold — a guy who sits around telling everyone else what to do. He's a doer, for sure.

While running, I happen across the Army JAG. He's back from Al Asad. We have quite the chat; he's a fun guy. I con him out of some cyalume light sticks — I figure that we will need them on the hump tomorrow at 0500. It will still be dark and we would hate for all of the doctors in TQ to be run over by accident.

After dinner, I return to find that my hootchmates are in a dither over getting their gear together for tomorrow morning's hump. I spend about an hour helping to square them all away, adjusting straps, making suggestions on how to load their packs, and so on. All this fuss for a 6-mile walk.

Been a quiet day today. Tomorrow is Referendum Day, I wonder if the locals are storing it up for then?

Saturday: TQ Day 223.

Up at 0430, drink coffee, and head over to the SSTP in my flak, Kevlar, gas mask and backpack. Unfortunately, we do not start the hump until after 0530, so I could have slept for another hour if they had told us this — but then, mustering early and standing around is definitely a military thing. I distribute yellow chemlights to put into helmet bands, so we don't get run over as we march along, and away we go.

We march in two columns, doing the 2-mile loop that I run every day. About a quarter mile into it, somebody comes shuffling up the side of the road like Yum Yum from *The Mikado*, screaming loudly, "This is not a f***ing race!" Except that it is. We have to do the 6 miles in 2 hours, a reasonably fast walking pace with all the crap we have on. The Marine officer setting the pace is unimpressed, and we proceed apace. "If you can't keep up, you can get in the truck…"

Our pear-shaped male ward nurse is in line right in front of me. He doesn't know how to do this — he's constantly "accordioning," that is, slowing down and then trotting to catch up. I keep telling him, longer strides or more of them. After two laps, he is ready to quit. But I won't let him — he has already gone over 4 miles, he has one lap left, so I grab his pack strap and start pulling his sorry ass along. I do the Gunny Hardiman thing from *Full Metal Jacket*, although I never actually refer to him as Private Pyle. Lots of pro-fanity, you're not giving up because I am not finishing this without you and I have no intention of doing this again, that sort of thing. If anyone is going to fall out of this hump, I don't want it to be him. We complete it with ten minutes to spare, well behind everyone else, but he finishes. No one failed.

We are done before 0800, and head back to the hootches, soaked in sweat, feet sore. No blisters fortunately, but definitely tired puppies — running six miles and humping it are very different things. Go shower and get ready for Grand Rounds at 0930, only to hear over the radio that it's cancelled because of construction. So we will have the FMFWO class at 1100 in the chapel, instead. Fine. I go check e-mail, arrive at the end of the class (as I have done all of the lectures), and head over to lunch with a few guys. Since I'm already in uniform and the chapel is halfway to the DFAC anyway, I may as well. And besides, I have a little errand to run over at the Texans' place.

As we finish lunch, I ask Phil if he wants to go for a little "walk." Yesterday, when I went to run another "errand," I came back with thirty rolls of paper towels and six cases of chemlights, so he's intrigued. I introduce him to the Army boys; they hook up on trading power tools and various sundry items, as Phil is into building things. He is quite impressed by the BAS, which was hand-built by the Texas medics out of scrounged lumber.

But now for the fun part. I go over to Habeeb, the JAG's, office; he has invited me to play with some new toys. Last night there were a number of raids in their battle space, and all sorts of things were picked up. One raid in particular was very revealing, in the courtyard of a house across the street from a school that was to be used as a polling station. Lined up on the ground and on tarps were dozens of well-maintained, well-oiled weapons: AK-47s, a lot of DPM medium machine guns, three mortars, RPGs. Plus thousands of rounds of ammo, grenades and so on. In addition, there were a number of combat-loaded vests, with full pouches of ammo, grenades, and so on. Someone was obviously planning something big for today's election. Phil and I get to play with all of this stuff. We have a blast (well, figuratively). Pictures of each other holding things, looking at the mortars, and so on. Phil is quite impressed with my connections.

Most importantly, I snap a great shot of Phil standing in the dirt, machine gun slung upside down on his chest, RPG falling off one shoulder, and a shotgun in his hands that has just fallen apart — the cover shot for *Soldier of Misfortune* magazine.

John also shows us a video they picked up — a box of recruiting DVDs that the insurgents have made. Lots of pictures of evil Americans, IEDs blowing up, Abu Ghraib, veiled people talking about American atrocities — and plenty of footage of Iraqis killing Iraqi policemen and soldiers. Nasty.

As we finish this, the radio says that Camp Manhattan is sending us a 4-month-old baby with an overwhelming infection of some kind. Phil and I start walking back, and we both think the same thing: Mom will be a female suicide bomber in a burka. When we get back (about a ten minute walk), the kid is already there, being worked on, and looks pretty sick. Nothing for me to do, not a surgical issue. The boss is pretty agitated, because of the position it puts us in: what are we supposed to do with this kid? She's not a trauma, and you can imagine the politics if she dies here. No family came with her, either. If we send her to Baghdad, still problems. Last time the family sees the kid, she's alive; the Americans take her away; a few days later they find out she has died. The Americans killed my baby, have stolen her, taken her as a slave, whatever. This is one of those humanitarian-versus-political-reality problems, and once again we are caught in the middle, forced to handle a mission we are not equipped to do, without support from higher up. The boss says he will report the Army guys. I tell him that this is what I foresee: an Army patrol has a sick kid brought to it; they radio higher for guidance; their commander says to bring the kid in, regardless of the rules; the Camp Manhattan BAS can't handle the kid and ships her to us; we ship her to Baghdad; Baghdad bitches at us for shipping the kid, and eventually sends the kid to Baghdad City Hospital (if she has not died); the Group medical planning people have no response, solution, or guidance except that "this shouldn't happen because it's not our mission"; the responsible Army commander says "I'm not going to let some little kid die before my eyes, screw the rules"; and things go on as before. Two hours later, the boss comments on my remarkable prescience.

The kid is intubated and goes to Baghdad; looks septic, overwhelming infection, possibly meningitis. Never hear anything else back from the Army bubbas, MSOC, or the Group Surgeon. What a surprise...

Monday: TQ Day 225.

Around 1800 we hear of two patients coming in. I then learn that they are coming in from Al Asad, which makes no sense as they are an Echelon II like us, and we are not on the way to either Balad or Baghdad from there. It seems that the weather has closed down in both Balad and Baghdad, so the EPW with the GSW to the head can't get there. Huh? We don't have a neurosurgeon either, what are we supposed to do? The PET (Patient Evac Team, the twigs that coordinate all medevacs in theater) is going to spin up a helo in bad weather to send a patient somewhere that can do no more for him than where he is already? That makes even less sense. Eventually, we learn that the weather is bad in Al Asad, too, and the helo was never able to take off. So why were we called in the first place?

I spend a good chunk of the afternoon working on PowerPoint presentations for our weekly officers' meetings. The first is the "2012 Iraqi Olympics," with assorted events like the 100m women's machine gun and combat "wabbit hunting." The second is an ad campaign for "Six Flags over Taqaddum." In the evening, the hootch sits down to watch a movie called "City of God," about Brazilian street gangs, which is an Iraqi pirated DVD dubbed in Korean with English subtitles. We also bandy about yet another topic for the weekly meetings, "Survivor — Iraq," in which every week we vote a member off the LSA (Logistical Support Area). Hmm, has potential.

Tuesday: TQ Day 226.

I sleep until 1000 today, first time in a while that I have gotten to do so. It was quite nice. Off to PT around noon. It is a surprisingly nice day today — a little breezy, a fair number of clouds, not too hot. Almost autumnal. Of course, it's still the dusty hellhole that is Iraq. Afterwards, I sit around on the Beach in the afternoon, started reading *Uther*, the fictional story of King Arthur's father.

I had sent off an e-mail to the Brooks running shoe people, with pictures of my bloody, defunct running shoes and me standing there in body amour and flipflops, forced to operate shoeless. They are sending me a free pair, quite nice of them. But they are the most comfy shoes I've ever had.

At 2100, we get an "All Ridgeways" call for an urgent surgical ... appendicitis. Uh huh. I ask the boss to call it off; he decides that no one needs to respond but the duty surgeon, which today is him.

Since it's been pretty quiet lately, I have time to write about my roomies. The boss, a colorectal surgeon from the Hospital, is a bike nut. He is turning out to be a good OIC; he has things in perspective and does not take things too seriously. He interacts well with the Marines, and he does not let the chiefs have their way. He's got a good sense of humor, and is pretty low-key.

Brian, a former enlisted Marine, is a psychiatrist from the same Hospital. He's a pistol. Always making one-liners and cracking us up. Today, he is going on about radio call signs and the incessant radio traffic we have to put up with. For some reason no one uses real names on the encrypted radios, unless we are doing accountability during rocket attacks where everyone goes by rank and initial. For example, I am "Oscar Five Sierra Zulu," O-5 Stockinger, Z., to distinguish me from "Oscar Five Sierra Bravo," which is Brian. He ad libs "Oscar Mayer Wiener Zulu" calls. He wants us to be renamed "WedgieWays" instead of "Ridgeways." It goes on and on.

Pat is the Lutheran Chaplain. He is definitely a "regular guy" and has a good sense of humor. His billet before this was as Chaplain at Camp David — yup, he was the President's chaplain out there. He has some good stories to tell, nothing inappropriate though — like Laura Bush frequently reading George the riot act to "keep him in line," forcing him to go bird watching, things like that. His first introduction to the President: "So, Chaplain, you any good?" "I can hold my own, Mr. President." "Well, that's okay, then."

Phil, the ortho P.A. (Physician's Assistant), looks like Marmaduke the dog. He loves to build things and can take and give a joke. He is a former IDC (Independent Duty Corpsman, like a mini–PA on subs and small ships) and Chief Petty Officer, which is why he shows them no mercy when they slack off.

So all in all, I have a good group of roommates.

What the trendy combat surgeon wears to work. With dirt everywhere and not enough scrub suits, it was usually USMC jogging gear (green shorts and t-shirt), sneakers or flipflops (depending on what you were doing when the patients arrived), and occasionally body armor if there happened to be incoming fire at the time. I'm actually overdressed in this picture, since I'm wearing a scrub shirt and ballistic goggles that can stop frags.

Wednesday: TQ Day 227.

I roll out of bed at 1000. A few minutes later, two casualties are dumped on the pad without warning, sending us all scurrying over to the STP. Fortunately, nothing serious. Two guys in a truck that tipped over, leaving them hanging upside down in their seatbelts. That would have been some photo op!

Thursday: TQ Day 228.

Out of bed at 0730 for a casualty, an Iraqi EPW shot in the ass. A flesh wound — yes, in the fleshy part of his ass. Wash the wound out and he eventually is sent to his reward at Abu Ghraib. I have Pat, our Lutheran chaplain, scrub in — he does fine until he gets a close whiff of the burning flesh smell that is electrocautery, then he wisely bows out and sits down outside. There is also a bit of confusion afterwards. The Army unit that brought him in and then left calls us to ask if we can take his picture and e-mail it to them. They think he is someone high on the "Most Wanted" list. Who? "We're not sure, that's why we want the picture." "But you captured him, don't you know what he looks like?" "Uuuuh..."

Do the AOM at 0930. Our Intel guy could not make it today, he had another intel meeting to go to, so in honor of Saddam's trial being in the news, I had to do the funny voices for the "Rock, Paper, Saddam" powerpoint all by myself. Too bad, the Army guy does the voices better.

I head out to run around noon, and am about four miles into it when the radio says we have five incoming. I take the shortcut back, and as I run past the DFAC, the Air Boss is pulling out of the parking lot, so I hitch a ride back to the STP with him.

The afternoon is busy. We end up getting nine more casualties (for a total of ten) and operate on two. One is an American soldier with a frag or GSW to hip who comes in looking shocky. He is the only one needing surgery at the time (we fly out a couple of head injuries), so we open his belly, suck lots of blood out, put pressure on everything to control it, and let the anaesthesia guys catch up with blood. We follow the bleeding way down into his pelvis, and out of it into his leg. The frag, or whatever, has trashed his artery right where it passes from his belly into his leg, a tough place to get to, but we do. Eventually we have control of everything. The guy's blood pressure is okay. But unfortunately, he has already received 22 units of blood, and his leg has had no blood flow for almost two hours. While I would like to repair the artery here, it is probably better if he gets the circulation going in the leg for a while before that is done. So I drop a temporary shunt into the artery, we pack him up, and then send him on his way. But he is still a "save." Brian, our psychiatrist, scrubbed in to help.

As I finish him up, some more casualties come in. One big guy has frags to his head and face; he will need a head CT. But despite having no obvious neck injury, his neck is swelling up. I tell them to intubate him before he flies out on the helo, to make sure his airway is not compressed while he flies out. Good call: when they try to intubate him, they can't see anything and he has lots of blood back there and he's spitting up a lot of it, too. Off he goes to the OR, where we crich him (cut a hole in his windpipe and stick a breathing tube in). He flies out, also.

By now it is 2000 so I eat the chow they have had delivered from the DFAC, something they do when we are operating. Then I head back to the hootch as I have work to do. The Grand Rounds lecturer for this Saturday has whussed out, so Tim asks me if I can give it. Hmm, this will be the new Team's fourth Grand Rounds since the RIP, and my third. They will need to find another speaker at some point. But sure, why not, I already have it prepared. But I have a few additional slides I need to work on.

First, Brian will be featured on the cover of *Unmilitary Medicine: The Magazine for Medical Mavericks*. It's the Combat Psychiatry issue. Second, Pat is in the *National Enquirer*— I have a nice picture of his hairy legs sticking out from under an OR gown — "Cross-dressing chaplain busted!" I manage to add a Gucci handbag over his arm, and pair it with a pic of Saddam with lizard eyeballs and the caption "Saddam trial shocker: 'My alien masters will come for me!'" These should liven up the Grand Rounds sufficiently.

Friday: TQ Day 229.

Up at my usual 1000. The weather has definitely turned, it's down into the 50s at night, and Phil has actually turned the heat on in the hootch this morning. I still wander around in shorts and t-shirt, as my roomies shake their heads. I run at 1200, after which I sit up on the driving range part of HESCO Beach, to soak up the sun. It may be 80 degrees max today, and very breezy, a lovely day.

My new unit's first BBQ starts at 1600, the same time we have to start wearing our body armor (1600 to 2000 every day). So I go in full "combat load": combat boots, cammie pants, green "HESCO Beach" t-shirt, Hawaiian shirt, body armor, helmet, dark glasses, and shoulder holster. Ammo pouches all hold bottles of near-beer. Six-pack in one hand, ammo can in the other. I'm ready for combat BBQing, Iraq style.

Sunday: TQ Day 231.

Interesting story today. Every patient who is medevaced back to the States needs various bits of paperwork. MSOC, the medical admin weasels who work 100 yards from us but never, ever, come by the unit, constantly badger our admin people about filling out the paperwork completely — ALL of the boxes need to be filled. We were sending back a young lady who discovered, a few weeks after getting here, that she was pregnant. The admin petty officer of the day, who is extremely literal and has no sense of humor, took MSOC's whining to heart when she did the forms. "Point of injury: vagina." "Personal Protective Equipment: not worn." MSOC was not amused and wanted heads to roll. The boss told them to bugger off; good for him.

Spend the evening doing data. My lecture for the corpsmen tomorrow is a no-brainer, I've given it many times before, no further prep required.

Tuesday: TQ Day 233.

At 1000 we get a patient flown in, advertised as a GSW to the leg. Well, sort of. Through the leg and into his ass, and he is in hemorrhagic shock. The bullet has transected his deep femoral artery and vein. We get to work and are done 3 hours and 32 units of blood later, but he's alive. He also had a GSW through his left hand, which Mike worked on while we did our thing. The case made a huge mess of my new running shoes. The guy flies out to Balad, as nothing is flying into Baghdad today due to the hotel bombing. They figure it's not secure enough to land helos at present.

Later, I'm off running in my squishy sneakers, to cover all the fresh blood with fresh dust — so they are now a nasty, rusty brown color, but better than red. The OR gowns were soaked through as well, so my PT gear was a mess. The boss was in his cammies, they were a mess. I keep telling him to wear PT gear but he won't listen. I plan to keep doing so, even when it gets cold. It's down in the 50s at night now, high in the 80s, still not bad, though.

Wednesday: TQ Day 234.

There is lots of really, amazingly, incredibly annoying irrelevant radio traffic at 0200. Then we get up at the crack of 0230 for a couple of casualties, two guys with various bits crushed by a truck. One has a badly ripped-up finger, it'll never work right again, and unfortunately for both him and the Marine Corps, it's his trigger finger. The other guy had his chest stuck between a truck and a trailer; we have to send him off for a CT scan because of severe neck pain.

By the time all this is done, it's 0430, so I go over to the trailers to call you. You are finally home, nice to hear your voice. We chat about what I can do in the Navy, as I am to call the detailer today. Afterwards, since it's 0530, I head over for breakfast for the first time since I came back from leave, then go back to sleep with my round little tummy.

My first jog in new running shoes was interrupted by casualties. I ran back and straight into the OR, where my new shoes soon looked like my old ones. They were ceremonially burned at the end of the deployment, just like the old ones.

Get up at 1000, because the heat/AC repairmen show up and make lots of noise. Go running. Another day, some more dust.

Thursday: TQ Day 235.

Around 1100, i.e., half an hour after a meeting I'm roped into is done, I hear the radio. "Ridgeway 19, we need an ambulance and driver down on the pad for a patient that was dropped off." This doesn't sound right, so I put on my sneaks and head over. The Air Boss is there. A Huey gunship picked up a patient from the soccer stadium in Ramadi, an Iraqi soldier who had his foot blown off by an IED. Looked classic for a landmine injury, the heel and the back of his leg are shredded. Mike and I get to work, but he ends up with a below-the-knee amputation as the foot was unsalvageable.

While I have been operating, there has been yet another weapons and bullet accounting. I get my weapon and stand by to be counted. As usual, I am shocked (but not surprised) at the complete disregard for safe weapons handling demonstrated by almost everyone, so when I get to the front of the line, I clear my weapon, lock the slide back, and attempt to show it to the clipboard commando. Who is not interested, all he wants is the number. "Oh, so you don't want to see if the weapon is loaded and I am about ready to shoot you in the chest by accident?" "Well, it's not loaded, right?" "We have had seven 'negligent discharges' in the last seven weeks on this base, all from weapons that were supposedly unloaded, including the guy who shot the top of his head off. You willing to bet your life on it?" I track down the earnest young Admin weenie who's in charge of this Charlie Foxtrot. I tell him that he had better start enforcing some safe weapons handling practices. How about using some of your enthusiasm for bullet-counting and making sure that your people don't catch one, instead?

Then five more patients arrive. An M113 armored personnel carrier, a big metal box on tracks, zips up, skids to a halt, and disgorges one patient. Cool. The driver obviously did not pay any attention at all to the signs posted around the base that say, "No tracked vehicles." Don't know why they are up, and if I was in a track, and in a hurry, I wouldn't care, either. Anyway, this guy has a badly broken knee and a broken hand, but is stable. The story, he tells us, is that an IED went off in front of them, covering their vehicle in a cloud of dust. So they didn't see the Bradley (tank) in front of them stop, and their Humvee ran into the back of it at about 50 mph — and then another Humvee rear-ended them.

The other four all come in a little later, for some reason they'd been taken to Camp Manhattan, instead. Three with open head injuries and the fourth with severe chest pain. So they all fly off to Balad for CT scans.

We ponder how much money, gas, and wear on helos we could save by having a CT scanner here. Someone (who will remain nameless) says that we would need a radiologist then, because they can't read CT scans. "That's OK," says I. "I can, and I don't need a radiologist telling me what injuries the patient had three days after I have seen them." Of course, the CT scanner would break in no time.

Friday, October 28: TQ Day 236.

Up at 0200, for an Iraqi soldier who has shot himself in the foot. Yup, never seen that before. I wash this out while Mike looks at some finger thing that came in unannounced on the milk run. Back to bed at 0300.

And awakened again at 0700, for the daily weapons and personnel accounting. Which amounts to someone from each hootch calling in on the radio and lying that they have seen everyone and their weapon. Guess we'll have to remind the COC that, when we are all up after midnight, we have mustered for the morning.

I get up for real at 1000, and at 1100 I'm invited for a group run. It quickly becomes clear that this is, in reality, a group start — everyone then trots along at their own pace. The 30-ish jocks tear off, the old guys hang back, and Pat and I hang in the middle, jogging and chatting.

At 1400ish, in the hootch, Brian, the psychiatrist, and I hear a loud "FSSSST!" followed by an earth-shaking boom. Put on the flak and Kevlar and stick my head out to see where it might be (if it's in the neighborhood, there could be casualties). I see smoke rising from over in the direction of the chapel. Again.

A minute later, Phil and Pat run in, looking pale. They were in the open-air wood shop when the rocket hit about 75 yards away. No casualties, fortunately.

I do some e-mail over at the STP for a bit. I'm surrounded by 8-foot HESCOs, but our Admin/Asst OIC is running around screaming that everyone needs to have their stuff on. Has he taken my safety talk of yesterday and run (overboard) with it? I ignore him.

Dinner was interesting. Chinese chicken. It was just "all right," but definitely a welcome change. At 2000, go over to Craig's (Greg's replacement) roof; he's having an early Halloween party. He has hundreds of purple lights up, candy corn that I can use as fangs, the works. Craig is a grade school gym teacher, so he's really into Halloween, and he has received dozens of letters and cards from his school kids. "Hi there. We all miss you. Do you kill a lot of people? My rabbit's name is Nigel..." But at 2100, the radio says we have another incoming, so I head back.

When I get to the hootch to change, I learn that the patient will not be here for a couple of hours. Great, but I'm too lazy to go all the way back. I spend the evening helping the boys study for an FMF test tomorrow.

Saturday, October 29: TQ Day 237.

The radio goes off right before the alarm does, at 0830. One patient, supposedly a GSW to the kidney. It turns out to be a rather chunky Iraqi (which in this area suggests "FRE," a "former regime element"). He ran a checkpoint and his car was shot up. One bullet has passed through the front of his belly from one side to the other. He is stable, though. Take him back to the OR, open his belly, take out two bits of intestine containing three pairs of holes, and close him back up again. He should be fine in the long run. The whole case takes 62 minutes, and at the end I send the boss (who has been helping me) off to FMF class — they have a test today. This case was no big deal. Well, okay, maybe for the patient, but not for us.

Off for a run afterwards, then check e-mails. My detailer tells me that I have the XO job at DMRTI in San Antonio. At least that's finally done.

Other interesting e-mails include some boondoggles. CLR 25 is completely unable to provide us with ammo for the pistol quals. I had run across Chief Warrant, the Marine who runs the firearms school at Camp Manhattan where I had gone to shoot AK-47s, in the chow hall — actually, he had run across me and came over to say "hi." I was surprised he had remembered me. I asked him if he could help us out, he said yes, and I got e-mail confirmation on it. Thirty officers, two groups of fifteen, doing two days each, 300 rounds apiece. In other words, 9,000 rounds of ammo, and instruction from the pros. Over on Camp Manhattan though, but still ... I get transportation worked out, too. I plan to sit it out as I have qualified, unless there are less than thirty people total that need to shoot. I also manage to get ten spots added for our Marines, as a treat for them (enlisted Marines rarely get to shoot pistols) and to show a little appreciation. In addition, I get word from the Texan CO that he can let me have 1,200 rounds of 9mm from their stock, too — so this can be a back-up hoard that we could use on the TQ range for anyone unable to make it to Camp Manhattan. These Green Team people owe me...

Monday, October 31: TQ Day 239.

At around 0400, another casualty, reported to have an arm in a cast. The boss is on duty and tells me to stay in bed, which I do. I get up for real at 1000.

Another gaggle run around 1100, but this time the group stays together. As we run through the engineers' parking lot, we see a blown-up Humvee, so we stop for group photos with it. And they wonder why I always bring a camera with me? We make it out to the pool, start heading back, but we are still about two miles out when the radio goes off again; one incoming patient will be at the SSTP in ten minutes. My colleagues start to run faster. Me, I run over to the road, flag down a Humvee, tell them that I'm the base trauma surgeon and we have casualties coming in, and of course they are happy to drive me back. Run smarter, not harder!

It's an Iraqi, shot in the upper thigh, with funny looking x-rays, so I send him to Baghdad for a CT scan. Can't really tell where the bullet ended up (is it in his large middle-aged ass, or his belly?). I don't want to give him an operation to find out. As you can imagine, my colleagues are a bit surprised when they arrive back, huffing and puffing, and see me there, already done.

Since I only did half a run today, I decided to run again. Swing by the Texans, try to make some deals to get even more ammo. It's time to work the unofficial channels. I know that almost everyone has spare ammo — since they are a combat infantry unit that does convoys, patrols, and goes outside the wire, they sign up for cases of ammo at a time and it's not accounted for bullet-by-bullet — they just get more when they run low. So, while the medics are supposed to have 30 rounds of 9mm each, most have 30–90 extra rounds. The guys with M4s/M16s are supposed to have 6 full magazines (180 rounds total) of 5.56mm, most have at least a dozen. As they get ready to RIP, they have to turn in their official "combat loads," everything else is dumped into the "amnesty box." If they dump it into an ammo can and give it to me, I can take my guys out onto the range with it and get them all qualified.

I head to dinner at 1700, everyone else heads over around 1900. Around 1915, we get two patients, a lightly injured American and an EPW shot through his knee. The EPW is in bad shape — in shock, with a broken femur and no pulse in his leg. Great case. I get him back to the OR and start shooting x-rays, getting him intubated, get IVs and blood into him. Eventually everyone shows up, including a visiting surgeon. I watch with horror as he manipulates the guy's broken leg, twisting it around. Great, if he didn't have a vascular injury before, he has one now...

Cliff and I scrub the case; we start at 2000. I am in professor mode, I ask him what he wants to do and we go to work. The visiting surgeon is standing directly behind me and says loudly, "If you can't feel a pulse, just make an incision where you know the artery should be." I turn around, look down at him (he is pretty short), pause briefly, and then say, "Thank you, sir," and turn back around again. No need to state the blatantly obvious, the merely obvious will suffice. Cliff and I discuss whether we will do a primary repair or shunt the patient; Cliff has never done a shunt, so he's interested in doing that; but he has also not done a vascular repair since he finished residency two years ago. As we work, I talk to him about when to shunt or not, based on the patient's condition. The visitor chimes in and says that clearly the patient should be repaired primarily, even though we have yet to find the injury and it will add an hour to the case. I say that we will decide that once we have found the injury, based on the patient's condition — right now he has a blood pressure of 70 after two units of blood, he needs to be doing a lot better than that if we are to do a primary repair. The guy does not hang around for long after that, and the boss has already told him that he will not be scrubbing while he is here. We clean out the wounds, put an external fixator on the femur to stabilize it, dig out his popliteal artery behind the knee. By this time he has had 6 units of blood but is now stable, good blood pressure, no more major bleeding. So we take vein out of his other leg and repair the battered artery.

We are done a little after midnight. I stay up to make sure he is packaged, get paperwork done, and check e-mail since I haven't done so all day. To bed a little after 0200.

Happy Halloween!

10. November 2005:
Sniper in the 'Hood

Wednesday: TQ Day 241.

Crawl out of bed at 1030, a major coup when one remembers that I have six room-mates, none of whom sleep late, and all of whom tend to forget that I do (or try to). Maybe I should stop staying up till 0400. I am about ready to make coffee when a casualty comes in, so I head over. An EOD Marine has been fragged in the head — he had just finished disarming one, when a secondary went off. He's in a bad way, a big hole in his left temple; I could easily put my finger into his brain if I wanted to. I take him straight back to the OR, we get him intubated as I throw a central line into him, and then away he goes on the helo.

Spend the evening putting the finishing touches on tomorrow's weekly case confer-ence. Included will be the old ad that says "I'd walk a mile for a camel," and a cartoon of a camel with a paper bag on its head with the caption, "The name of the camel has been withheld to protect the innocent." Followed by a "Sponsored by Diet Coke" slide.

I learn that our Marine Sergeant knows the head-injured Marine; he's from our base, assigned to the engineer unit where my FRSS IDC now works. They had two others killed yesterday, one a corpsman, and have had three more casualties in the past week. I hear later that this patient had a craniotomy in Balad, and then was sent urgently to Ger-many, with arrangements made for his family to meet him there. That suggests that he is expected him to die.

Iraq sucks.

Friday: TQ Day 243.

The day starts badly. Roll out of bed at 0830, up to the pad for an incoming U.S. casualty. About twenty minutes later, we hear that the patient, who is "not breathing," was dropped off at the HQ BAS. Ronnie, our ER doc, jumps into the back of an ambulance and zips over there — without any equipment, so he ends up not being able to do anything, either. A couple of minutes later he arrives, with the patient getting CPR.

I take him straight back to the OR, tell the techs that we are opening the chest now. He's not intubated — doesn't matter, he's not going to feel it anyway. I let Cliff do this while the boss drops a line into his other side. When we are open, the kid's heart is not beating, and he has massively bruised lungs — classic blast/pressure injury. I start doing open cardiac massage while the anaesthesia boys push drugs. He has barely a mark on him, just a little cut on his chin (not even through skin) and a puncture on his knee. He has a big belly, the ultrasound shows lots of blood in there. But not much point in going there if his heart is not going. I spend about fifteen minutes massaging his heart but, as expected, it never starts up again and he doesn't make it.

I go out to talk to his guys. He was hit by an IED. They were in a place where it wasn't safe to land a helo, and it took an hour to get the guy to us — with an M1 tank in the lead clearing the way. Who knows what might have happened if he had gotten to us an hour sooner...

Saturday: TQ Day TQ Day 244.

It's extremely windy and dusty, so I eat lunch with the boys instead of running. We get back, and Cliff and I decide to go to the bat cave, as it's his last day here before he goes to Ramadi. As we walk up to get the keys, we hear that there may be five Iraqi Army casualties coming from Camp Manhattan. A few minutes later it's confirmed, four incoming. Go change and wait.

First guy "looks bad." The boss (who is primary) tells me to take him back. He's already intubated and has blood all over his head. I get back into the OR with him and take a quick look. Big hole in the left side of his head, one eye full of blood, other pupil blown, blood pressure of 60, coma score of 3 (as low as it can get) — not good, he won't make it. The boss sticks his head in the door and asks what's up. I tell him, and he says we have other things to do, so I make him "expectant." He is moved out into the PACU (the "post-op" area between the ORs), where we expect him to die fairly quickly. The boss has a neck injury to operate on in the other OR, and he asks me to help Cliff in the ER tent with one of the other patients that Cliff's having trouble deciding what to do with.

I go in, look the guy over, and get quick x-rays of his chest and belly because he has a frag hole around the level of his diaphragm, on the left side. Frag is on the right side, where his liver is, and the trajectory would go past the heart. We need to operate. I walk over to the stretcher and announce, "We need four litter-bearers to move him to the OR now," turn around, and head over there. A couple of minutes later, still no patient, so I go back. Another doc is standing there, trying to talk to the patient with their little DOD English-Iraqi phrasebook. The litter-bearers are standing there, not moving. "NOW!!"

The frag has gone through his chest wall, into the left side of his liver, all the way through it, and out the right side. I feel the frag poking out the right edge, and leave it there, telling Cliff (who is new to Iraq) to take a feel. He does, and pulls it out. "Okay, so what would you have done if the frag had been followed by a huge gush of blood?" Don't pull stuff out until you are ready to deal with the consequences... Fortunately, it's better to be lucky than good. Repair the diaphragm, do a pericardial window (peek at the heart through a small hole in the diaphragm) which is negative, fix the hole the frag made in the diaphragm, then pack the liver injury and close. No massive bleeding, but a good case. We then washed out some frag wounds and his broken leg. We finished about the same time as the other case, and they both flew out on the same helo.

Meanwhile, the expectant Iraqi has failed to die. He has no cortical function, his blood pressure is now down to 50, he is breathing 4 times a minute, but he's still technically alive. Eventually, though, he succumbs to the inevitable. We had called the Air Force neurosurgeon in Balad about this guy; he had agreed that there was no point in sending him.

Sunday: TQ Day 245.

Did not get to sleep in, got up at 0900 for a casualty. A Marine K-9 handler was walking his dog around a secured IED site when he was shot in the arm. The puppy, a German Shepherd named Chang, was smart and hid under a truck when the shooting started. His handler had a hole through his shoulder, but amazingly the bullet did not hit his lung. Washed it out in the OR. He'll be fine, eventually. Did not get to meet the dog, though.

A little later, another casualty, an M1 tanker who was ducking into the turret as an RPG was fired at him; it hit the turret and put some frags in his hands. He'll be fine, too.

Went running, then at 1400 the officers played the enlisteds at volleyball. The enlisted won, many games to one.

Monday: TQ Day 246.

Had planned to sleep in again, no luck there. It was a busy day.

Started with three Iraqi casualties from an IED at 0700. First one comes screaming in by ambulance; he has a frag that has gone in one side of his head and out the other — dead on arrival. The other two come in by Bradley (a "small" tank), which was pretty cool. They both have their left eyes ruptured and head injuries. They fly out by helo. Get some nice pics with the Bradley; I shoot pics for other people, they just don't carry their cameras around — and they wonder how I get all of the cool pictures? Talk with the tank crews a bit. We learn that these Iraqis are from a unit informally known as the "Nissan Brigade," i.e., they drive around in unarmored or lightly armored Nissan SUVs and pickups. There is also a "Mazda" and a "Toyota" Brigade. I tell our chief to get two of the tankers new uniforms since theirs are covered in blood; we also give them a gallon of bleach to clean out the inside of their tank where the Iraqis bled.

I then go back to the hootch. It's 0900 so I try to get more sleep. Ten minutes later, the radio tells me that I have a telephone call. No idea who it's from, but I find that it's butt pus from my Texan friends. I am not on duty today, but whatever. He comes over, the boss and I look at him (he is the colorectal surgeon and on duty, after all). We decide he needs to go to the OR. But he has just eaten breakfast and he will need to lie on his stomach for the case, so it will have to wait until the afternoon so he won't barf under anesthesia. So, since I'm already up, I run with the boys. We do about 3.5 miles as a gaggle.

Shower, change, and then more casualties. Three guys with frags from mortars in

Habbaniyah. One has facial injuries and needs to go out for a head CT. The second has some little holes in his leg, no big deal. The third needs a lot of work. First, we ex lap him for a spleen injury and a hole in his diaphragm. I put in a left chest tube while the boss closes the belly. Meanwhile, Mike and Phil work on his right leg, which has a fracture and needs fasciotomies. Then I do a left neck exploration for a big hole in his neck. Then explore a hole in his shoulder for bleeding. So four cases on one guy — but he should be fine, ultimately. He flies out.

I get cleaned up and go to dinner. I had planned to take the SUV this afternoon and go ammo shopping for the range, but we've been too busy. Maybe tomorrow. Afterwards, we rearrange the hootch so that the end with the TV and fridge has more space. That way we can sit around, and chat, or play cards, or whatever. It's pretty cozy in here now, but it works, and with Cliff gone to Ramadi, I get my top bunk back for storage.

Today was supposed to be the day the detailer talks with the CO at DMRTI about my next assignment. We'll see what happens. Either way, I am ready...

Tuesday: TQ Day 247.

Despite the usual 0700-ish radio traffic, I manage to sleep past 1000. It's always good to accomplish one's goal for the day. I check e-mail and discover that my plan for the pistol qualifications has gone awry: Gunner tells me that he couldn't get the ammo to train my guys, the Division will not pony it up for non-division assets. He suggests that I ask the G3 (Ops Officer for the General, under whom training also falls) to cover this. I tell this to the boss. He will ponder it but I am not going to make any official request like this on my own. Meanwhile, I still plan to scrounge ammo from anywhere that I can.

At 1300 I take the SUV and go visit the Texans. All of the new medics from the unit slated to replace them are there, including their new PA, who apparently is a surgical PA in real life, so he's quite eager to help out if the opportunity arises. I make the rounds, and get about 1,000 rounds of 5.56mm (M16) ammo signed over to me from various places. Not 9mm, so it won't get my guys qualified on the pistol, but we can still go out to the range and have some fun with it by ourselves. Our Marine sergeant is qualified as a Range Master, and his Marines need to have a little fun. I also plan to use this to let the enlisted corpsmen qualify, if possible, starting with the most junior and working my way up. And if I want to shoot, that means that everyone else has to shoot first. We'll see how much I can get from my friends before they leave.

Thursday: TQ Day 249.

Happy 230th birthday to the United States Marine Corps. The 0700 radio traffic is disgustingly chipper, with lots of "Happy Birthdays" passed back and forth. Good thing this doesn't happen every day.

There's a new sniper in the 'hood. An unfortunate soldier at an observation post at Camp Manhattan got one round through the back of his head and out the ear. He arrives alive but looking very bad. I get him packaged very quickly and he flies out. I don't expect him to live; I'm right.

We go back to our weekly meeting, and are again interrupted, again for a GSW to the head. This patient, from the same Army unit, ends up bypassing us and going straight to Mortuary Affairs — he had died en route. His unit shows up, we give them the bad news, as expected some of them do not take it well. Yep, this war is getting really old, really fast.

By now it's almost noon, so I head over to lunch with some of the guys. Afterwards, I enter some new patients into the database for follow-up, and at 1445 the boss and a few others go over to Lakeside for the official Marine Corps Birthday Cake Cutting Ceremony. As usual, I am on duty when this stuff happens, but such is life. I would have liked a picture or two. They get back in time for dinner, which I also attend as it is, after all, the USMC Birthday, and I go ahead and get dessert today. No dieting on birthdays.

Afterwards, I check e-mail and discover that the detailer has come through and I have the San Antonio spot. Most likely will move down there as soon as I get home. I go ahead and call you to let you know, since of course you have been waiting just as I have been. Yes, we are both excited to finally have some sort of answer.

Saturday: TQ Day 251.

Up at 0030 for two Iraqis brought in from Habbaniyah. It turns out that they are two Iraqi Policemen who claim to have both been shot in the leg while "on patrol." The odd part is that our Intel bubbas say that the Iraqi Police disappeared in this area months ago and that none have been seen since. Still, they are not EPWs, so we treat them like everyone else. I operate on one guy's broken leg while Mike and the boss start on the other guy's leg; then when I am done I do the other guy's broken arm while they still are on the leg; not that I'm faster, their leg was more complicated. In bed around 0400. Our Ops guy later tells me that these guys were probably trying to shake someone down and were shot.

At 1730, I take the SUV over to the Texans as I've been invited to what may be their terminal BBQ. I also take a Humvee and two Marines with me, as I'm "acquiring" an exam table with gynecologic stirrups for doing pelvic exams. Why, you ask?

Apparently the issue of what we would do if a rape case came up has become a hot topic this week at high levels. Not that this has actually occurred. We have pointed out that the BAS's have the SART (evidence) kits and the GMOs have all had to take SART training, whereas we have neither the equipment nor the trained personnel. It's really not hard to do, but you have to do the official training in order for the evidence collected to be legally valid. However, doctrine has been that the SART exams are to be done only at Echelon III hospitals (i.e., Baghdad and Balad in Iraq), but now they are changing it to Echelon II (i.e., us). So we get to deal with yet another problem that is not a part of our training or equipment. Fortunately, I know someone who has two gynie exam tables in a shipping container, so that part of the problem has been solved.

As my Marines are loading the thing, I go over to the BBQ. Of course, at that moment the radio goes off and, since I'm on duty, away I go. Just like the last time I went to one of their BBQs. Oh well.

It's a TCN from Sierra Leone who was run over by a motorcycle on Camp Manhattan, and sent to us with a broken hip that he doesn't have. But man! Does he yowl! Eventually we shoot every x-ray known to man and get him sorted out, but by then it's almost 2000, when I have to return the SUV anyway. So no BBQ for me.

Sunday: TQ Day 252.

Around 2000, I head over to the Texans again, I've been invited to a "burning." Specifically, they are going to incinerate various things that they don't plan on taking back with them, assorted files and so on. I will miss these guys, most of them have an irreverence combined with common sense that is too often lacking in the active duty side of the house. Their admin officer dropped his broken laser printer into the burn barrel with glee.

Tuesday: TQ Day 254.

An entertaining day today. I wake up at 0700 for radio traffic, and decide to get up to do e-mails and patient follow-ups. Discharge a kid observed for appendicitis — he didn't have it. At 1000, I had reserved the SUV and I head out.

Meet up with Geoff, one of the Texans, and get about 500 rounds of 9mm ammo signed out from him. The scouts are still out, so hopefully I will get more when they come back from their forward patrol base for good. I then pick up Habeeb and the new Illinois PA (the "cool PA"), and we go play golf.

Yup, golf. The "Golf for Ammo" program to be exact. We drive out onto one of the headlands overlooking Lake Habbaniyah, and shoot off a bucket of balls. I have never done this before and demonstrate some remarkably bad form, but what the hell. We all have a great time though; it's just one of those bizarre things that you need to do from time to time. Of course, I have a picture of me with the Hawaiian shirt. We even play "Combat Golf," where you are thrown a ball every three seconds and have to drive it off. I have the worst form, but end up being the only one who manages to get them all off in the allotted time.

Then lunch, and a trip to the MiG. Out by ECP 1 there is a partially buried MiG 21 fighter. We park behind a berm so we cannot be seen from Habbaniyah, and climb all over it taking pictures. On the way back, the Illinois PA says that he should be able to get us some ammo, too, which would be very cool, indeed.

We spend the evening watching *Wonder Woman* DVDs. Don't know why, it just seemed the thing to do.

Thursday: TQ Day 256.

As of today, I now have 966 rounds of 9mm. Already gave 1,500 rounds to our Marine sergeant, and he has another 150 or so lying around. So we have about 2,600 rounds to get the STP officers qualified; that's over 100 rounds apiece. That should be

The mesa overlooking Lake Habbaniyah was the perfect spot for a driving range, if one over-
looked the old Iraqi minefield off to one side. My Texas Army National Guard buddies and I
would head out there on occasion to hit a few balls. This photo clearly demonstrates that I am
one of the few doctors in America who knows nothing about playing golf. But I'm willing to
try anything.

enough, if they take the training seriously. We make some plans; we may be able to start running ranges at the end of next week. Our Navy officers need to qualify on the 9mm pistol to get their Marine warfare qualification.

Sunday: TQ Day 259.

The 0700 radio muster... But I go back to bed, and finally get up at 1100, which is a "win." Phil and I then go window-shopping. We go to the blown-up vehicle lot to pick up an armored Humvee window. Phil plans to put it in Brian's wall so our resident shrink can look out and see the birds. He's been feeding them daily, and they now will only eat biscotti crumbs... I also buy a swagger stick for the boss, and a stuffed camel that plays Arabic music over at the Hadji store.

Afterwards I run, and then watch volleyball from HESCO Beach. Then off to dinner. Spend the evening going over the paperwork and rules for the pistol and rifle quals we will be doing. I want to shoot but already have the expert marksman medal, so I will shoot last. That means I will need to find more ammo...

Monday: TQ Day 71 or 260.

Up at 0700 for casualties, an Iraqi EPW. Well, four EPWs actually. Well, they are actually Iranian refugees, who were trying to scoot back to their "off limits" refugee camp. The most interesting one is a guy who was shot off his motorcycle while riding away from where he had just planted an IED. Bullet went through his ass, trashed his hip, and traveled inside his leg to his knee, which makes sense because he was shot from behind in a sitting position. The other three were less surgically interesting.

As we are finishing this up, we get word on five American casualties coming in from the field, from an IED blast. This IED had a can of kerosene buried on top of it, so the blast had an accompanying fireball. We get four patients, all badly burned on their heads and arms, all get intubated and sent off, mainly because we hear that we are getting at least two more casualties. I handled or supervised three of these guys, and as they are getting packaged, I go into the boss's OR to see what he's up to. His guy is like mine, but he says that he needs to do escharotomies on him because the skin on his arms is very tight (this cuts off blood flow). I tell him that all of the patients need escharotomies, that will add an hour to each one, and once you start doing that sort of thing they all bleed, get coagulopathic, then we'll start the walking blood bank, and in the meantime they will get sicker. Send them now, while we still can. Burns always get a lot sicker in the first 24 hours, which makes them harder to move later. He agrees and we get all four out on the same Marine helo. Just as well, two of them were already doing badly on the vent when they left, and there's nothing we can do about that here.

I'm glad we don't see many of these. The frag wounds were actually fairly minor in comparison; it's the burns that will kill these guys if they don't make it. Later, we learn that the fifth guy never made it out of the vehicle — he burned up, but probably never felt anything because the top of his head was taken off by the blast. Iraq still sucks.

During all of this, the Illinois medics had been called, and they had responded promptly, led by their PA. Unlike with the Texans, the Illinois PA is also the Medical Platoon commander, which makes things easy. He's a PA for a surgeon in the civilian world, and his wife is an Ob/Gyn, so his assistance will be quite welcome. We talk a bit as we wait for the next batch, and I deliver on a trade we had set up yesterday: I sign over to him three "roll-downs," canvas/plastic rolls that can be filled with medical equipment and hung from the wall of a building or an ambulance, and some soft white hospital blankets. In return, we will pick up some patient wool blankets later. The expected patients never materialize, so they head out.

While the exchange was being made, our twig had observed me giving the roll-downs to them. He gets into a major tizzy and asks if the boss knows about this trade. The Chief chimes in, too. I ignore them both. The gear is old and dirty, we'd planned on disposing of them, and we have new ones on the way. The twig doesn't get it. He's a "by the book" kind of guy. We had also run out of Versed, a sedative. The Army guys called over to their BAS and an ambulance drove over with ten vials, which they signed over to us for free. When I asked the twig what his solution to the problem would have been, he says, "We should make sure that we order more in advance." Yeah, we did, but that doesn't solve our problem now. You do favors for people, they do favors back. If they have too much, it expires, and you just end up throwing it away.

I head over to the Texas BAS (Illinois BAS now, I suppose) in the SUV to say "adios" to the Texans. Get the patient blankets signed over to me, plus some anesthetics and thermometers. I also work out an amazing deal with the new guys from Illinois: their XO is willing to requisition ammo to train 30 medical personnel on the pistol (about 120 rounds per person). Unbelievable, but I'll take it if offered. That means that I can use the ammo that I have scrounged to train our Marines and enlisted. It would be great for the kids to come home with pistol and/or rifle ribbons as well as the usual "I went to Iraq" medals.

The real purpose of my visit, though, was to look for various people to say goodbye to. The JAG has all sorts of goodies for me: 200 rounds of M16 ammo, a number of pistol and M16 magazines, chocolate crackers, spray insulating foam (goes great around the A/C in the walls), and about twenty pounds of *Starbucks* (oh baby!). Unfortunately, the one thing that I really want, I must refuse: a World War I–era British Webley Mk.IV .38 caliber revolver. This is a classic, extremely cool, and would go well with the World War I Lee-Enfield I already have; but I've no way to get it home. Officially, it could be given to me by a sheikh, and taken home as a unit trophy to put into a unit museum. But that's a lot of red tape, and I still wouldn't get it. So I must regretfully decline.

Then the radio goes off and I have to zip back. One patient is already there by the time I arrive (actually, he arrived unannounced a while ago but the boss was there and handled it). A 14-year-old Iraqi kid with frags to his belly and finger from a mortar, who looks very stable. He is waiting to go to the OR until we hear what else is coming in. Three more from frags, all American. One has a hole in his shoulder with "blood squirting everywhere." The boss (who is on duty) has me head straight to the OR with him as he looks the sickest. The second has a mangled leg; he and Mike go to the OR with him. I have them call the PA at the 2/130 to come over. The third has an eye injury and will be flown out.

The shoulder is bad, but not as bad as advertised. He's not actually bleeding a lot, at least not from any major blood vessels. The frag went through his shoulder joint, destroying most of it, but missing the nerves and blood vessels. The PA and I wash it out, pull lots of bone and metal frags out of it, and pack it up. He will need a lot of work on this, probably a shoulder replacement (prosthesis), but he should keep the arm. When I am done with him, the boss and Mike are still working on the leg, so I do the kid with the belly, which fortunately missed everything important. They finally finish up the leg and we are done around 1900.

A busy day for all. At 2000, I go over for the last Texas bonfire; they are burning all sorts of crap: uniforms that they don't want, stairs, signs, towels, a wooden trash can (which, as it goes up, looks like a giant torch, so I get a shot of the "Iraqi Olympic torch" for the slide show). Hang out with the boys until 2200, then back home, a shower, and off to bed.

Mondays are historically our busiest days. Yup.

Wednesday: TQ Day 262.

Wake up at 0830, am tempted to go back to sleep but don't do it. I go to the gym for the semiannual weigh-in. Then spend the next several hours working on the database and putting together tomorrow's patient Q&A conference. I include a slide on Mike and the orthopedic productivity (now measured in negative numbers by one yardstick), and a case presentation on a fly I killed in the OR when it landed on a patient's abdomen while I was operating. The question is, was the fly "Killed in Action," or did it "Die of Wounds" because it arrived alive in the OR?

When I check e-mail, I find an extremely irritating one from the twig. It states that no one is to barter or trade anything any more without his or the OIC's permission, for legal or accounting purposes. Anyone doing so will face "appropriate legal action." There is a Marine Corps supply system in place, that is how we must do business.

I ponder many responses to this, and choose to make only one, that I hope he discussed this with the OIC before threatening the unit at large with legal action. But Man! Is this guy clueless, or what? He clearly has no idea how things work around here; if the system functioned perfectly, we wouldn't need to be doing this. (We might anyway, just for fun, but that's beside the point.) I believe that he had absolutely no idea that anything was going on at all, until he saw Ronnie drop off two roll-downs with the Army guys during the mass casualties a few days back. And it's all legal, we do the paperwork.

I search the internet for some good fly pictures, then head to dinner. I even get to sit right next to the young twig at chow, although he has very little to say. I leave fairly soon after finishing, because I still have to finish up the presentation for tomorrow. I am told that on the way back, the twig talked to the boss about the chain-of-command thing, and was told that (a) he is not anywhere near the top of the food chain; and (b) the supply system is broken, so we will continue to get what we need, however we need to get it, as long as it's not illegal.

That evening, I am called to the COC because I have a visitor. An Army guy in a Polaris (a little 6-wheel ATV) has driven up with "a box you left in our BAS, sir." The twig just happens to be there when I sign for it—about 600 rounds of M16 ammo and some spare magazines. No comment is made. We are now up to about 2,700 rounds of pistol ammo, which should be enough to get the 30 medical officers on base qualified, plus our Marines, plus some of the Navy enlisted; and about 2,000 rounds of M16 ammo, enough for the Marines to do their yearly re-quals and get some range time for some of our Navy enlisted.

Can't wait to see how the supply issue plays out at tomorrow's meeting, it's on the agenda.

Thursday: TQ Day 263.

Happy Turkey Day. I run the patient conference, as usual. We have an "antiterrorist" video (a humorous VW ad), the fly thing, and the KPI—K's Productivity Index (our orthopod). One of the stats I track is the average number of surgeons per case, and operations. I do this in part because the medical planners continue to insist that one surgeon can do one case every one hour, for 24 hours. Our stats show that an average of about two surgeons can do one case every two hours, with each case (or patient) getting 3.5 separate surgical procedures. Our average number of surgeons per case for the first rotation had been about 2.5, so we had always joked that the orthopod was the 0.5, and made comments every week as the fraction went up or down. Well, over the last couple of months, the number had gone down to 1.8, which makes the orthopod a negative 0.2. But it occurred to me that, previously, we had three general surgeons, now we have only two. So, when we had 2.5 surgeons per case, the 'pod was really negative 0.5, as he was detracting from the work of three. Now, with only two surgeons, he is up to negative 0.2, so he is actually getting better!

Monday: TQ Day 267.

...We're still looking for some windows. We have had a running gag going for about two weeks, that Brian, our psychiatrist, needs a window in the wall where his corner of the hootch is. He feeds the birds crumbs every day and likes to watch them, so Phil and I have decided that he needs a window so he can watch them from indoors. Besides, we have diagnosed him with AL ASAD (All Latitudes, All Seasons, Affective Disorder). Originally we had thought about plexiglass, but Brian has a thing about death by rocket, so (even though the plexiglass is about as tough as the plywood), we decided that an armored window would be the way to go. So we drove over to the MAIS (Marine Armor Installation Site) to look for some armored windows in their junk pile; our previous trip to the Humvee graveyard was unsuccessful as all the good windows had been stripped out and the remaining windows were broken. Found two absolute beauties, about 12 by 8 inches, armored glass with metal frames that can be bolted into the wall. We are set. We also do a little sight-seeing, crawl around in some of the Marine EOD Cougar armored cars, go by the buried MiG for a photo op, and play on some old Iraqi antiaircraft guns. A good time was had by all.

We get back, then after dinner the fun really starts. Brian had thought that he was humoring us by agreeing to the window thing, but we were not. By the end of the evening, we have decided that not only will we put in a window, it will need a shelf for the birdfeed, and a phone next to it to make it look like a prison window. Pat, our Lutheran chaplain roomie, is also starting to get worried: he had bet me "two large" ($2 in pogs, those cardboard tokens we get at the PX instead of change) that the window would not happen.

We have quite an entertaining evening, discussing all sorts of bizarre things: Robert E. Lee, the Abominable Snowman, Post-traumatic Stress Disorder, residency programs...

Tuesday: TQ Day 268.

The day gets off to an incredibly annoying start. We are awakened by the radio at 0730, telling us that there will be an "all hands" muster at 0800. The boss knows nothing about it. We all get up, go pee, get dressed, and head over. To discover that the 72 people in the unit have been gotten out of bed because seven of us have been randomly selected to pee in cups for the monthly urinalysis. Brian is livid and ranting. Actually, he was livid and ranting before he even got up there. He has become thoroughly disgusted with how un-militarily things work here. He and I are two of the lucky ones and, of course, we have both just emptied our bladders. We have until 0930 to comply.

So we go back to the hootch, drink lots of coffee and water, and go back. We walk into the tent where the Chief, one of our four chiefs, is sitting there, running this. I ask him why we have to do this before 0930. "Well sir, it takes an hour or more to get the samples over to CLR 25 and logged in properly, and I don't plan to miss lunch like I did last month." "So the entire unit was pulled out of bed and annoyed this morning, then told to pee on command, for your convenience?" "Yes." Not even any pretense about it. Brian starts to turn very red and leaves, he is so enraged. It turns out that the urinalysis can be done any time during the month. The boss is pretty steamed, too, and he plans to have a meeting with some of our senior enlisted to ream them all over their general lack of professionalism and lack of leadership. Me, I would have fired some of them by now.

Wednesday: TQ Day 269.

The day gets off to a bad start, but at least not early. At 0930, roll out of bed for four incoming U.S. casualties. Get up to the STP and a couple of minutes later a Humvee rolls up with a guy lying across the hood looking pretty dead, with his corpsman in a panic, screaming, "He's not breathing!" Unfortunately, the corpsman is not "breathing" for him, either. I take him straight off the pad and into the OR. There, he is not breathing *and* has no pulse, so I do CPR while he is being intubated and lines are placed. His EKG is flat, and on ultrasound his heart is motionless. He's dead. Not a lot of marks on him, except for a big bruise up under his right armpit. I surmise that he may have a torn aorta and died immediately.

I go into the next OR, where the boss has arrived and taken in a guy with an impressive open humerus fracture, the bone is sticking way out of his upper arm with a lot of mud plastered to it. He is very combative, probably a head injury, so he's also intubated as four people hold him down. While his arm is a mess, his head may be a mess too, so he will fly out. His arm won't kill him, but his head may. We have another guy out in the ER tent with a big bruise on his belly, but stable. He will need a CT. The fourth guy has a broken wrist and won't be going back to work. They all fly off.

These are Marines from our air wing. They were driving down MSR Michigan, and a car was poking along on the road and wouldn't get out of the way. The Rules of Engagement state that they need to honk, shoot flares, and so on up the escalation of force. When they drove up behind the car and bumped it, they lost control of the Humvee and rolled it. So, one dead, one or maybe two seriously injured — all from an idiotic traffic accident.

But not much we can do about it. A few of us go running after this, about four miles. It's a beautiful day, fairly warm, so I sit out on the Beach, catching rays, for about three hours, reading T.E. Lawrence (of Arabia's) *Seven Pillars of Wisdom*. I find a great quote: "Opinions are arguable, but convictions need shooting to be cured." Or, to put it another way, the difference between convictions and opinions is the difference in the contribution made by pigs and chickens to breakfast.

We drive to dinner, as we have to pick up near-beer for the inauguration of the SSTP MWR (Morale, Welfare & Recreation) tent. I have mixed feelings about this tent: yes, we can set up an MWR tent for movies, a monthly newsletter, and a website, but the same people who did this have not managed to fix our x-ray monitors or the cold-storage freezer for three months. They are still "working on it."

During dinner, there is some discussion on how busy we have been. "Al Asad Surgical Company," as they style themselves, although they are nowhere near a company in size, has started putting out a monthly newsletter, of which Mike obtained an electronic copy. Everyone is all atwitter about how busy we are, versus how busy they are. They say they have seen 1,200 patients (they do sick call, we do not), have done 75 operations, and 133 surgical procedures. There is much speculation on what they count as procedures, if putting IV access lines in is considered an operation, and so on. I tell them, quite frankly, that we have operated on fewer patients (67), but done more trauma surgical procedures (177), and that it doesn't really matter. Why not? Because no one out here is doing anything special. We are doing what we all have to do. It's not like we are going out and drumming up business, or going "above and beyond." Compared to prior wars, like Vietnam and Korea, which had much higher casualty rates, we are doing much, much less. "We are not doing anything that those before us have not done, or anything that those after us will not have to do."

11. December 2005: The "Sundays with Psych" Show

Thursday: TQ Day 270.

Phil and I have some fun. We install Brian's window in the hootch while he's out, and it is a thing of beauty. People from all around come by to marvel at it, and more importantly, I collect my "two large" ($2) in pogs from Pat. Who's your pog-daddy, Pat?

Later in the afternoon we have an Iraqi brought in, shot in the back. He turns out to be a local sheikh, who is pro–American, and has even allowed U.S. forces to live in his house. He looks very stable but has a nice round hole in the right side of his back. Eventually, Ronnie, the ER doc, puts in a chest tube. Pat, the chaplain, says the guy would have been long gone if we'd just taken him back to the OR and done it there. The counterintelligence bubbas come through, they are adamant that the sheikh not be sent out until their bosses come through to apologize, we are equally adamant that what they want does not matter. Not my day, so I was peripherally involved.

In the evening I get follow-ups on our patients from yesterday's Humvee wreck. Besides the death, the guy with the mangled arm also has a serious brain injury, another guy has a broken back (fortunately his spinal cord is okay), and the fourth has a bad wrist fracture. What idiocy, from a car wreck. As if the IEDs weren't bad enough...

Friday: TQ Day 271.

The Marine GMO brings over a guy who shot a nail into his hand with a nail gun. We have a great time with this, including taking pictures of us pretending to pull it out with a claw hammer. Even the patient is having fun, since the injury doesn't really hurt. As we work on him, we note that he has a smashed thumb as well, from whacking himself with a hammer a couple of days ago. Hmm, maybe he should stay away from the tool box.

Saturday: TQ Day 272.

At 0930, our weekly Grand Rounds. Brian, my hootchmate psychiatrist, gives a talk on spousal abuse. He does it all *acapella*, no slides, or A/V, and it's a blast. He is the

185

Brian, the "combat psychiatrist," peers out of his new armored SWA hut window. The window itself is the most robust part of the hut — it can stop an antitank rocket, but the rest of the hut is just plywood!

"Robin Williams of Psychiatry." He does imitations of teenagers, frumpy housewives, cowed husbands, Valley girls, you name it. Goes into a lot of the psychodynamics of it all, and how a lot of it stems to regressing back to the level of a three-year-old: if you handle most people like three-year-olds, you won't go far wrong. We were almost rolling in the aisles.

Spend the evening watching *A Christmas Story* on AFN. Surprisingly, neither Phil nor the boss had ever seen it. They'd never seen *Bad Santa*, either, so maybe this will be a Christmas to remember.

Monday: TQ Day 274.

Am up at 0730 or so, check mail, and get ready for pistol class at 0900. It goes pretty well, overall. A couple of people were annoyed when I took their ammo away, even though I had told them that they should bring only empty magazines to class and that any ammo they have will be secured until after class is over. If you don't have live rounds, you can't shoot anyone by accident, can you? The Marines did a good job, and they had fun with it, too. They enjoy anything related to the brotherhood of arms.

Phil, the unit carpenter, seems pleased with his handiwork — Brian's new armored window! Phil and Zsolt went to a great deal of trouble to ensure that Brain wanted for nothing — even when Brian wanted nothing.

At 1100, I went running in a gaggle, and then sat up on the Beach catching some rays. Around 1500 I went to check e-mail, and while I was doing so, yet another Army guy comes by to sign over another 900 rounds of M16 ammo. I called my Marine sergeant to lock it up, and he, another sergeant, and two of his corporals spent the afternoon happily putting rounds into magazines (yes, I have procured about fifty empty magazines as well). Happy as pigs in swill they were, doing Marine stuff, with the prospect of eventually getting to go out and shoot things.

Tuesday: TQ Day 275.

Up at 1015, the day is already off to a good start — meaning that I slept until 1015. I sit around and drink coffee for a while, eventually go running. In the afternoon, I help Phil install our second window, and of course do up a home improvement PPT presentation entitled, "Windows by Phil™." After dinner, I put together the weekly conference for Thursday.

I learn that we are all expected to go to eight hours of TMIP training over the next few days. This system is designed for outpatient care; it can be used to order labs, x-rays, and put in clinic notes. It is therefore completely useless out here: it's not connected to anything; we cannot print out anything we put into it; and the "smart cards" (little data chips for it) are not available, so we can't put anything into the system and send it with the patients. And of course it can be used only by the doctors, so it does nothing to save us any work. In fact, it gives the work of others to us. Much like every other "advance" in Navy Medicine of the last two decades, I hear.

Friday: TQ Day 278.

Up at 0800. Right after this, I hear on the radio that Pat has to report to the SSTP by 0930 for a command urinalysis. Oh, great, this again, but at least they didn't muster all 70 people for it. Still, Brian is pretty pissed off, and Pat is not happy either. It's not that we have to pee in cups, that's just part of life in the Military (although we had never done this during my first tour here). It's that the Chief arbitrarily sets a 90 minute time limit on it, for his convenience. Of course, Pat has already peed for the morning and has nothing to offer, so to speak.

At 0900, we start our pistol dryfire training, with me and Pat as RSOs (Range Safety Officers), and two of our Marine corporals as instructors. At 0915, Pat is called on the radio to remind him that he has to go pee. I mention this to the boss, who is on the "firing line," that Pat is an RSO and, in principle, we cannot run the course without the two of us. So he radios in to say that the LtCdr will not be available until after 1115.

Saturday: TQ Day 279.

I had planned on getting up at 0745 to run with Eric, our young nurse, who must do his Marine PRT today. But I don't even wake up when his alarm goes off, although Phil does and goes with him for moral support. I sleep until 0900, and head over to Grand Rounds at 0930. Afterwards, lunch, and then I spend the afternoon working on my next PowerPoint on TMIP. We have a new mission statement: to be "turnkey providers working as transformation advocates to champion groundbreaking initiatives in medical informatics." I even come up with a new program to complement the BMIST system being fielded, i.e., the Battlefield Traumatics Handheld Device. Or, B-MIST and BT-HD, for short. Of course, I will have the appropriate desktop icons shown on the laptop screen.

Sunday: TQ Day 280.

At 1300 I get the SUV and head over to the IECI camp where the poll workers for the Independent Electoral Commission of Iraq work. The G3 (Ops) for Special Projects has been involved with this quite a bit, and has invited me over there for lunch. I pick up her, and a couple of her Marines, and we drive over to the compound, which is a large area walled off with 8-foot HESCOs topped with barbed wire, since it has Iraqi civilians living in it in the middle of our U.S. base. The poll workers will be here for a few days before and after the election. It's great food, lots of well-cooked rice with sauces, spices, chicken, pickled veggies — definitely different from what I usually eat here. It's a good meal for the day, and leaves one with a nice full tummy.

Another day with no trauma. It's been quiet everywhere it seems, but I know it will be too good to last. I can't imagine that they won't try something for the election. The insurgents have put up fliers in Ramadi saying, "You vote — you die."

Monday: TQ Day 281.

Up at 0800 to drop my sleeping bag off at the laundry. Pistol dryfire at 0900. This was made entertaining by what was going on next to us. Our "dryfire range" is a row of three shipping containers next to the new K-span (metal hangar) that will house the "hospital" once it's built. Pat and I stand at either end on large heaps of gravel looking out for pedestrians who pass through the construction site, acting as Range Safety Officers. Even though we make sure that no one has any ammo on them during the training, and everyone has to show empty weapons and magazines, we still treat it like a real range. Also, we don't want to freak anyone out when they walk by and twenty pistols are pointed at them.

So I have the perfect vantage point to watch something incredibly stupid. There is a small formation at the far end of the hangar. I watch the engineers go up onto the roof of the K-span, which is like a huge Quonset hut with a curved roof, and put ropes down the sides. Then we watch three guys go up the ropes, weapons flapping, and stand up there. No safety harnesses and no helmets (the ropes are hanging three feet from the "hard hat area" sign). Well, this is an accident waiting to happen. So, during a break, I walk over to the formation and ask what's going on. "Promotion ceremony, sir." "Who is in charge here?" "The Colonel, sir." "Where would I find him? " "He's up there, sir," the gunny says, pointing up onto the roof. And that was the end of that.

Tuesday: TQ Day 282.

At 1400, I go to the "MCMAP" briefing. This describes the Marine Corps Martial Arts Program, which is actually quite interesting. It teaches the Marines hand-to-hand combat and how to fight dirty. Only problem is, we have been seeing a lot of McMap injuries out here. It looks like something I would be interested in doing, but not out here. Last thing I need is to hurt myself and not be able to operate, and we don't have a lot of surgeons to spare.

It's been quiet. Real quiet. Too quiet. I have spent all week feeling like the sword of Damocles is hanging over us, waiting to fall...

Wednesday: TQ Day 283.

At 2130, we get a "duty Ridgeways" call for an incoming pregnant Iraqi. Head up there, find out that this is essentially all the info we have. The patient arrives, the report is that the baby is breech (i.e., butt first). I take her back to the OR and examine her. Yup, ass first, but not ready to come out yet and the kid seems to be doing fine, otherwise. She is packed (we had warned the Air Boss in advance) and flies off to Baghdad, where they have two Army obstetricians.

I get the story from the Army guys who brought her in — from one of the CMET guys in fact (these are the U.S. military advisors to the Iraqis). An Iraqi patrol was going through Kaldiyah, when a man comes up to them saying his wife is in labor and dying. They go and have a look, and she is certainly in labor. There is lots of excitement, she has been in labor for ten hours. A crowd of about a hundred people gathers to see what is going on (what with the yelling husband, screaming woman, and Iraqi army patrol, it's the best show in town). The Iraqi lieutenant tells the U.S. Army advisor that the woman may die; he needs to call for assistance. The advisor calls his Brigade, which calls HQ at Camp Manhattan, which says that their BAS can handle it, bring her in. Of course, they can't, and she comes to us after a brief stop there... We'll see how she does.

I get an incidental follow-up on a previous case from the CMET guy. A few days ago they saw the kid I operated on a couple of months back with the big frag hole in his chest, the one with his liver and lung hanging out. He was playing in his yard and they gave him a soccer ball. He had been transferred to the Baghdad hospital and eventually sent home. That kid was a real save. I ask how his wounds looked. "Man, his scars are ugly, looks like a big snake across his belly and chest." "Yeah, but is the skin healed up?" "Yup." Success! The surgical macramé I did on him worked.

Thursday: TQ Day 284.

Election Day for the Iraqis. I hope they appreciate it. Somehow, Phil had convinced me to get up for breakfast before the conference, as it is reputedly the best meal of the day. While it wasn't bad, it wasn't great, either. Omelets made to order, but not cooked quite the way I like — I prefer my omelets fixings pre-fried, and then chucked in the eggs, not all done at once. Still, you don't go to war with the omelets that you want, you go to war with the omelets that you are issued.

Election day and no trauma. Have we turned a corner? Maybe it's not a dust storm that has settled in outside, maybe it's the winds of change.

Friday: TQ Day 285.

At 1700 we have a unit BBQ. Good ribs, chicken, dogs. I skip the steak. Afterwards, a bunch of us decide to gaggle down to the hootch for coffee and biscotti. As I walk through the front of the SSTP, I see a stretcher being brought in from some humvees out front. An Army guy is brought in, without warning, from an IED blast. The front fender had been blown off their Humvee and they had driven the 30 km to the base in it, apparently because they couldn't get their radio to work. The guy is deaf in one ear, and has severe neck pain, so he's sent off for a CT scan, but has no obvious external injuries. We leave our big arc lights on over the pad so the Army guys can work on fixing the Humvee, which has a number of leaking hoses.

Saturday: TQ Day 286.

I play "combat badminton" for a while this afternoon, then off to dinner. At 1900, we go up to the SSTP to drive over to the Marines' mandatory PME (professional military education). The General will be speaking on how the Marine Corps is transforming logistics. At the start of the lecture, the General is up there making some opening remarks. He then looks out into the audience, straight at me, and says, "Where have you been the last few weeks, doc?" "Hiding, sir, it's the next best thing to staying out of trouble." "Thought you would have made it home by now." "No sir, I can't seem to find a ride out of here, maybe next year." Most of the Marines in the room seem taken aback that the General even knows who I am; but of course, I have been here three times as long as they have, and I live on his side of the base. 'Sides, I've given him the guided tour of the chest cavity in my OR...

It was an interesting, yet scary, talk. The amount of jargon and buzzwords was incredible — some necessary, some not. I could see what he was talking about, but the problem will be, as always, that these changes will require that everyone do what they are supposed to do. If they were already doing that, then a lot of things in the system would not have to be changed. The General is actually an engineer by trade; I'm told that he was only

Desperate times call for desperate measures. Two Navy doctors do not allow the threat of incoming fire to deter them from a vigorous game of badminton.

assigned to logistics once he made full colonel, and he seems to know his stuff all right. However, I can already imagine the huge piles of jargon-laden documents being generated by people who want to prove that they are on track with the program, which of course defeats the purpose.

But he said some really good stuff. (1) We do not want efficiency, we want effectiveness. Often, what is effective is inefficient. (2) We do not have customers, don't use that word. (3) It's not enough to say that stuff is "in the system" on order, and we will wait for it to fall out the other end. We need to be more interested in what comes out the other end, and when. I wonder if the Medical Service Corps officers (my friend, the twigs) were paying attention?

At the end of it, many of my medical colleagues are looking confused. Not that they had been particularly interested, anyway. Brian, ever the master of the inappropriate question, confesses that he had been tempted during the Q&A period to ask the General who invented sausage...

Sunday: TQ Day 287.

Up at around 0800, make coffee. Mass at 0930. Afterwards, the coffee klatch meets and we spend two hours bantering about all sorts of bizarre things. We also learn that someone had dimed Brian out to the General. The boss, the General, and Brian all sing in the choir at Mass and, at the start of the Mass, the General had asked Brian if he had ever heard of some obscure German doctor. No, he hadn't. "Oh, he's the guy who invented sausage." Brian's jaw certainly dropped at that one!

Hang unwanted candy canes all over Brian's bed because we can. We also learn that there might be some action in Ramadi tonight, so better get some sleep. To bed at 2300.

Tuesday: TQ Day 289.

Having no particular reason to get up today, I make it until 1000. Around 1300, we get in a soldier who dislocated his ankle playing football. Very ugly x-rays but nothing broken, we reduce it and splint it. About an hour later, an Iraqi civilian is brought in, shot through the left knee. We get three versions of the story: the Iraqi Army shot him, or he shot himself, or they were celebrating the election and someone else fired in the air and the bullet landed in his leg. The latter is the least likely of the three possibilities. Anyway, we have to wash out his knee, which is trashed. A few days later we learn that the Intel boys figured it out eventually — he was a bad guy and was ultimately sent to Abu Ghraib.

Thursday: TQ Day 291.

Up for the 0800 meeting, where I royally mocked Ronnie, the soon-to-be White House physician. I have fakes of him with the President, the First Lady, the Veep, the

Secretary of State, the President of South Korea, and, of course, with Miss Beasley and Barney, the Presidential dogs. I also include a picture of him doing something interesting with Gold Bond Medicated Powder.

Friday: TQ Day 292.

More dryfire practice today at 0900. Around 1000, a patient comes in, an Iraqi girl supposedly shot in the abdomen. She arrives with a wound under her ribs on the right, looking scared but okay. No exit wound, but no bullets or frags visible on x-ray, either. Whatever hit her either fell out, just nicked her, or doesn't show on x-ray. We take her to the OR and explore the wound, which does not penetrate all the way, and she gets to go on her merry way. Her grandfather had brought her to our ECP, and tells us, through the interpreter, that his 7-year-old grandson was killed by random gunfire last year. He is happy that we "saved her." Let's hope he's sincere.

Saturday: TQ Day 293.

After dinner, I try calling you. Thirty seconds into it, we hear that casualties are coming in. First report is that it's two or three of our unit Marines, burned when their Humvee was blown up by an IED. One is reported to have third degree burns to his face, which is very bad. After an hour, we learn that they have not even left the scene yet, because three other IEDs were found, and the area has yet to be cleared to allow the casualties to be moved. Bad news for the facial burn, if true. After another hour, we hear that they are finally on the way, and eventually they arrive by helo, a little more than three hours after the event.

The Marine with "third degree burns to the face" turns out to be a Sudanese interpreter with a burn on the tip of his nose and on his right hand. The other patient, a unit MP, has burns on both hands. Neither needs surgery, but both will need to fly out for wound care. Neither will be going back to work any time soon. The XO has come by, and eventually the General does too, and I get a couple of photos of them carrying stretchers. Eventually they fly off, by which time it's about 2230.

At 2330, Pat does an "unofficial" nondenominational Christmas service for the STP. Since he's our chaplain, that is, assigned to our unit, we don't see what the big deal is about doing a service, but the base's Chief Chaplain sees it differently: it will compete with other services being offered elsewhere. Except that no one else is doing a Midnight Mass-type of service. So Pat does it anyway.

Sunday: TQ Day 294.

Up at 0800, we start drinking coffee at around 0845, and then off to Mass at 0930. Afterwards, more coffee, then the ever-popular "Sundays with Psych" show, a.k.a. "B.S.

with Brian," and "Brian's Place." At 1100, a call for an incoming casualty, which turns out to be a guy sent by Combat Outpost for possible appendicitis. The boss, who is duty surgeon, thinks it might be a kidney stone. We wander back to the hootch and drink more coffee.

Brian is in rare form today. He starts by telling us that he woke up at 0300, attacked by a starfish. He had noticed the snowflakes that I had stuck to the roof of his bunk, but had said nothing. Early this morning, one of them fell off and stuck to his head. He awoke startled, disoriented, and he claims, nearly incontinent, flailing at this thing attached to his head. Finally he got it off and tried to toss it on his desk, but it was sticking and wouldn't come off his fingers. I would have paid money to see that…

Then I give him his Christmas present, a possessed camel. It's a stuffed camel about a foot long, which when you squeeze it plays a recording of Arab kids chanting, and its eyes glow bright red. Brian almost pees himself with delight, he keeps playing it over and over again. Feeding the inner child…

It actually rains today, a couple of times for about 5 minutes, total. Not impressive, but unusual for here, and the clouds were nice. A wet, if not white, Christmas.

We head over to lunch at 1300. Pretty good food: turkey, roast beef, ham, stuffing, pecan pie *à la mode*. Then we wander back to the hootch and sit around watching the Fox "Who was Jesus?" report, and contemplate taking a nap. The boss is called to see the kidney stone guy again; he has a fever, and a few minutes later I hear him call for the OR crew over the radio to do an appy. After about a half hour, I wander over to check e-mail, and then go to the OR to see what's what.

I walk in to see him looking at a normal appendix surrounded by yellow fluid. "I'll go scrub," sez I, and he nods. Perforated gastric ulcer presenting as appendicitis, an uncommon but well-known phenomenon. Open his belly, find a nice hole in his stomach, fix it, and then set him up to fly to Balad and eventually home. Back to the hootch for me. Merry Xmas, kid.

No luck calling you tonight. I had really looked forward to it.

Monday: TQ Day 295.

Get up at 0900, but decide I can do better and go back to sleep until 1030. After lunch, I check e-mail and pick up snail mail: the portable hard drive and lots of musicals, cool! I race back to the hootch to try out the hard drive, only to discover that it won't run on the laptop I'm using. So much for that plan … I will have to think of some other way to transfer stuff off my 8-year-old laptop. Will probably have to borrow a laptop from someone. The new drive works on other people's computers, though.

In the afternoon I get a consult for an incarcerated hernia, or a testicular torsion, or something. It ends up being none of the above, but he will need to see a urologist eventually for his very impressive varicocoele.

A little later, we hear that there is a wounded soldier coming in by Bradley (tank), shot through the neck. Head up to the STP, where I learn that he's coming in from Kaldiyah, which is a few miles away and will take a while. This does not bode well for him, the delay will likely kill him, assuming that the injury is even survivable. A few minutes later I learn that he has died en route so he most likely would not have made it, and we stand down. I tell the guy's company commander who is here with us, waiting for him. A little later, Pat (who is also the chaplain assigned to Mortuary Affairs), goes over to the Mortuary when he arrives.

Try calling you again, you're out. Maybe later. At 2100, I get through, and it's good to hear your voice. Miss you a lot. It will be good to get home many months from now. The boys are entertaining, but it's just not the same.

Wednesday: TQ Day 297.

Another successful sleep-in until 1000, then lunch. Later the boss, Phil, Pat, and I go running. We are about a mile out when we get a call that "5 or 6 patients are coming in by ground, unknown nationality, unknown injuries, unknown ETA." We turn around and start running back. I tell Phil to call the COC (he's the only one carrying a radio) to send a vehicle out for us. We then hear that there is already a patient on the pad. A minute later a Humvee ambulance zips up and we pile in and go. Arrive on the pad, pile out, and I run into the STP tent.

Ronnie is standing with an oxygen mask on the patient's face. CB is trying to put in a chest tube. Mike has his hand under the patient's back, holding something. Tim is trying to put a central line for IV access in the guy's groin. I walk up to Ronnie: "What's going on?" He tells me the guy came in with agonal respirations and a big hole in the left side of his back. Mike is holding pressure on the back wound. "Is it bleeding?" "I dunno, but it was bubbling a lot." Okay, let's start over. A — Airway. He needs one, but is awake enough to fight it, so he needs IV access to push drugs (Tim is working on that). He does not appear to have a head injury; his eyes look okay, although he has blood in his nose. B — Breathing. Chest tube is in, that works. C–Circulation. Get a blood pressure. Still no IV access, Tim can't get it, so I go to the other groin, harpoon the femoral vein, and put in a big central line. Push the drugs, intubate the guy. As Tim does this, I say loudly to the room that, as soon as the tube is secure, we will lift the patient and get a chest x-ray, then ultrasound him. We do this with some pushing and yelling (people have a tendency to just stand there and do nothing unless you tell each one personally what to do). That's done. ABCs taken care of, he has a blood pressure. Roll him over and he has a hole in his back which I (of course) stick my finger into. It goes into his lung through his shoulder blade, but no major bleeding. Also a hole in his ass, but it looks superficial.

Ronnie wants to know when I will take the patient to the OR — "to check for bleeding in his pelvis or something." The boss tells me that we may have 3 or 4 more coming (we have had a couple of minor injuries arrive in the interim meanwhile) and we might need to make room for them. So I tell everyone that I have no plan to take him to the OR, yet. I want to see his chest x-ray to see where the frags are. In the middle of his chest, great.

Pat comes to x-ray to get me. "They are taking the guy to the OR." "What?" I go back there and tell them to stop. Look at the guy again. Now he has a "raccoon eye" (a big black eye) on the left, blood coming out his left ear, and his left pupil is twice the size of his right one. Bleeding into his brain. Can't do anything about that here. I look over to one of the Marines: "Tell the COC to call the Air Boss. Tell him we have a no-shit head bleed here and when we drop the 9-line (the official request for a helo), we're gonna want it immediately, and it HAS to go to Balad" (the only place with a neurosurgeon). Then to the corpsmen: "Package him. Make this the fastest 'hot pocket' you've ever done, his life depends on it." In less than 5 minutes, he is gone.

We get no other significant injuries. The group turns out to be civilian security contractors, many of whom are former Australian SAS, so we have quite the accent-fest going. I tell "Bloomer," their boss, that it doesn't look good for the guy we sent out. He tells me that this bloke, Mac, had been hit by four IEDs in the last four days, this is the first one to injure him. Hmm ... Bad luck, or did they not learn anything from the first three? But they sound like they know what they're doing, SAS usually do.

I learn later that when he arrived at Balad, he went to the CT scanner, the scan was aborted, and he then went to the OR to evacuate a massive subdural haematoma. They took out his left brain's temporal lobe for massive swelling, and he died an hour later. The left side of his skull was crushed like an eggshell from the blast, no penetrating injuries at all. Good diagnosis on my part, but a bad outcome.

Of course, I didn't know this until the next day. We finish our run as the sun goes down. (Okay, I probably would have run anyway.) Afterwards, as I'm putting my stuff away from the shower, a piece falls off my bed. It is some curlicue metal ornamental bit, about a foot long, which of course is immediately put to use. Phil and I drill a hole in the rafter over Brian's desk, shove it through and bend it so it can't come out, and then use it as an ornamental hook for the bird cage. Did I mention the bird cage? I have a wire box that J.J. sent me biscotti in. I put a stuffed parrot in it, some popcorn, and a little metal bell. The whole thing is then hung over Brian's desk. Brian has, of course, already seen the bird cage, but he did not notice the new hook (which allows the cage to hang much lower) until he whacked his head into it, twice.

After the boys get back from dinner, we watch *Pirates of the Caribbean* until midnight, sit around making "Arrrrr" noises for a while, and hit the rack.

Thursday: TQ Day 298.

Up for the 0800 case conference. Not too many cases to discuss. The boss reveals the super-secret RIP dates (i.e., when we get to leave). I suppose I could have looked this up myself if I had ever bothered to activate my "secret" clearance computer account 11 months ago; I never seemed to find a good reason to do so. The dates always change anyway, and the less I know, the less I can give away. We also discuss how the Marines do awards. I end with some "new" bogus ribbons that I found somewhere to present at the next meeting: the "never deployed" ribbon, the "everyone went to the Middle East but me" ribbon, the "never moved from home" ribbon, and the "never been on a ship" ribbon, to name just a few.

Afterwards, our internal awards board meets again. Finished all the medals we are

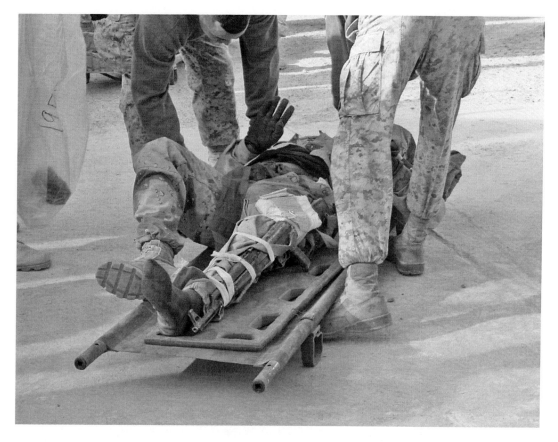

Everyone, including the Iraqi Army, learns to make field-expedient splints out of whatever is at hand in order to stabilize broken limbs. This time, what was at hand was an AK-47. Of course, it would have been better if the leg had actually been broken, and the AK-47 had been unloaded first....

submitting, at least the first drafts, anyway. Then back to the hootch, where we chat with Brian for a bit. He made the comment that he is running out of space in his corner for all of his "stuff," that is, all the stuff we keep giving him. Phil and I tell him that he needs a loft, and immediately work on measuring things and drawing plans. Brian, of course, insists that he does not need a loft, even though we point out that he can even sleep up in it if he wants to, or store things in it. We can put in a spiral staircase. Pat mentions that a cellar might be better, because of the rockets. A cellar? No, no, no — a spider hole! Over lunch, plans for Brian's new spider hole are drafted on paper napkins and left on his desk. He is, of course, ecstatic. Well, maybe ecstatic is not the word I'm looking for...

"Why don't you just build a tunnel from the hut to the new hospital?" he cries out in frustration. Hmm... Okay, so we can't do that. But we can berate him for his constant neediness. He insists that he needs none of this, yet he keeps demanding more and more! Brian, what kind of psychiatrist are you, anyway? Me, me, me. More, more, more. Some people!

Get a call for two "severely injured" Iraqi soldiers coming in by ground. One is on his side, awake, with a bandage on his jaw. The boss, who is primary today, sends him into the SSTP while the second guy, with an AK-47 attached to his leg as a splint, is evaluated on the pad. I go with the first guy.

I take a quick look at the bandage on his jaw. Well, I look at the bandage where his jaw is supposed to be; it has been blown off by an IED frag. Time to go to the OR; he needs to be intubated before he aspirates and drowns in his own blood. Away we go. Get in there, things go remarkably calmly compared to yesterday, probably because we have fewer people and there is not too much confusion about who is in charge. I tell the OR crew to get a trach set ready. Tell them he is NOT dying but he needs to be tubed. We will get his clothes cut off, then start an IV with him lying on his side. Once that is done, push drugs to put him out, lay him on his back, and tube him. Tim is worried about tubing him because of the injury, I tell him it should be easy; after all, most of what makes an airway difficult (the jaw) is not a problem as it's no longer there in the way.

Everything goes according to plan. He's tubed; I sew the tube to his upper lip. He has small frag holes high up his neck and will need a CT. Has a hole in his ass, but it is superficial. He would be a good case — tracheostomy, interesting facial injuries, butt wounds — but he really needs a CT first for his Zone III neck injury, so no case for me. I get him packaged to go.

Friday: TQ Day 299.

I am finally forced from my bed at 1015 by the incessant radio traffic. First, Mike is called to tell him that there is an ortho patient up there who came in on the milk run last night. (I dimly recall that the duty doc had been called to see this very patient, around 0300.) He tells them to cut the cast off, get x-rays, have the IDC start the paperwork, and he will be there in twenty minutes. Fifteen minutes after Mike's interchange, Phil is called about the same patient, by someone else. Come on guys, we all have the same radios and hear everything, why are you calling?

Pat, Phil, and I go running at 1200. It is around 45 degrees and very windy, so we only go a couple of miles. On the way back we see Eric, our young roomie, and torment him into doing pull-ups. Well, a pull-up. Okay, almost one. Two months of "working out" and he is incapable of doing a single pull-up... I have bet Pat one large ($1) in pogs that he can pass the Marine PFT before we leave (more as moral support than because I think he can). I tell Eric it's coming out of his hide if I lose.

...(sometime later) The patients (now two) finally show up. One has some broken teeth. The other has bandages on his face and both legs, I take him straight back to the OR while Ronnie looks at the other one. My guy has a hole in his head, and is blind in one eye (so he needs to fly straight out), a hole in his neck (which needs an operation), and broken ankles bilaterally. So lots of good surgery for me and Mike, except that he needs to fly out to get his head CTed and an eye surgeon to look at him. Damn! He goes to sleep, I tell Brian (our FP) to put a central line in his groin while I ultrasound his belly. When I'm done, still no central line. Now Tim is trying, too, and hits the artery. Ronnie, who is finished with the other Iraqi, tries in the other groin, still no luck. So I grab another kit and stick one in under his collarbone on the first attempt, and he's ready to fly. Who's the man? (Heehee.) I need to have these guys do a few more of these on less urgent patients.

But then we learn that he can't go just yet. We get word that he might be an EPW. One of our corpsmen in the COC was called by a Casevac (helo) corpsman from the squadron, who was radioed by an Army medic in the field, who says that these guys might have blown themselves up setting the IED that went off. So the PET (the twig weasels up at Ramadi-Blue Diamond) insists that the guy go straight to the military prison at Abu Ghraib (which has a hospital with an Army general surgeon). Even though they have no eye surgeon and no neurosurgeon. I convince them that they are wrong; then they insist that only the one guy can go to Balad, the other must go to AG. Two helo flights? I point out that we have already loaded both of the patients onto one helo; the twigs finally agree that sending both to the same place is okay, and they leave.

Saturday: TQ Day 300.

Day 300. And it doesn't seem a day over 250. Up for Phil's 0930 talk on hand injuries for Grand Rounds. "Windows by Phil™" made its reappearance, presented by Phil, with some new additions: miniblinds and birdfeeders. We have plans to add doors and spider holes, but that's for another day.

At 1830, we head to dinner. But it's not the usual dinner. We had been invited, by our favorite Iraqi-American interpreter couple from Detroit, to a New Year's dinner. Specifically, the boss, Mike, Phil, and I have been asked over. There is red rice (saffron rice), assorted odd salads, lamb curry, turkey, chicken, and steak, all of it very tasty. A phenomenal dinner was had by all, and we sat around telling various stories and chatting. Most of the interpreters are female: one from Damascus but now Canadian, one from Baghdad, one from L.A., and a couple of others. One reminds me of a short, chunky Emma Thompson, she has that incredibly straight nose. There are a couple of men, including one who moved to Scotland in the '70s when Saddam came to power. Also Talia, the new NCIS agent, Patrick and Dave the CI guys, and a few other folks. A good time was had by all.

A few minutes after we left, around 2130, we get a call for a patient coming in, an Army guy goofy after he had his bell rung by an IED. He gets flown off for a CT scan of his head. Then back to the hootch. We watch *1776* until shortly before midnight, and then switch over to Fox's New Year's coverage. They had some snippets on the year's top stories including, of course, Iraq. A fascinating interview with some European-dressed 20-something Iraqis at a lakeside resort in northern Iraq who state: "If everyone would just forget the whole 'Islam thing,' this country would be much better off." Right.

At midnight we tooted horns, wore party hats, blew bubbles, and toasted with near-beer. Twenty minutes later, we're in bed. Another year bites the dust.

12. January 2006: The "Overflow" from Ramadi

Sunday: TQ Day 301.

I walk into the hootch after doing e-mail, it's around 1400. The boss, Pat, and Phil are sitting around, drinking coffee. As I walk in the door, there are two "booms." I walk to my rack and start putting on my body armor. "What are you doing?" "Those were rockets." "Oh, come on, we hear stuff all the time around here." "Yeah, I know, 'There's always something blowing up in Iraq' is my line, but those were rockets on base." The scoffing continues. A minute later, the "Big Voice" sounds for the first time in over two months. Told ya' so. Later, it's rumored to be two mortar rounds out by the engineer unit, but we are pretty well out of mortar range. I'll try to find out more later. (It turns out to be 107mm Chinese rockets.)

Because the dog-and-pony show took up the morning (Chief of Naval Operations and the Master Chief Petty Officer of the Navy came by for a visit), Father Tim had offered to do Mass for us at 1700, which we take him up on. Phil, the boss, Joe (the psychologist), and I have our own little Mass with him, and then go have dinner with the good Padre. He's a very down-to-earth priest, something you would expect after 30 years with the Navy and Marines. He's the originator of the phrase "Iraqi T&A," i.e., toes and ankles.

Wednesday: TQ Day 304.

Head out for a four-plus mile run with the boss, Phil, and Pat. When we get back, we force Eric from his bed (he was up late) and he actually succeeds in doing two whole pull-ups. There may be hope. The "last chance" Marine PRT for us Navy officers is in 10 days.

I put in the finishing touches for tomorrow's conference, including checking the latest American College of Cardiology recommendations on the treatment of myocardial infarction (heart attack). As I consider showering before dinner, we hear of a TCN truck driver coming in by helo, hit by an IED. As I get to the pad, a Humvee drives up and disgorges an Iraqi-looking guy with bandages on his arm. All right... Turns out this is some other patient entirely, ours is still coming. The one helo patient then becomes two, one "walking wounded" and one with "severe facial and neck injuries."

200

When they arrive, the "severe facial and neck" injury guy doesn't look that bad, so the boss (duty surgeon) has him go in the ER tent. The "walking wounded" guy has a little piece of gauze taped to his neck. Lift it up and see a big hole. We walk him straight back to the OR.

I leave the boss in the OR, getting that guy organized, and go back to the ER to see about our other guy. He has some strange findings: a very impressive laceration over his left eye, and his pupils are both oddly shaped and nonreactive to light—injured? Or has he had eye surgery? But he's looking around and talking. No interpreter, so no idea what he's saying or whether it makes any sense. He will need a CT scan of his head. His left hand has lots of lacerations. His belly is rather poochy and hurts a bit, but nothing on ultrasound. When I ultrasound his heart, something just doesn't look right—there is no abnormal fluid around it, all I'm really looking for, but his heart just does not seem to be contracting uniformly. Maybe a cardiac contusion? Shoot a chest x-ray and one of his mediastinum, including his heart. It's rather abnormally shaped. Okay, he gets to go away now. He needs at least a chest CT.

Back to the OR, where the boss and I open the guy's neck up, fix his bleeding jugular vein, and look around for any other injuries. A nice case.

Thursday: TQ Day 305.

Hear over the radio of incoming casualties, unknown number, unknown ETA. Head for the pad.

I'm the duty surgeon and so get the scoop. Mass casualties, we can expect a helo with 3 or maybe 6, possibly a second helo with 6, possibly a third. So anywhere from 3 to 18 patients, all Iraqi civilians. This is the "overflow" from something in Ramadi, so they are already full. The fun begins. First six arrive, all need surgery, all have many frags to many places, none are actively dying except for one guy with a head injury who needs to be intubated. Nothing more at present, but we're not sure, so I send the boss back to the OR with the first and most obvious belly case. I am making the rounds, trying to keep tabs on what is going on with all the patients, making suggestions such as throw in a chest tube, etc. The big question is, what else is coming? We learn that we are getting another six in a few minutes. That settles it, the stable ones can fly out with the head injury guy, and we start packaging them.

We send four stable patients out as another six come in, same drill, only now we have one surgeon (me) and several very nasty surgical cases, but most are, for the moment, stable. I have told the PET that we cannot take any more patients right now if they can avoid it, but four times in fifteen minutes I'm told that the PET has called again, asking when we can reopen. Crap, they are looking for somewhere to send more patients. Call the Air Boss and PET, work it out: as soon as you can get me a bird to fly most of the stable ones out, I'm open for business again; we have at least six surgical cases backed up, two looking pretty bad, so our two ORs will be full if I go back to operate. If I can get them out, I will have an open OR. However, if you have to send patients from the field to somewhere and no one else can take them, send them to us and we will work it out, somehow.

Unfortunately, there are no helos available for me to send anyone anywhere, so I head to the OR with a crashing patient with literally about a hundred small holes in his ass and right leg. I get to work on him, open his belly, fix his colon, and see that he has a massive blood clot in his pelvis; but it's not getting bigger and he has pulses in both legs, so he doesn't have a major arterial injury. Leave that alone! Opening the clot to look for the source will often produce uncontrollable bleeding from inoperable veins.

I have an additional problem. While I cannot see one, this guy may very well have a rectal injury in his pelvis, which I don't want to get into because of his pelvic clot. Normally I would divert the guy, meaning give him a colostomy so no poop goes into his rectum and it stays relatively clean. But I have a couple of concerns: because of his massive resuscitation, his belly will swell up, which may stretch the colon I used for the stoma and cut off its blood supply (I have seen that a couple of times). Also, I think this guy will need a second look tomorrow, anyway, to look at the colon repairs I have made under less than ideal circumstances. Finally, he is very labile, and if I was the receiving surgeon, I would probably take him back to the OR anyway to look for missed injuries to explain his instability. So I decide to leave things be for the moment. The boss sticks his head in for a minute to see what's up and tell me what he's got, and I ask him what he would do. He would do the colostomy and close his belly. Nah, I decide to do neither. "You know, boss, I asked you so you would agree with me."

Finish him up and talk to Mike about getting to work on his leg, which is a mess. But I am plus/minus on this versus just sending the guy out, as he has already received 12 units of blood and his blood pressure is still quite labile. Sending him out might be better, and we have a lot of other work to do.

During the case, I remember looking up and seeing our Marine CO standing in the back corner. As I was working alone (well, an elderly Army PA had scrubbed with me), I was too busy to really chat. A few minutes later, I look up again, he's still there. A little later I look up yet again and now it's the General. "Oh, hi, sir. How's your day been?" "Fine, doc, how about you?" "Not too bad, I'm almost earning my pay today."

Unfortunately, the patient has another problem. Someone has put a central line, a huge IV, into the guy's chest under his right collar bone. Gerry had pushed three units of blood through it on a pressure infuser, without the blood pressure getting much better. He had checked the lines, to discover that he could not draw blood from the central line; so it may be malfunctioning. Three units of blood may have been pushed into the guy's chest instead. Oh ... bother. So he puts in another smaller IV and makes do with that for the case. Afterwards, I get a chest x-ray, see a huge mediastinum filled with blood, but his heart works. I put in a central line that works on the other side, and Gerry is happy again.

Outside, we have reopened for business as our second bolus of patients has gone out, but now both Balad and Baghdad say they are full and cannot take any more patients. So the only place to send casualties from here is to Tikrit/Mosul way up north, where there is another Army Combat Support Hospital. Out of helo range, but the Air Boss is working to get a C-130. The PET, who is supposed to be handling this, has clearly demonstrated that they are in over their heads and the Air Boss has taken over. An Air Force C-130 is going to Al Asad to pick up patients, and will then come here to pick up our patients and the patients coming from Ramadi by helo to meet the bird (Ramadi's airfield handles only helos). The C-130 is on the way now. The PET says, "What C-130?" But it won't arrive for an estimated 55 minutes.

Meanwhile, another "crashing" patient has been diverted to us and will be here in a couple of minutes. The boss is closing and will then be available to take him. I go back to my other guy. He ends up taking this new patient to the OR for a liver injury which was surprisingly minor.

Walk back into the OR, ask Mike how long it will take him to do what he has to do. "An hour." "A real hour or an ortho hour?" (We have both joked about surgeons not being able to tell time.) "Okay, ninety minutes." This guy needs to be on the ambulance out to a C-130 in 55 minutes. I point to the Chief in the room and tell him to tell us to stop operating in 30 minutes. We get to work. Fasciotomies to right thigh and calf, control bleeding vessels, and put on an ex fix (erector set) from hip to femur to tibia, as his femur and calf bones are all shattered. We are done in 45 minutes, a case that would normally take 2–3 hours. We don't wash the wounds out as much as we would like to; that will have to be done by the next guys along. The guy has received over 20 units of blood now, his pressure is better, but he needs to go to an ICU.

It is 1730, we have been working for only four-and-a-half hours. Hell, I've only operated on one patient, although I have done a lot of other stuff outside the OR, and the boss has done two cases. We work on getting the patients ready for the C-130. Eventually it arrives, and they leave. Only one case left, a knee and leg washout that Mike and Phil do after dinner. This guy can stay with us for a couple of days and then go home.

Quite a day. But, as usual, I'm not satisfied. Despite all the questions about "when can we reopen," we only received one more patient, and he was supposed to be going to Baghdad when he was diverted to us for instability. When I get to the bottom of it, it turns out that the PET only called once and there were no more casualties to send at that time; but four different people came to me at different times with four different stories. If I had known that there were no more patients expected, I probably would have kept at least four or five more of them for surgery here. Cases for us, and it takes some of the pressure off the Echelon IIIs, that end up getting most of the casualties from everywhere eventually anyway. Such is the "Fog of War."

One of my non-surgical colleagues continues to insist that his central line could not have been the problem. "It flowed great. How could that be?" "Easy, you lacerated the vein and it bled." "But it went in easy." "I watched you put it in, it wasn't that easy. If you have to push that hard to get it into the vein, there's something wrong." "But this has never happened to me before." "Well now it has, so you can now say 'In my experience.' Learn, and get over it."

But the night isn't over yet. A guy with a crushed finger, and then a request to do post mortem surgery.

Yep, post mortem surgery. I am called to the COC to talk to some spook. There were two Marines killed in Fallujah by a sniper, now in Mortuary Affairs. He wants me to dig the bullets out of them so he can get ballistics. Why? They want to see if several deaths over the past few days are all from the same sniper. Do they have someone detained that they need this evidence for? No. Is this going to help track down the sniper? No.

Who authorized this? Well, his boss got the call from some "bigwig" somewhere, saying it needs to be done. Got anything in writing for this, since, after all, this will alter the forensics when the guys get real autopsies when they arrive back in the States to the Armed Forces Medical Examiner in Dover, DE; and they will no doubt have a cow and this will come back to haunt us? No. Fine, get us your boss's and the bigwig's phone numbers and we will talk to them, but this is highly irregular. He says okay, but one way or another, the slugs will come out, sez he, patting his Leatherman. The guy clearly has no idea what he's asking.

He heads out, we make some calls. Talk to the General's Chief of Staff. "Hell no." The spook comes back, all apologetic. His boss has backed off, the suggestion was made by some JAG, somewhere, who looked at this as a "typical" murder case and had told them to "pick up the bullets from the coroner." Except that we don't have a coroner.

We also learn that we all have to go to a mandatory safety briefing on the other side of the base at 0930 tomorrow. What fun...

We learn on CNN that today was quite a bloody day in Iraq with over 130 dead. Five soldiers in an Army vehicle were killed on patrol in Baghdad, two Marines in Fallujah, and two more soldiers on patrol in Baghdad. A suicide bomber blew up a crowd at a shrine in Karbala, 49 dead. And another suicide bomber got into a crowd of people signing up for the Iraqi Police and Army at Ramadi: at least 56 dead (plus two U.S.) and 70 wounded — that was our particular disaster. And, oh yes, one injured bomb-sniffing dog. We also hear through the grapevine that an hour after the Ramadi bombing, people were lining up again to sign up. Amazing.

Quote of the day from the COC, courtesy of one of our corpsmen: "Who is this Sharon girl they keep talking about who's in a coma?" Meaning, of course, Ariel Sharon, the Israeli Prime Minister...

Friday: TQ Day 306

We have a mandatory safety brief to go to on Lakeside with CLR 25, so everyone piles into a bus while the select few (me, the boss, Phil, and the twig) drive over in the SUV. We get various other briefings also, the most interesting being on the election. In Al Anbar province, our little slice of heaven, voter turnout for the October referendum was 0.005 percent, with 96 percent voting against the constitution. For the December election, it was 55 percent, that is, 11,000 times higher. Overall turnout across the country was in the 70 plus percent range (final count is still not in). All parties — Kurds, Shi'ites and Sunnis — are claiming election fraud, so I suppose it all cancels out and was fair? The U.N. certified it, for what that's worth.

I wonder how many Americans would turn out to vote, under threat of death?

Afterwards, I drive us to a couple of scenic sites, like the top of the tallest bunker on base. Yes, I parked on top of the bunker, it has a long sloping side. Nice view of flatness covered with shipping containers, our home-away-from-home.

After lunch, I got to work sorting out the mess from yesterday. We have almost no names to go on, missing data; it's going to be a lot of fun trying to track these people down...

Around 2100, a call for an incoming Marine casualty, coming by ground. We stand down when we learn that the Army medics met him at the gate and took him to their BAS instead. Good on 'em.

Spend a couple of very entertaining hours chatting in the hootch before bed. Brian was in rare form!

Saturday: TQ Day 307

Up at 0830 for the 0930 Grand Rounds. Check mail as I leave, got a box. The plastic birds have arrived! I carefully glue them to the ledge outside of Brian's window, facing inwards so he can look out and see them.

After lunch, I'm in the hootch when Brian comes back. On his way over he saw the birds up on the ledge from outside and thought they were real. So he carefully crept around the hut and came in through the back, then crept up to the window and peeked outside — to see two birds staring back at him through the window. Priceless. For a while, he was worried that the birds were scaring away the others (real) birds outside, until he realized that the other birds had been off their popcorn for a couple of days and these had been there for only an hour. Well played!

No one knew when the window ledge and bird feeder were put up that the local birds were all ground-feeders and would not fly up to look for food seven feet off the ground, in view of Brian's window. When we finally figured it out, ringers were imported. Brian, an avid bird-watcher, was thrilled one afternoon to discover two birds roosting on his window ledge — until he discovered that they were Styrofoam.

Then off to the COC to do e-mails. As I sit there, lots of radio traffic goes back and forth about getting an ambulance to the pad, now! What's going on? He's leaving. Who's leaving? Mike. Mike's leaving? Yeah, he's being medevaced. Turns out that Mike had developed back pain and now he can't feel his foot. Probably a slipped disc, but he needs to go out before it gets worse. So he's packaged, put in the ambulance, and off he goes. That fast. One minute he's here, the next he's gone. It's possible that he won't be back. My last words to him as he left: "Mike, can I have your stuff...?"

Of course, this becomes quite the topic of conversation in the hootch. Mike will probably be okay, and we wonder how it will affect the way we do business. Realistically, while it was nice to have an orthopod around, we didn't have to have one, other places certainly do not. We will get by. I note that this is turning into "Survivor: TQ, for Surgeons." So far, John, Cliff, Peter, and now Mike have come and gone through TQ. Just me and the boss left. Who will go next? Given that I already survived Round One, you know who my money's on...

It rains quite a bit in the afternoon, things start to flood. Water pours through the door we have not sealed around (it used to leak at the other end last year). Mud everywhere (since we have dirt here and not sand).

Around 1800, we get in a casualty from Combat Outpost. During the changing of the guard at one of their OPs, a guy got sniped and was hit in the back of the right arm. Several tiny frags, possibly from a ricocheted bullet or whatever the bullet hit, no broken bones. But despite the tiny holes, he has a devastating nerve injury; all three major nerves in his right arm are nonfunctional, his right hand is useless and insensate. Pretty surprising given the external injuries, but there it is. Nothing for us to do, either; one usually waits a few weeks to see what comes back, and then possibly operates to do a nerve repair if it seems feasible. I plan to fly him out on the milk run, but it's delayed due to weather. Later in the evening, around 2230, I am called because "his hand is getting numb-er." A little odd, because it's already completely numb. Go over and look at him and it turns out that it's not numb but tingly. Getting better! Two of the three nerves have regained some function, the third is still gone but not entirely. Hopefully it's all just neuropraxia (bruising) and not really nerve laceration. Lucky him, perhaps. He still needs to fly out, though. The patient still wants to go back to his unit, though!

Sunday: TQ Day 308.

Take a run around 1600 and do a "mock PFT" with Eric. After six weeks of working out, he is getting ... worse. His run time is 45 seconds slower than he was when he started, and he couldn't do the required number of sit-ups or pull-ups. I may lose that "one large" in pogs to Pat after all.

Go to dinner with Brian, Phil and the boss, mostly for company and soup. Afterwards, we watch *Operation Petticoat*. I would argue that it, and *Mr. Roberts,* are the two classic World War II Navy movies.

By the way, Brian cannot get over the "racing vulture" I've put up over his desk. It's a little stuffed "Air Force" eagle that I found at the exchange. I painted the tip of the beak black, and drew a ruff around its neck, and then cut a sock into a little t-shirt with a number on it (15, same as his radio call-sign). I ripped a hole in its little wire cage, and he's now breaking out of it. Got the idea from a *Ripping Yarns* episode.

Monday: TQ Day 309

A major coup today, I sleep until 1130. Okay, so I was up doing crosswords until 0200, I got up at 0815 to go to the bathroom, and the radio kept waking me up, but still quite an accomplishment. I spend the afternoon doing lots of database stuff, I am way behind still. I want to know what happened to our patients.

Go running at 1600 with Phil, Pat, the boss, and Eric. The boss gets a call from Mike today, from Germany. He's there getting bed rest and steroid injections in his back, what we had predicted. However, he says they plan to send him back in a week or so, which is a bit of a surprise. We will see how that really goes. It's a good thing though, because even though we are down to about 6 weeks before our replacements arrive, the "powers that be" want to send out a replacement orthopod now. Exactly where they are going to get one from at the drop of a hat is anyone's guess, but there you have it. We don't think we need a replacement, we can get by, but then they have never, ever, listened to anything that we've suggested. Ever. With Mike's info, we can put off the ortho replacement issue for a couple of weeks and then, if he doesn't come back, we'll be so close to the RIP that it will no longer matter.

Tuesday: TQ Day 310.

Up at 0830, lecture to corpsmen at 0900. Roger, our senior nurse, had reminded me a couple of days ago about an e-mail he had never sent me: I was supposed to educate the corpsmen today. Good thing I've got lots of canned talks. I also learned that I'm giving the last Grand Rounds of the deployment, at the end of February. Lovely, my fourth one. That's what happens when I say, "If you can't find anyone else to give one, I'll do it..." For the corpsmen lecture I talk about shock, but mostly about medic-type things, like tourniquets and so on.

After lunch, pistol dryfire for the Marines and junior corpsmen. Kinda scary, because while these kids are no better or worse than the officers when they were doing it, they are like kids with toys and therefore less careful. We even had one kid who looked like he was straight out of East L.A. He's a twitchy kid, won't stay still, and was holding the pistol like a gangsta. I had a little chat with him, and he calmed down a bit. "If you don't play nice with your toy, I'll take it away from you."

Wednesday: TQ Day 311

I get to bed around 0200, as I spent the time reading and have nothing to get up for in the morning. At 0500, the radio says we have an incoming patient. He finally arrives around 0630. The PET had put out on the computer system that we were getting a patient, but neglected to tell us that the patient is actually an ortho consult, and was not coming urgently. So he arrives, we all look at his sprained knee, and I go back to bed. Sleep until 1100.

One of our docs has a hissy fit during this, up in arms about why we are getting an ortho consult when our ortho doc is gone. Why? Because the boss has told the PET and the Group Surgeon that we still have our full orthopedic capability: Phil, the orthopod PA, can do all the nonoperative ortho evaluations, and we can do any orthopedic surgery that needs to be done in this environment. Anyone who needs an elective operation will either have to wait until they get home, or get medevaced out, and Phil can handle those decisions, too. Phil is a damned good ortho PA.

Dryfire training is interesting. Now that people are settling in a little bit, it's fairly easy to identify who the problem children will be. Not from the standpoint of who will qualify, but from the standpoint of who might be dangerous. Most of the corpsmen, and all of the women, take the instruction seriously, follow the rules, and concentrate on what they are doing. The loud kids are the ones to watch: they talk, joke, do not concentrate, and so do stupid things. I relieve one kid of his pistol and make him stand in the corner for fifteen minutes when he pulls his weapon from his holster to show another shooter something, without instructions to do so. Our way, or the highway. Overall though, I think they will do fine.

Thursday: TQ Day 312.

Up for the Thursday case conference. The Army Intel officer makes it today and we get the scoop on the Ramadi bombing. A suicide bomber wearing an explosive vest packed with ball bearings was in the line of police recruits. The military working dogs got suspicious and he blew himself up. They assume that he was trying to get into the building itself, which would have been full of Iraqi Police and Iraqi Army personnel. Two U.S. dead, 2 injured, 4 dogs hurt. Thirty-two dead Iraqis at the scene, at least 74 wounded that we know of, probably a lot more who went to Ramadi General Hospital or elsewhere for care.

I discover that my orders to San Antonio have finally been "cut," i.e., they are official. I now need to get an electronic copy. Also find out that housing on Fort Sam looks very nice and we can probably get some. Cool! I'm ready to come home, and ready to move!

Friday: TQ Day 313.

Despite my firm resolve to vacate my bed no earlier than 1000, I am rousted out at 0830 for an "urgent" telephone call. I call the new reservist doc for the Army supply battalion on base. He tells me a story that sounds absolutely classic for appendicitis, and then tells me that he thinks the patient has "an acute abdomen, or a kidney stone." I tell him to send the guy over. Figuring that it will take a while to get him here, I tell the

HM1, the duty IDC (Independent Duty Corpsman, sort of like a PA) to see the guy when he gets here, and then call me. With real doctors here they do almost nothing and are getting no clinical experience at all, so we are trying to encourage them to use their skills. Unsuccessfully for the most part, I might add. When I tell him, he says, "Do you want to get x-rays when he gets here?" "No, I want you to examine him and decide what you want to do to make a diagnosis. Then, when you're done working him up, call me." Hope springs eternal...

I go back to bed. About thirty minutes later, the radio tells me that the patient is here. I am tempted to ask if the IDC has seen him, but just head up there, instead. Not surprisingly, he's nowhere to be seen; in fact, the boss is seeing the guy, he just happened to be getting back from a meeting on Lakeside when the ambulance pulled up. The IDC had also neglected to tell anyone that he was coming.

I look the guy over, he has appendicitis, and I take him to the OR. Pretty straight-forward case and the appendix pops right out. I am done in about thirty minutes, with Phil helping me. It turns out that Phil has never scrubbed on an appendectomy. I feel pretty happy, because I love appendectomies. You take a young, otherwise healthy person who develops a disease which, untreated, would normally kill him. You make the diagnosis by examining the patient, usually with no other testing required. Do a simple operation which the patient quickly recovers from, thus giving him back the remaining 50 or so years of his life. And he goes off on his merry way, typically oblivious to the potential catastrophe that has been averted. One of the few truly life-saving operations done by a surgeon on a regular basis, and probably the most underappreciated. But that's okay.

Afterwards, I check e-mail, to find that you have bad news, your mother has died. Yes, we both knew it was coming, but that's not the same. From what you describe, I would bet that it was a pulmonary embolism — broken hip, immobility, blood clots form in the legs or pelvis, when the patient finally gets up and moves around (e.g., goes home) the clot breaks loose, shoots to the lungs, and causes death very quickly, sometimes instantly. There are a lot worse ways to go, let me tell you.

So it tempers the joy of the appy and of finally receiving my orders. Seems to be a pattern: my birthday, Moof dies. Get my orders to DMRTI, your mother dies. Both happen about two months before I go home, and I'm not there for you. I am really ready to go home now, and I'm ready to not go anywhere (at least, not without you), for a while.

Call you in the evening, you sound a little stressed out, but also resigned. I suppose we knew this was coming. You're a lot tougher than you look, I must admit. Lucky for me.

Saturday: TQ Day 314.

My appy patient is a little whiny, so I will keep him for one more day, and then send him back to his unit. After lunch, Phil and I go shopping. We plan to remove a hatch from a wrecked armored car in the junkyard but, unfortunately, are unable to remove the hinge pins despite whacking at them with a hammer. Instead, I find a nice metal cover from the side of a crane; we will use that, instead. Why? For Brian's spider hole, of course.

We also find a metal cylinder to make a bell out of; that'll teach him to make *Hunchback of Notre Dame* jokes. Of course, those particular jokes were in response to our offer to build him a little tower in his corner of the hootch, but still...

It pours for about fifteen minutes this afternoon, enough to refresh all the mud we already have. Lovely. At around 1600 the radio goes off, an incoming Iraqi soldier who has managed to shoot himself in the left foot. Gee, never seen that before. When he arrives, the bullet has grazed his heel and has not even broken the skin. What are they doing? I give him a scrub brush, make him clean his own feet, and tell him to treat it like a blister and it will be fine.

We go over to the interpreters' for dinner, another delightful Middle Eastern meal. They are fun folks. Then around 2100, another guy from Camp Manhattan, with a puncture wound to his right forearm from barbed wire, billed as an injury to the radial artery. The duty doc takes a look at it and is unimpressed, as the hole is not over the artery and is not bleeding. I, on the other hand, notice that the guy has a fair amount of dried blood on his arm. I squeeze his arm in a couple of places, and blood squirts about a foot out of his wound. The "Probing Finger of Death" does it again. I had knocked the clot off the hole with my manipulations. We go to the OR, find a hole in the radial artery, and fix it. Nice little case.

Tuesday: TQ Day 317

I spend a fair amount of time working on the database. Also, Mike is heading back from Germany, his back's better. He went from here, to Balad, to Germany; but apparently is coming back through Bahrain, Qatar, Balad, and then here. I have been working on an incriminating series of slides on his unauthorized vacation. This should be good. Pictures of him drinking, partying, smoking a hookah, flying on "Hooters Air," it's all pretty bad. Should be fun, if he's back by Thursday.

In the evening an Iraqi soldier comes in with a mortar frag in his ass. I take him to the OR to wash it out and check for a rectal injury, which he does not have. Lucky him. He should be able to go back to work tomorrow.

Wednesday: TQ Day 318.

Freezing last night, I actually zipped up my sleeping bag. The temp was down to 35 degrees and our heater kept tripping the circuit breaker and shutting off.

At 1730, we hear that a GSW to the abdomen is on the way in. It turns out to be an Iraqi translator, and he's a mess. A single bullet enters in front and exits out the back. We expect a few holes in the bowel, possibly a renal injury. We get a lot more than we bargained for. This was one helluva bullet.

On opening the abdomen, I see something I have never seen before: a fully formed turd floating freely in the abdomen. The bullet has completely transected his colon and the turd dropped right out of it. I scoop it out, change gloves, get back to work. Three hours and 35 units of blood later, we have removed his left kidney, repaired his vena cava, ligated the left common iliac vein in the pelvis, repaired the left common iliac artery, resected the sigmoid colon and two feet of small intestine, and packed off his open lumbar spine fracture. I hope he lives, but don't expect him to. The boss, who's in uniform, has his pants and boots soaked in blood when he takes his gown off. My shoes are already disgusting, but my shorts and t-shirt are in good shape. "You people might make fun of me for wearing this, but I have the lowest laundry bills in Taqaddam!"

Thursday: TQ Day 319.

Up at 0700 for a "patient at the SSTP, injuries unknown." The duty doc happened to be up there when the KBR ambulance had pulled up and disgorged a patient. When I walk in a couple of minutes later, he tells me that "the guy has a heart attack, or a dissecting thoracic aneurysm, or a GI bleed, or something." Gee, now that narrows it down a bit... All I can conclude is that it's not traumatic; but I can see that the guy is lying there, talking, does not look like he's in distress, and has decent vital signs. So I cut to the chase: "So he's flying out?" "Yeah." I go back to bed. I later learn that the boss had done essentially the same thing that I had done when he arrived later, but it took him about ten minutes longer to decide to leave. I sleep until almost 0900.

The conference is a lengthy one, almost 100 slides, it even has a few related to patient care issues. One on the FMF board, the critical difference between "McP.P." (Marine Corps Planning Process) and "McPooPoo" (picture of Phil with a brown roostertail up his back, from biking through the mud). One of Eric doing pull-ups to pass the Marine PRT, after which I force Pat to come to the front and ceremonially hand over the "one large" ($1) in pogs he lost to me betting Eric would fail. About two dozen fakes on Mike's adventures in Germany and Qatar: beer drinking, hitting on women, playing with an oompah band, more drinking, more women, some belly dancers, etc. Finally, a series on tattoos that I have seen in Iraq, including Pat's "Popeye Chaplain" tattoo and a fake Irish tattoo that I claim belongs to Brian.

This gets us to around 1100. I spend the afternoon working on more patient follow-ups and then officer fitness reports; I have four to write, plus two more to chop, then I give them all to the boss. As the sun sets, Phil, the boss, and I attach a urinal filled with the phosphorescent fluid out of chemlights to the HESCO opposite the Frat House (where the younger med officers live), since there is a rumor that they have been peeing against it rather than walking all the way (75 feet) to the toilet. It just seemed like the thing to do.

Friday: TQ Day 320.

At 1700, two Army casualties come in. Odd story. Their Bradley is sitting by the side of the road in Ramadi. Cars drive by slowly, checking them out. Then the locals disappear, which tells them that something bad is going to happen. Then they are simultaneously attacked by mortars, RPGs, and machine guns with armor-piercing bullets. Why didn't they move when they figured something was up? My guess is that their mission commander told them not to while he thought about it, or called his higher ups, or something. Maybe they were there as bait. Dunno. Anyway, these guys are regular Army, they should know better. One guy was reportedly knocked out completely; we send him off for a head CT which I suspect will be negative. The other guy has frag holes all up the left side of his body, but miraculously has no broken bones or holes in his belly. Four of us scrub to wash out all of his wounds, and then we wrap him up. He goes out with the routine patients tonight, headed for home.

Saturday: TQ Day 321.

I am awakened around 0330 by rain on the roof. Lovely, we are supposed to go to the range today, it could be a mudbath. Am up at 0600, make coffee, head over to the STP, where we all muster at 0645 and head over to the range. Despite the rain, the range is dry. However, it is cold and we get the wind straight off Lake Habbaniyah, so everyone is miserable. At least I get to wear gloves, since I'm not shooting, although as usual I am not nearly as cold as other people. Ah, the advantages of being well-insulated!

We have a dozen people firing today, including the last two officers who need to do the pistol qualification — one of whom is Eric. He had shot with the CLR 25 ammo previously, and had done miserably, the only one not to qualify. I have saved 320 rounds, enough to fire the course eight times. If he can't do it with that, he's hopeless. A perfect score is 400, passing is 245, and on the first course he gets 180. Aargh. Second round, 250. Yes! He is done! Not by much, but it doesn't matter. Hoo-rah! Since everyone has finished their FMF oral boards, he is now done and can get his pin. In fact, everyone is done.

The range goes rather well, although two of my corpsmen do not qualify, but 10 out of 12 isn't bad. I think that part of it is simply that the officers, who are somewhat older, wiser, and mandated to do it, took it more seriously. These kids are doing it because it may be fun, and so some will put more effort into it than others.

We get back at 1300; I'm hungry and go over to lunch with Eric. He gets assorted attaboys from various people. I hope he is learning something from all of this: that he needs to apply himself to succeed, not that other people will bend over backwards to pull him through.

Phil gets good news today. He is being interviewed for the job of White House Physician's Assistant, as the "wild card" (they normally interview three, he is the fourth). Even better, the interview is in three weeks, which means that he has to be home before then to get his uniforms and so on. And of course, since our replacements arrive not too long after his interviews, there is really no point in having him come back. The lucky dirtbag! He will go home six weeks early, not have to jump through all the "postdeployment training" hoops with the rest of us, and he may land a cool job.

Around 1900 a patient comes in with an impressive laceration to the bottom of his foot, several tendons are severed. Mike and I are going to fix it, but Phil really, really wants to, so I let him scrub. Phil's specialty is hand orthopedics, and as they say in ortho, a foot is just a dumb hand...

Sunday: TQ Day 322.

Up for Mass by 0930, then the usual "Sunday with Psych." Around noon the radio calls "Attention all Ridgeways: patient with appendicitis coming from CLR 25." The boss is on duty and he tells them over the radio that the duty surgeon and ER corpsmen should suffice. He gets a brisk "Roger that"—and then they proceed to call everyone else, anyway.

After lunch, I spend the afternoon catching up on patient stats and e-mails. Around 1500 there is a loud boom, followed by the Big Voice. I continue on with e-mails in the COC, what else is there to do? Chiefs and others are running around madly, radio messages are sent in by panic-tinged voices. Jeez, get a grip, guys, this is nothing that hasn't happened before; we just call in by the numbers for accountability. If there are casualties, we will hear about it.

Monday: TQ Day 323.

Up at 0600 to go to the range. We are there a little after 0715, set up targets, do the safety brief, and "go hot" at 0815. There are a dozen shooters, plus coaches, Range OIC (me), Range Masters, and so on. We shoot for about 4½ hours, by which time all but one of our shooters have qualified. The one is a nice, but ditzy, lady who, on her first string of fire, scored 22 out of a possible 400. You get 4 points minimum if you hit the target, 10 max. She hit the target 5 times out of 40 rounds. The target is two feet by two feet. She is obviously quite frightened of the weapon; but by the end of the day she is up to 172 points, hitting the target almost every time, a vast improvement, and the whole time she has failed to be a danger to anyone. Smart girl.

By now, it is 1245; the range must close down at 1300. I have told one of our Marine guests from the head shed to load all of our empty mags (about 35) with ammo. When the last course of fire is over, I tell all of the shooters on the range to take three full mags and stand on the 7 yard line. Our dozen shooters get on the line with three mags each. "Shooters, with all the remaining ammo that you have, lock and load. Fire!" We all blaze away merrily. We all finish, check empty weapons, and check out the targets.

I look around, figuring that everyone has blown away their targets. Think again ... there are holes all over the place! My target has the middle blown out of it, two shots not in the black, that's all. My Marine corporal and firearms instructor walks up. "Holy shit, sir! That's a helluva target!" Nah, got a 9 mil at home that I practice with. But it's cool for the Old Man, having fired not a shot in the weeks we've been practicing, to just walk up and blast the hell out of the middle of a target.

Unfortunately, there is one small thing that mars the day. Phil had gone out to reshoot, as he had the previous high score for officers at 339 (need 345 for Expert). Pat, who has lost "3 large" ($3) in pogs to me on two previous bets (the window and Eric's PRT), decides that we want to mess with Phil by betting on his score. I bet he will score Expert on his second course of fire, "2 large." Pat says no. Score: 342, three short. Sonofabitch! Double or nothing? Sure. Phil chokes, gets in the high 200s. I am out 4 large to the chaplain, just great! But we get lots of mileage out of it so it's worth it.

We head back to the SSTP after range clean-up, around 1400. Afterwards, I talk with the corporal about how we want to do the M16 training. This will be more difficult, even though we have more ammo (about 6,000 rounds, 4,500 of which is already in magazines). We only have the Marines' M16s to work with, and with some Marines having to stay behind on duty, we'll really only be able to have eight Navy shooters. Will have to be very careful about who we offer it to, as the training is 5 boring days before the range, and half of our corpsmen had expressed no interest in learning how to use the weapon they have been carrying for 6 months (the pistol) or had dropped out of the course. Will go over possible candidates with the boss.

Tuesday: TQ Day 324.

I am awakened at around 0830 for a telephone call, so I wander over to find out that it's from the battalion surgeon for one of the units on base. I had done an appy on one of his guys a week ago and they'd decided that they could allow him to recuperate here; so I had kept him for a couple of days on the ward and then sent him back to his unit. With very explicit instructions on what to do with the surgical wound, which they did not follow. So now there is a problem. "I think the wound is coming apart," sez the Colonel. "Send him on over," sez I.

When he gets here, I see that there is, in fact, no problem at all, except that when they took out his wound staples, they had neglected to put tape on the wound, so there is now a little gap in the skin. Which is why we tell them to put the tape on. I solve the problem by covering the wound with steristrips, which are little tapes that take a week to fall off. This way, there will be nothing for them to mess with.

We watch *The Great Escape* tonight, and we know exactly how they feel. Living behind barbed wire in a hostile land, in wooden shacks, finding creative things to do with our time. We debate whether "the cooler," or solitary cell, is better or worse than our SWA hut. Pros: no roommates, doesn't leak, room service. Cons: can't get out. Debatable...

Try to get to bed early as I have been getting up early all week. I am cracking under the pressure. Not.

Wednesday: TQ Day 325.

Around 0100, a radio call for an incoming U.S. casualty. No ETA or injuries, but it is from an IED to a patrol "just outside the base." The Army ambulance has gone to get the guy and supposedly will be here in a few minutes. A half hour later, we are told that

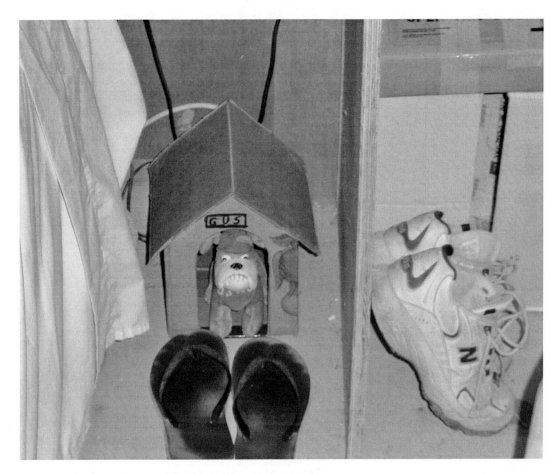

One of Brian's many pets that he acquired during the deployment, besides the "possessed" camel, the parrot, and the racing vulture. Despite peeing on the floor and eating Brian's flipflops, Gus made it home and continues to guard Brian's house to this day.

it might be two patients, one with a head injury, and the other with a leg injury. Another half hour, now we hear that the ambulance has just arrived — arrived at the scene, that is. A half hour after that, the patient finally gets to us; only one, the other is just shaken up but has no injuries. The casualty we see has a scrape on his knee, one on his shoulder, and a small cut on his nose from where he hit his machine gun. Back to bed at 0300.

It pours off and on all day today, turning our little slice of heaven into a mudhole. On the plus side, the Iraqis don't like mud either and therefore don't go out much to blow things up. Which is good, I want to try for an early night tonight.

Phil happens across a stuffed bulldog today. Which is great, we had been telling Brian that he needs a dog to greet him when he gets home every day. We badger him incessantly all afternoon with the question, "If you had a dog, what would you name it?" and finally settle on "Gus." After Brian leaves, I make Gus a nice doghouse out of a cardboard box, and we put him under Brian's desk, next to his slippers of course.

To say that Brian appreciated all of our efforts does not begin to describe what occurred...

Friday: TQ Day 327.

A long day today. Up at 0830, drinking water so I can go pee in a cup for the monthly command urinalysis; I get to be one of the lucky random ten percent selected. As I finish that up, I go into the COC to see if I can get onto a computer to check e-mail, when I hear some confusion from the watchstanders. "H&S doesn't answer." "Who's going to get the casualties?" "Well, it's their job, they are the BAS that is over there." It turns out that a Humvee ran into a 7 ton truck, right by Base Ops, which is about 300 yards away. "Why don't *we* go get the patients?" Duh...

But by the time our ambulance is crewed, an SUV has already arrived with the one "seriously injured" patient, whose knee hurts. He hops out of the SUV and the corpsmen try to force him onto the stretcher. Whoa, why don't we get his body armor and blouse off while he's standing up, it's so much easier? Then I tell the HM1 to get stretcher bearers, which he does by yelling loudly. Now why didn't I think of that?

The casualty is carried into the STP tent. Since the COC never called for the duty crew, I'm the only doctor there. This looks like a great training/practice opportunity for an IDC. "HM1, who is the duty IDC?" "Don't know sir, they're not here." He turns and starts to walk out of the tent. "Well, feel free to jump in any time." I get a most unpleasant look, and he then proceeds to do the most disorganized and perfunctory trauma assessment that I have seen in ages. Still, the guy is not badly hurt, which is why I had him do it in the first place.

Afterwards, Phil and I have some work to do; going over to the Seabee workshop to make Brian a bell. Used the heavy metal screw top from an oxygen cylinder, drilled a hole through it to hang a clapper, and voila! "Captain (select) Brian, arriving." We know he will be so thrilled.

Following this, Phil and I head back to Base Ops to finish Brian's *pièce de résistance*, the long-awaited spider hole. We had pulled the metal cover off a gear box from a derelict tractor in the vehicle graveyard, we build a frame for it and screw the lid hinges to it, then put it under Brian's desk. We just know that he will be so happy...

Right as we install it, word comes that in addition to Phil's orders coming through to go and interview at the White House, there's 'Space Available' on a flight out this evening. It is now 1700, so I help Phil pack all of his gear. As we are getting ready to leave, Brian walks in, in a foul mood. It's not improved when Phil rings him aboard with the new bell. The man stomps out in a huff. Phil tries to tell Brian that he is leaving, but he's gone. Our psychiatrist has been pretty moody the last few days, usually at the end of a day after dealing with Army admin. all day long. He says that it's not the patients, it's their commands' near-total lack of responsibility for them once he has seen the patients. Anyway, Phil does not get to say goodbye.

Phil and I drive over to Air Ops to check in. Yup, there is a seat available, the plane will be arriving soon, and will leave in two hours, so don't go anywhere. So I drive Phil over to the Lakeside DFAC for his last meal in Iraq. "Hey, it's not my last meal. I'll eat in Kuwait tomorrow." "Phil, Iraq tried to turn Kuwait into a part of Iraq in 1991 and we wouldn't let them. That's why we're here now." "Oh yeah..." Then back to the Air Ops hanger, unload his gear, and he's off.

Just that fast. And he won't be back. He interviews in 10 days, and by the time he would get back here we would be getting ready to leave; so he was cut orders terminating his assignment to Iraq. He goes back to Lejeune to turn in his gear, and then back to the Hospital.

Or maybe not. I've been back at the hootch for about an hour when the radio tells me that Phil is requesting me to pick him up, his flight's been cancelled. I start to get dressed, and suggest that Brian come with me. In fact, "Brian, you need to come." "Why?" "There were some things that Phil had wanted me to tell you, since he didn't get to say goodbye, and you really need to hear them before we pick him up." This generates quite the stir in the hootch, but I refuse to elaborate and away we go.

As we drive along, I tell Brian how upset Phil was that he did not have the chance to say goodbye. "He tried to tell you, but you stormed out in a huff. He was so worried that you were mad at him and that you would be parting on a bad note..." On and on like that for a few minutes, quite the sad story. As we near Air Ops, Brian suggests that I drop him off before we get there, so that we can pretend that he's not been seen since he walked out and that everyone is out looking for him. "But do you think you can tell him that with a straight face?" "Brian, I told you the story about Phil being distraught over your parting of ways with a straight face, didn't I?" "Oh, you mean...?" "Yup. Gotcha."

I drop Brian off on the road just outside Air Ops, then pick Phil up. Plane cancelled, never even came in, but there are six flights out tomorrow. I tell Phil that Brian has not been seen since he stormed out; that he apparently has his radio but is not answering. We have looked in the chapel, the DFAC, phone trailers, everywhere. "We could do a 'Code Red' drill for accountability." "Phil, we did. That's how we know he's missing." As we are talking about this, I am slowly driving up the road when, in the headlights, we see a man wearing body armor, wandering in small circles by the side of the road. "Hey, is that Brian? What's wrong with that guy? Is it Brian? It is Brian! Man, he's messed up. Hey, wait a minute..." Brian shines his flashlight into Phil's window, and Phil finally gets it. We really had him going, and we were all laughing our asses off as we drove back.

It's been a good day for me. I pulled a fast one on Brian, a fast one on Phil, and I collected 5 large in pogs from Pat for the completion of both the spider hole (4) and the bell (1), neither of which he thought would be done before Phil left. He tried to weasel out of the spider hole bet, though. "There is no hole in the floor under the hatch." "Pat, that wasn't the bet. I was very careful on the terms: the hatch has to be big enough for a man to fit through, it has to open all the way, and it has to have a handle. No one said anything about a hole in the floor..."

Saturday: TQ Day 328.

Drop Phil back off at Air Ops at 0715, a line is already forming. There are six flights out today, he should be able to get one. I do assorted bits of paperwork while I wait for the 0930 Grand Rounds on combat stress. We get the "Official Story," which is that we all have to do various debriefings, questionnaires, etc., before we can go home. Then the "unofficial" version, which is that there are no real data showing that OIF veterans are any more psychotic than their civilian counterparts, when one takes into account the age and socioeconomic background of most of these kids. There are no data supporting that preemptive debriefings and "crisis interventions" decrease long-term psych issues, there are even data that suggest the opposite. But this is a box that the Military can check, saying that they did what they could.

Speaking of which, the poor CLR 25 GMO has to do 1200+ PDHAs (post- deployment health assessments) by herself. So we have volunteered to help her out. It's a shopping list of all sorts of things: what were you exposed to, do you feel stressed, would you like to kill your family, have you developed any health problems while you were out here, that sort of thing. Checking any "yes" box requires an interview with a medical officer, and a lot of people believe that checking "yes" to everything "gets it in the record" in case they ever have any problems later. Which generates a huge amount of work for everyone in the end. Of course, some people check "no" to everything because there is a rumor that they can't go home if they check "yes." "Were you exposed to dust?" "No." You get the picture...

We hear in the late afternoon that Phil is still at Air Ops waiting for a flight, but by 2200 he is not back here yet, so I assume that he finally made it out. Then at 2215 he walks into the hootch to get his laundry. The boss and the twig had driven by Air Ops after some meeting to see if he was there, he was, so they drove him back to get it. Another round of handshakes and he's off again, hopefully to get Space A to Kuwait City International Airport tonight, and from there, commercial tickets to the States. His problem is that, while he has orders, they state that he detaches "on or about" 4 days from now and he has a booked a seat out of TQ for 3 days from now. Why the S-1 did the orders this way, we don't know, but they can't get changed, and if he leaves then, it'll still take him a couple of days to get back to the States; which gives him two days to get home, get his uniforms and so on squared away, give the missus a quick "tickle pickle," and then off to the White House. If he wants to get out before then, it's Space Available only.

Learn later that Phil flew out on a C-130 around 0400, the one that carries bodies to Kuwait for return to the States. A quiet flight, at least.

Sunday: TQ Day 329.

Up at 0730 to attend the enlisted muster. I call out a list of ten names to see me in Ward 1; the ten enlisted who will be offered the chance to do the M16 qual. Two are not interested, and I tell the other eight that, if they want to do this, they have to show up for all five days and pay attention. We'll see if it happens.

After mass, we spend a delightful two hours with Brian ranting about the silly briefings we have to endure before we get home. "Do you own a motorcycle?" "No." "Well, you have to endure a one hour motorcycle safety briefing anyway..." Then, as we get ready to go to lunch, we get a couple of casualties, two Iraqis shot in the leg. Our guess is only half right: they did not shoot themselves, one of their friends shot them. He was trying to clear his jammed weapon and fired a burst into the ground. The frags peppered their legs. They have no significant injuries though, so we put on the Band-Aids and get ready to send them on their way. I make it back to the hootch, when we get another one, an Army soldier with a "blast injury." He also comes over from Camp Manhattan, and has nothing really wrong with him. So we hold the ambulance and send all three back at once.

By now it's around 1500, so Pat and I run four miles. Read for a bit, then shower and dinner. Around 1830, I hear a "pfffft" overhead. Brian: "Did you hear something?'" "Yeah, a rocket going by overhead. It's a dud." "A rocket? You're kidding. How do you know?" "It sounded like a rocket and since there was no explosion, it must be a dud." "No, really?" "Just wait, the Big Voice will go off in a few minutes." And three minutes later, there it is. Us Old Timers know these things... It turned out to be a dud; hit the basketball court between the chapel and the Hajji shops. It smacked the asphalt, broke into pieces, then bounced over the chapel and ended up in some HESCOs on the other side.

Monday: TQ Day 330.

Could not manage to sleep past 0930. Put together a presentation for the corpsmen for tomorrow, then am considering whether to go to lunch or not, when we hear that there are two Iraqis with gunshot wounds "on the pad." We run over and get the story. Two Iraqis in a car were driving towards a checkpoint, did not stop for the arm waving or the flares, so their car was shot. It then crashed into the armored Humvee. One old guy has some scratches on his leg. The other has a broken humerus, broken foot, and bullet frags in the other arm and leg. He goes off to the OR for an erector set for the broken arm and washouts for everything else. Guess he won't be crashing any more checkpoints any time soon.

And oh, by the way, even though they crashed the checkpoint and had fake IDs, they are not detainees...

We have finally received the list of who is coming out from I MEF to replace us. One hundred and seven people, including six surgeons here and two for Ramadi. TQ will be divided up as three FRSSs, two mobile STPs (ER tents), with 17 admin people for all this. Of course, we do not have enough gear for three FRSSs, or two complete STPs, or berthing for 107 people. What are they thinking? Apparently some folks are thinking that this is OIF I all over again, and that they'll be gallivanting all over Iraq like a traveling circus. And here I was, thinking that the U.S. presence is downsizing.

Dinner is rather unappealing: greasy fried chicken, turkey stew with stale breakfast biscuits on top (masquerading as "turkey pot pie"), or spaghetti with meat sauce. Brian, who normally eats at around 2000 with his "peeps," skips dinner and eats potato chips with Cheez Whiz on them.

A word about Brian's peeps (or Brian's "people"). At the end of every meal period, the TCN (Third Country National) workers in the DFAC eat, and they really pile it on. I expect that they are not used to seeing so much food. Several tables usually fill up with them, and Brian likes to eat late in the evening, right before the DFAC closes, sitting at one of their tables by himself. "I like to be an anonymous face in the crowd," he says.

Yeah, the only white face and the only person over 5 foot 6 in the crowd. His quotable quote on the peeps: "They're pricey little guys, but I like them." They are certainly polite and cheerful.

Tuesday: TQ Day 331.

Busy day, today. I am up at 0800, to give the corpsmen a lecture at 0900. Halfway through, we have a casualty come in, a 50-something Army Reservist who had been getting something off the top of a shelf in a warehouse when the shelf fell on him. He has severe back pain and, when I carefully roll him onto his side to look, I can see that there is a lump in his spine, as if the bones are no longer aligned. One of the docs hanging around wants to push on it while they examine him; I tell them to stop. We fly the guy out for a CT scan.

Right after that, a patient with belly pain is driven over from Camp Manhattan. Turns out that he has had this pain for three days, was seen at Fallujah, his labs suggested bile duct obstruction, and the PA there treated him for "ulcers." So, big surprise, he's no better. I decide that he has a hot gallbladder; but the best thing for him is a laparoscopic cholecystectomy, and we don't have a laparoscope. So I admit him for IV antibiotics and he will go out on the milk run.

After lunch, I am called over to the ACE for another belly pain case. This guy has had diarrhea for a week, got better, and then got a lot worse. When I examine him, it feels like he may have a mass in his belly, possibly diverticulitis. So he's also admitted on IV antibiotics, to be sent up for a CT scan. Another case I have to give away. Still, I prefer to operate on people that I *know* need an operation.

At 1600, we hear that we will be getting two Iraqi soldiers, hit by an RPG. When I get to the COC, I learn that Camp Manhattan had called to say that they are getting the two patients, but they are letting us know because they will send them to us. Okay, so let me get this straight: they have not even examined the patients but have already decided that they need to move to us. Why even take them there? Unfortunately, this is a recurring theme.

They finally get to us at around 1700. One has frags to his leg and no pulse, the other has frags to his face and is blind in one eye. We then hear that we will get a couple more in a few minutes, and they eventually arrive. Another one with frags to the head, and one with frags to the leg. I work on packaging the two head cases and tell the boss to head back with the pulseless leg. The fourth guy will need some x-rays but can wait, if he has anything we can do it later. Ultimately, he turns out to have nothing.

I head back to the OR. One of the other docs has ultrasounded the guy's belly and says there is blood in it. In addition, the guy's scrotum is a bag of blood from a frag wound, highly suggestive of a urethral injury, so he needs a tube placed directly through his abdomen and into his bladder. While I start on his belly with the boss, Mike starts to work on cleaning up the frag holes in his right leg. Into the belly — no blood or other injuries, the other doc was wrong. But he can't understand it, there must be something there. Sorry dude, the Mark 1 Mod 0 eyeball test sees all, and you were wrong. I sew in the bladder tube. As this goes on, Mike says "There's a little bleeding here." Yup, blood is pouring out of the thigh incision he has made. He keeps his finger in the hole while I finish up the belly, then the boss and I start on the thigh while Mike works some more on the calf. I dissect out the femoral artery and see that about three inches of it is shredded. Time to do a graft, so we take out a piece of vein and sew it in to replace the missing piece of artery. He gets a nice pulse again. We finish up the case, cleaning out the leg and closing the belly. But at the end of it, he has no pulse in his foot, although he has a great pulse in his graft and at his knee. The guy needs an angiogram to see if there's a problem, which we cannot do, so we pack him up and ship him off to Baghdad.

A less than satisfying case. Fun operation, but not a straightforward good outcome. I will be interested to see what the follow-up is: a problem with the graft, or something else that we could not see. I learn the next day that the graft anastomoses were fine. Clot was removed and everything worked again. Still a mystery, though.

13. February 2006: A "No Shit" Head Injury

Wednesday: TQ Day 332.

I manage to sleep until almost 0900. Unfortunately, it's the 1st of the month so we have to re-encrypt radios this morning. I crawl out of bed to do so, then do e-mail. Afterwards, I take the SUV over to the Post Office to mail home five boxes, mostly books and clothes that I have no further use for here. I plan to go back with one seabag of crap that they had issued me and that I have to return, one seabag of my own crap, and one backpack to live out of for the trip. Everything else can be mailed.

Friday: TQ Day 334.

Roused out of bed at 0400 for an incoming patient, someone shot in the leg. It's raining. I traipse up there to find that he's expected to get here at 0430. This is based on the PET's estimate that the helos will leave TQ at 0415, then fly 20 miles, pick up the patient, and be back by 0430. In other words, they are idiots. At 0530 he finally arrives. He turns out to be a sad case.

The kid is awake and talking, has a round that has passed through the front of his right thigh and out the back of it. No broken bones or other major injuries. I see muzzle burns on his thigh, though. "What happened?" "I shot myself." "Was it an accident?" "Yes and no." "We'll talk later." I take him off to the OR to wash out his leg, and we leave him on the ward to recover. This is the first American I have ever treated with a self-inflicted wound to get out of combat. I go back to bed after telling the COC to find out the number to his command.

Get up at 1030 or so, go up and see the kid. He is barely 19, was sent to Iraq a week after finishing SOI (School of Infantry, the basic grunt training after boot camp). He has been in Iraq for a week, has a pregnant girlfriend, and is scared to death. A couple of days ago, half an hour before he was supposed to relieve a sentry, that sentry was shot through the head by a sniper, and all he can think about is that it would have been him 30 minutes later. Or, as I point out, the sniper might have moved elsewhere during that time. Anyway, he's freaked out and just wants to go home. He clearly has very little idea of what he has gotten himself into, either in joining the Military, or by shooting himself.

From a medical standpoint, he would be ready to go back to duty in a few days. There are two questions: first, is he mentally capable of doing so, for which I will have him see our psych guys (Joe is the duty guy today); second, does his command want him back? I call his unit GMO at their base south of Fallujah and talk to his doc, who knows the circumstances of the incident. He will get back to me as soon as he can with his CO's decision, and I will let him know what psych thinks as soon as Joe has seen him. If he's going to be returned to duty, the standard management for combat stress cases (shell shock, battle fatigue, whatever you want to call it) is "three hots and a cot"; the soldier is pulled out of the front line for a day or two to rest and sleep, with the expectation that he will return to the front. It helps to prevent any guilt about leaving one's comrades from settling in too much. It's been found that the farther they are removed from their unit, the more psych issues they develop as a reaction or excuse to justify why they cracked. It is therefore best treated as "stuff happens," with the expectation that some rest will get them through it. And when they go back, most actually do better.

Eventually Joe tells me that the guy has no major psych issue except for an acute adjustment disorder, i.e., he is freaked out. This would not make him unfit for duty, although Joe does not see the point in sending him back, but that will be up to his CO to decide. Since I live with Brian, I've told him about the kid, and while Brian agrees in principle, it is never that easy. Giving the kid what he wants gives him the lifelong mental burden of knowing that he has failed, quit, abandoned his buddies, whatever. If his unit goes all the way in punishing him, it's jail time and a bad conduct discharge, which will follow him for the rest of his life and limit his employment and educational opportunities; or his CO may want to send the message that doing this will not get you sent home, and may return him to duty. We'll have to wait and see.

Saturday: TQ Day 335.

Another brisk day. The rain has stopped and the sun is out. After the 0930 Grand Rounds, our first casualty for the day, a guy with bumps and bruises from an IED. After lunch, a lot of confused radio traffic about patients who are incoming, but are already here, but have already been seen, but are on the pad, everyone has to come now, but they are already taken care of, but where is everyone? Proving once again that, when all about us are losing their heads, we can, too.

I also learn today that the kid who shot himself in the thigh will be going back to his unit. They will not put him back in the line, but they plan for him to handle all the admin matters at his base. The kid is happy that he will not be going back into the line. I still don't think that he understands how much trouble he's in. Wonder what will happen to him? Jail time? Big Chicken Dinner (Bad Conduct Discharge)? Who knows? He lies around reading cheap thrillers, looking like he doesn't have a care in the world. That won't last much longer, I plan to send him back tomorrow. (A couple of weeks later I learn that he's been court-martialed and sentenced to 14 months in jail, reduction to E-1 with loss of all pay, and then a bad conduct discharge.)

Sunday: TQ Day 336.

I'm up before 0800 to go to the enlisted muster so I can finalize the shooting lists for the next range. We pull aside the lucky shooters. There's whining, of course: "How come I don't get to shoot the M16?" Simple, we don't have enough M16s and we are only doing this once. And of course there are people who had no interest in learning how to shoot the pistol that they've been carrying for 6 months, but they want to shoot the rifle, which takes twice as long to learn.

I end up with a list of 17 pistol shooters and 9 M16 shooters. Nine is all I can do for the rifle in one day, but I still have open slots for the pistol. The whiners don't want to learn or practice, they just want to blow holes in things. The prevailing opinion in the "frat house" is that, while some do want to shoot, they don't want to get up early to do it. Sure, whatever, I know that we all have so much better things to do. Not.

Monday: TQ Day 337.

The Chief had decided that, because the Superbowl started at 0200 our time, the enlisted would not have to muster. They would still have to be accounted for, however. My prediction that this would result in 30 minutes of annoying, sleep-destroying radio chatter is confirmed, so I get up around 0800. Spend about an hour at the COC doing e-mails of various flavors, and then I drive the boss and Joe over to the Army 230th Finance Battalion, which is on the other side of our junkyard, far off the beaten track. The Marine finance unit had announced, without warning last week, that it would no longer cash checks for the next 3 weeks, as it's getting ready to RIP. So a lot of people who need cash to mail things home can't get cash. Fortunately, I know my way around, and drive them over to the Army disbursing office, which is still open. Ain't I clever?

Wednesday: TQ Day 339.

Get the message that we have 3 or 4 incoming, including an EPW. They eventually arrive, which is pretty cool in itself— they show up in Iraqi Land Rover ambulances, blue flashing lights and sirens blaring. Brian's comment: "I was expecting clowns to come piling out..." They have assorted stories. The EPW had walked up to a checkpoint and shown his ID, which was on the "detain immediately" list, so they tried to arrest him but he ran, and they shot him in the leg and butt-stroked him in the face with a rifle. In addition to the gunshot to his leg, he has a huge bruise on his face and head, so we are obligated to fly him out for a head CT.

The other three are Iraqi soldiers. Two were shot in the leg in a firefight. They go to the OR to get their legs washed out. Our initial guess, that they shot themselves, is close: one of their colleagues was trying to un-jam his weapon and shot them by mistake. The third broke his leg jumping out of the back of a truck, he will need a cast.

Thursday: TQ Day 340.

Yet another busy day today. First, the usual Thursday patient follow-up conference. Afterwards, Pat gives us our official "Warrior Transition Brief," so we can check that box on the long mandatory checklist to freedom. Afterwards, we go to lunch. Following lunch, as I'm getting ready for the M16 "dryfire" training, we hear that there may be one incoming U.S. patient; but the problem is that there are dust storms everywhere and the helos can't fly, so the patient will probably be coming by ground. The boss is duty surgeon today but has PDHAs to do on Lakeside; I tell him that I'll call him if I need him.

About 45 minutes into it the patient arrives. Another sad case. A 20-ish Marine private on foot patrol, hit by an IED on the opposite side of Lake Habbaniyah. Both legs and his left arm are a mess, full of frag holes, as is his ass. He can't move his legs, most likely a spinal cord injury as he has a frag hole in the middle of his back. But that's not what worries me. He arrives almost two-and-a-half hours after the injury, because of the weather. When he arrives, even though his head does not have a mark on it, he acts very goofy. He cannot stay awake, his eyes are pointing in opposite directions, and he keeps nodding off. I suspect that he has a significant head injury; he needs to fly out. Call the Air Boss and tell him that "...we have a 'no shit' head injury, this kid will die if he can't get out of here." Impossible for the helos to fly, but the Air Boss comes through and in minutes has arranged for a C130 to come down from Al Asad to pick the kid up and take him to Balad—if he lasts that long. Plane will be here in 45 minutes.

A few minutes later, as we are resuscitating him, his head injury seems confirmed when he suddenly starts "posturing" (holding his arms in an odd position, classic for a brain injury) and then has a seizure. Even though we have already put 5 units of blood into him, his blood pressure is dropping. While all of this had been going on, I had ultrasounded his belly and seen no blood and his chest x-ray has shown no blood. I've assumed that he has lost some blood from the various extremity injuries. But I have to be sure, and since his pressure is almost gone, I open his left chest and look at his heart, which is okay, his left lung is okay, and I clamp his aorta so the blood flows mostly to his head and not his belly. Open his belly to look for a bleeding source, and while he has a bunch of bowel injuries (no surprise), no significant bleeding. Extend the chest incision to the right side, again no major blood loss.

So he's screwed. No major source of ongoing blood loss, no blood pressure, we keep giving him blood but eventually his heart stops and it's over. Killed by an IED and bad weather. I go out and talk to his CO, who was in the convoy that brought him in, and give him the bad news. Turns out that there was a KIA as well, and they've had three others killed in the past week. They are the same unit as the kid who shot himself in the leg...

As usual, I have no heartburn over what happened, although I am sad that it did. We did what we could. As a thought exercise, we ponder what might have happened if the helos had, in fact, been flying. He would have been picked up at the scene and flown somewhere fairly quickly. If he had arrived without sign of a head injury, he would have been put to sleep for surgery and been under anaesthesia for hours, during which he very likely would have died from his brain injury anyway. Hard to say. I later get a call from the battalion GMO, asking what they might have done differently, I tell him nothing. IED and the weather, wish I could have saved him. (Like all U.S. casualties, he went to the Armed Forces Medical Examiner. I eventually saw the autopsy report, which showed no brain injury. My best guess is that the kid died from the sequelae of two-and-a-half hours of hemorrhagic shock; he probably lost a lot of blood from all the various holes throughout his body, and not from a single injury.)

Friday: TQ Day 341.

I had reserved the rifle range for the entire day, so we could start a little later when the sun is up and it's a bit warmer. We head out to the range, get set up, post road guards. It's a lovely day, around 70 degrees, a slight breeze and sunny. A great day to shoot. Only problem is that we can't. In order for us to "go hot," we need to establish radio communications with our road guards (done), HQ at CLR 25 (done), and TQ Tower (who tells us when to shut down for overflying aircraft) — not done. No one on the base can get in contact with TQ Tower. We can all talk to each other on the net, but no one can get anything from TQ Tower; who of course insist that the problem is not them, even though everyone else's radios seem to work. They work on the problem all morning, but by noon it's still unsolved, so I pack it in. All was not lost, however, as the kids treated it like a day at the beach. They slid down sand dunes on cardboard, wrestled, rolled down hills, laid in the sun, and generally acted like teenagers. On the way back, Pat and I find a nice orange traffic cone sitting half buried in the desert on the range and we rescue it. It has "Brian" written all over it, don't you think?

Get back and decide to go for a run. I am about three miles into it when the radio asks if "any provider" is available to give the new Group Surgeon, an ER doc, a tour of the STP. Of course we have already met him, and he has already had the tour, but I say I can and run back. When I get there, I run across the Army sergeant I know who's my hook-up for another pistol range. We chat a bit and confirm that we are good to go for four days from now, all day, starting at 0800. He will bring the ammo, we do everything else. And oh, by the way, would I mind if he brought out their machine gun and shotgun? Well, all right, just this once ... I also get him hooked up for treatment for reflux, a little mutual back-scratching.

Have incoming, an Iraqi civilian shot in the shoulder. He had not stopped when approaching a convoy, had ignored the escalation of force (flares, shots at the engine, then shots at him), and he took a round in the back and a round through the arm. His humerus is destroyed, but amazingly all the nerves and blood vessels are intact, a bloody miracle. I can look into the hole in his arm and see them all sitting there, uninjured. Mike and I take him to the OR. I walk Brian, the Family Practice doc, through a chest tube; Gerry walks him through a central line; then Mike and I put an ex fix on his arm. As we finish that, a Marine is brought in with "fumes." His Humvee supposedly had fumes in it and someone is worried about smoke inhalation. This gets us to about 2000.

Get back to the hootch to discover that Brian has taken the orange cone out of his corner and put it outside. Humph, some gratitude...

Saturday: TQ Day 342.

One of our OPs noticed a car stop by the side of the road just outside of base — possibly dropping off a package, they can't be sure. A patrol was sent to investigate. An NCO, on his last patrol in Iraq before getting on a plane in two days to head home, was leading the patrol with his replacement. Just as they spotted the package, it was detonated. Severe brain injury among other things. We sent him out, but he will probably not do well.

At 1500 we go to Lakeside for a formation, the General's farewell speech to his Marines. You done good, don't do anything stupid when you get home, look after each other. Short, sweet, to the point.

Sunday: TQ Day 343.

Up at 0800, check e-mail, find out our head injury patient from yesterday is alive but doing badly as predicted. Afterwards, sit up on HESCO Beach drinking coffee with some Marines until Mass at 0930. This is actually a theme, we have a number of Marines who come by to "get away from the Marines" for a while, like the Air Boss and the Civil Affairs Officer. After Mass, it's the General.

Yup, the General came by after Mass for "Sunday with Psych." Managed to get Brian going on a few things, like redeployment ("I'm not redeploying, I'm going home!"), but it was a somewhat PG-13 tirade. Still, we figure that the medical people are about the only ones on base that the general can sit down with and not be "The General." Sure, he is our boss, but we are "The Docs" and no one expects us to act military. We are *Different*.

He had quite a good time relating to us Father Tim's tormenting of Brian. Brian happened to mention, during choir practice, that he had watched *Life of Brian*. Unbeknownst to him, I had primed the good Father about this; it turns out that he's an "L of B" fan, himself. He looks at Brian, thunderstruck, tells him that the movie is sacrilegious, and that the Pope had issued a Papal Bull condemning the movie. He really gets Brian worried. "But they made me watch it, I didn't want to..." Got him. Then the good Father laughed his ass off.

After the General heads out around noon, I go running. Get a call for a patient, run back. It's an EOD guy, been here for three weeks, out with an Army unit. They find wires to an IED, trace them back, and the secondary IED blows up in his face. The only part of him injured was his face — he wasn't wearing eye/face protection. The EOD teams have the best protective gear around, and he wasn't wearing it. What can you say? I fly him out to the eye surgeon in Balad; he can't see out of either eye.

We have an unannounced BBQ at 1700; it was pretty good. Around 1930, another patient comes in, this time an EPW. A scout-sniper team in Habbaniyah saw a couple of guys digging a hole in the road and shot this guy through the neck. It takes about 50 minutes to get him to the BAS at Camp Habbaniyah, another 40 to get him to us. When he gets to us, he's not moving anything. But I don't think he's paralyzed, I think it's worse. He is moving nothing, not even his eyelids. I think that either his carotid arteries were hit and his brain has had no blood flow, or he was paralyzed and unable to breathe and he has an anoxic brain injury. Either way, he's screwed. But he still has a blood pressure. I am tempted to operate on him because he would be a "good case": bilateral neck explorations with probably either vascular repair or airway repair, but it's futile if his brain is gone. So he flies out for a head CT.

About an hour later, one of the nurses comes into the hootch, all atwitter. She happened to be in the COC when it shows up on the "MRC-chat" (real-time medical e-mail) that the Medevac helo (which is carrying one of our nurses) was fired on and the escorting Cobra fired 120 rounds back at something. The MRC says no personnel casualties, they don't know about the helo, which is not back yet. So here's the problem. The MRC-chat is supposed to keep all medical assets up-to-date on what is going on medically in theater; who is where, who is getting casualties, where the medevacs are going, and so on. What it's become is an on-line rumor mill. According to the Air Boss, helos are fired on all the time, usually a few rounds of small arms fire that rarely hit anything. If the escorting gunship can determine where it's coming from, it returns fire. As expected, the helo lands about ten minutes later and everything is fine.

Monday: TQ Day 344.

I sleep until 1000 for the first time in a couple of weeks, it was quite nice. Eventually wander off to lunch, and then afterwards Mike and I go over to CLR 25 to help Marcia with PDHAs again. Somewhat entertaining today. I had one Marine who answered "yes" to the question, "Are you concerned about any exposures you have had that might affect your health later?" His concern is that "if I go back home and get married and have kids, Agent Orange might make them have three heads or something." "Um, that was Vietnam." "Yeah, whatever, man." Duly noted...

I spend the afternoon taking care of finishing touches for the Army pistol range tomorrow. It should be good. Pat and I also spend some time watching Olympic curling. It's that sport where you slide rocks with handles into a bulls-eye, somewhat like bocce ball or shuffleboard on ice; you knock the other team's rocks out and yours in; and the closest wins. Mesmerizing in its own way, and the Scandinavian women's teams were pretty cute. The U.S. women's team was knocked out of the competition, so that's probably the last we'll see of that.

We also learn this evening that we have acquired more SWA huts for the turnover. So we will move out of our SWA huts into other SWA huts a hundred feet over, so that the new guys can move into ours. No, it doesn't make sense to us either, but what can you do?

Tuesday: TQ Day 345.

Happy Valentine's Day! Another busy day. Up around 0630 to go to the COC and make sure we are set for the range. Then breakfast at 0700. At 0800, we gaggle together and head to the range. It's a little overcast but not a bad day at all. Get there around

0830, the Army guys are already there with the ammo, cool. We get set up. Comms works, everything is ready to rumble.

Well, almost. Even though I had given the children (my two corporal-instructors) a checklist of all the things they need to bring with them, they didn't bring tape to stick the targets up with. I had brought enough to get us started, but I need to head back to get more, while they start without me (since technically the Army is running the range today, I can get away with leaving for a bit). I am back before 1000.

The range goes quite well. End up with five experts, four sharpshooters, and three marksmen. Two of my shooters (one corpsman, one Marine) did not qualify. They hadn't on their previous attempt, but they are just good kids and I had let them come out and try again. At the end, we all load up two magazines (well, okay, I had hogged four) and we blaze away for a minute to blow off the excess ammo that we can't return. My second time to shoot during Tac Two, at 10 yards, and again the middle disappears out of my target. "Damn, sir"...

An odd thing had happened during the shoot. An SUV had come up and three Marine pilots got out. They walked up to the range with weapons and started to prepare to shoot. Of course I asked them what they thought they were doing. "Oh, we just thought we'd check out the range and tag along with someone who's shooting." They were hanging out in the Crack House when they heard us checking in with TQ Tower to "go hot," and had decided to wander over.

That's nice, think again. They shouldn't even be on the range without permission, and the range is already double-booked with us and the Army guys (who do some M16 rifle zeroing while we prep between shoots). No room for anyone else, especially when you plan to do something different from the rest of us. "But we just came out from Pendleton and didn't get a chance to shoot." Listen, if you want to schedule a range, then schedule it, complete with comms and everything else that's required. However, to be nice, if you show up at 0800 tomorrow and we have room, you can come out then. Plan to spend the whole day, and bring your own ammo. And stop driving through the middle of a live-fire area unannounced...

Wednesday: TQ Day 346.

We plan to step off for the range at 0800, so I'm up at 0630, go to the COC to ensure that we have everything we need (including tape), then head to breakfast with Pat. I get the SUV loaded and it's a few minutes before 0800, when it gets very dark very quickly, and starts to pour. While we can shoot in the rain, I have a group of novice shooters and I want them to concentrate on shooting, not on being miserable. Moot point, as lightning flashes overhead. Marine Corps regs say we can't train if there's lightning. In addition, TQ Tower shuts down operations. I call them and the weather weasels claim that it will look like this until at least noon. So realistically, the range is cancelled.

I call range ops, but they say that there are absolutely no open range dates available until we leave. In the last week, everyone has booked everything. So it's today or nothing. At 0900, still dark and raining. Time for some executive decisions. If we get out to the range at noon, we will only have three or four hours to shoot. This is not enough time to get the Navy folks qualified (it takes almost an hour to shoot one course of fire, most will need two, three, or even four to qualify) and still expend our excess ammo which we have no one to turn over to. The corpsmen will shoot off about 1,000 rounds and we will still have over 5,000 left. No way. So the new plan: I will head out to the range at 1100 with the Marines, and we will wait out the weather. As soon as it's clear and we can go "hot," we will have an organized shooting frenzy. If we are going to blow off that much ammo in half a day, I want experienced shooters we don't need to keep a close eye on. Especially if I'm the one who will be responsible.

We are at the range a little after 1100. By noon, it's bright blue skies, 70 degrees, and a beautiful day. Funny place, this Iraq. I have invited along the oral surgeon from Dental, as he has an M16 and is an experienced shooter, and I borrow the other dentist's M16 for myself. So everyone has a weapon. Cool. We proceed to spend the next three hours blasting away at water bottles, empty ammo cans, playing cards, silhouette targets, bits of wood — all safely, of course. Single fire, 3-round bursts. Standing, sitting, kneeling, prone. Shooting from the hip. Every rifle drill you can imagine.

Then the extra treat. Oh look, where did this extra 9mm ammo come from? We have two pistols, one is mine, and we take turns firing those, too. Even get some really dopey shots of us blazing away with a gun in each fist. Too much fun! Back from the range around 1600. All the kids can talk about is how much fun they had. A good way for these Marines to end the deployment, I think. Too bad the corpsmen couldn't qualify, though.

Thursday: TQ Day 347.

Up for the 0930 case conference. Not too exciting. Afterwards, lunch. It's a little cold and windy today so I decide not to run; besides, my legs hurt from all the kneeling and shooting yesterday, dunno why. Must be getting old ... er.

Early in the afternoon we get one patient coming in, an Iraqi civilian "shot in the head." We hear lots of radio traffic between Witchdoctor and the ECP that the vehicle will be coming through. Apparently their ER doc is calling for all sorts of equipment to be brought to the checkpoint so he can intubate or do some other procedures to the patient as he comes in the gate. Wait a minute, the gate is less than two minutes from us, and he is going to hold the patient there and play? I call their BAS and tell them that I suggest that if the patient is really badly off, they leave him on the incoming vehicle and just let him come on through. Eventually the patient arrives. He has a big laceration on the top of his head, whether it's from a bullet or from hitting his head on the inside of his car, we don't know. I can feel a skull fracture on him, so we intubate him.

That is another issue. Gerry, our anaesthesiologist (doctor), is over at Lakeside doing PDHAs. That leaves Vic, our CRNA (nurse) as the only gas-passer. I've brought the guy to the OR because that is where the gear is. He tries to intubate the guy but it's a difficult intubation. Vic gives it a couple of tries, no dice. "What do you want me to do?" he asks me. Whatever you want, you're the airway expert. But it's not a big deal, I tell him. We can bag him and he has no airway injury. "Do you want me to let the drugs wear off and have him wake up?" No, just intubate him. Do your thing, man.

Vic came to Iraq almost straight from CRNA school, so he's very junior, but he's been doing a great job. I try to keep the pressure off him. Just relax, take your time, the patient is stable, we can breathe for him with a mask while you get everything set to do whatever you need to do next. Unfortunately, the boss arrives and asks Vic if he wants to call Gerry back. I tell him that there is nothing critical going on here, there is no need to. What I want to say is look, it's not really an emergency, and even if it was, by the time Gerry got back it would be over; the guy would either be intubated through his mouth by Vic, or by me through a hole I cut in his neck. But he calls Gerry back anyway, which I see as a vote of "no confidence" to Vic. About a minute later, the tube is in courtesy of Vic. The patient then flies out for a head CT and whatever else he may need.

People get way too excited during these things. There is a time to rush, and a time to wait. You know, like the song. Time expands, seconds seem like minutes. Just relax and look at the bigger picture.

I spend the rest of the day working on my Grand Rounds for Saturday, our last one ever. As the Bible says, the first shall be last and the last shall be first. I was the first and the last.

We learn a couple of interesting things about our replacements. We medical types from our coast belong to specific Marine units who are supposed to look after us. This is both good and bad. One particularly good thing is that, since ultimately we have to rely on the Marines for everything, they end up making our housing arrangements and travel to and from Iraq. They run our schedules. The replacements from the other coast are coming out as their own distinct surgical companies, and will not belong to any Marine unit in particular. In fact, the three Navy surgical units will all be one "company," and Al Asad, Al Qaim, and KV will be another. So they will have no one specifically looking out for them, it'll all be up to them to make their own arrangements — assuming that they know the system.

Well, here are the fun parts: first, they have not arranged their own housing, and second, they have not made any travel arrangements past TQ. All the people for Ramadi, Fallujah, and TQ will show up at TQ as a group, and then two-thirds of them will have to figure out how to get to where they need to go. Every Marine coming in has a ULN (specific travel itinerary) to his final destination, but these guys either have not figured it out or don't know that. With 30,000 people moving in and out of theater in a one month period, they expect to just hop onto a convenient flight to get to where they want? And oh, by the way, temporary housing at TQ is already 200 percent booked with people the Marines know will be coming, and these guys are not on that list.

So of course the twigs from the other coast have asked our twig, as a fellow twig, to handle it for them. They have not told him who is coming, or when they will get here, so it's impossible for him to get them ULNs, but they want him to do it, anyway. This is going to get very interesting...

Saturday: TQ Day 349.

I'm up around 0830 so I can give Grand Rounds at 0930, our final one for the deployment. It's on military ballistics, complete with lots of gross pictures, and it goes over very well apparently. After this, lunch, followed by PDHAs at the Marine RAS. I see 20-something patients, and in fact we let Marcia, the GMO, do sick call stuff while we handle the PDHAs. She is getting really tired of them. On the way back, I hit the Post Office and mail off the last of my unnecessary stuff, including the combat coffee pot.

When I get back, I learn that tomorrow is moving day, as there may be some replacements arriving on Monday. We can't be sure, even the new Group Surgeon, whom they belong to, does not know who is who. So I finish packing up my stuff in the evening into mobile packages (seabags, footlocker, backpack).

I also finally get around to making Brian's end of tour medal: the Combat Smiley Face. A Rainbow ribbon and a big smiley. I will give it to him tomorrow during "Sundays with Psych," as it will be our last Sunday coffee klatch in the SWA hut; or at least, in the custom SWA hut with the armored windows, miniblinds, spider hole, bell, and racing vulture. (Hey, there's a name for a pub, "The Bell and Vulture.")

Sunday: TQ Day 350.

Our last "Sunday with Psych" in the old hootch this morning. I present him with his Combat Smiley Face, complete with certificate. A thing of beauty. People of course ask where I got it from, and I, of course, tell them that I simply ordered it from the on-line uniform store. From where else would one get medals? After this, Brian heads off to clinic while we move our stuff. It's only about 100 yards but we use the SUV and do it in three loads in about an hour. Then make it somewhat habitable for 3 weeks, set up the coffee and TV corner, make beds. I am fairly well packed at this point and could easily be gone in an hour if need be. Better than a tent, anyway.

A word about Brian's clinic. He has quite an active psychiatry clinic going as he gets referrals from bases all over. So, unlike the rest of us, he actually has to work all day, every day. Most of the referrals are completely inappropriate—behavioral and discipline problems that the command (typically some senior enlisted) wants "checked out," without ever going through their own medical people or chaplains. Those folks are supposed to weed out the crap and send the true psych cases only. Naturally, it doesn't work that way.

Eventually Brian gets back and we all pitch in to get him moved. It's fairly rapid. He has a tendency to get attached to wherever he is, so we just up and move him all at once. We had finished moving, and are tidying up, when we hear of two patients coming in, hit by an IED. One has neck pain and one has back pain. The duty doc has the guy sit up so he can feel his back. Exactly what you do not want to do to a possible spine injury...

Monday: TQ Day 351.

First night in the "new" SWA hut. It's fine. I am awakened by the incessant beeping of Eric's alarm clock at 0700, since he's not there to turn it off. Note to self: kill Eric later. Pat and I rip his rack apart trying to find the damned thing and shut it up. We then go back to bed until 1000, when there is an incoming patient. Who finally arrives at 1100. A Marine who jumped across a canal and broke his leg, silly man.

After a year, it's finally starting to feel a little "short," since we have moved and the new guys are due in soon. I can hardly wait to get home.

Tuesday: TQ Day 352.

The first batch of our replacements had arrived last night, and they had shown up for the casualties. There are three officers: their "XO"—a LT (O-3) twig, a PA, and their preventive medicine guy. Also about twenty enlisted, half of whom are Marines. Not much for them to contribute since none of their docs are here, so they just stand around, in the way.

At 1430 I'm supposed to give them a guided bus tour. I was "volunteered" for this as being the person who knows his way around the best. We ride around in a minibus while I point out the few sights. Twelve hours in TQ and they are whining already: "This base sucks" being the most eloquent of the complaints. Some of the enlisted had been here a year ago and are quite vocal about it. Okay, so why didn't you volunteer to go somewhere else instead? You know, somewhere where the Iraqis are much more able to kill you? As we pass the white metal 2-person "spam cans" that are slowly replacing the SWA huts as living quarters, lots of loud complaining that they will not get to live there, instead. They know that they can have a lot more "fun" living in the TQ trailer park as it's more private. Sure, move over there if you want, just sprint the half mile to work whenever there are casualties...

Around 1800, we hear of another patient coming in, ETA 15 minutes, a TCN truck driver with severe chest pain. After an hour, still no patient. I have them make some calls, and the story goes something like this: a TCN truck driver was being searched at the convoy ECP when he complained of chest pain. The convoy commander called us to say he was coming over, and then sent the guy to the medic at the convoy marshalling yard. He was given ibuprofen, and then it gets confusing. Yes, we sent him to you. No, we didn't. Yes. No. Yes. No. Oh wait, that convoy has already left, he probably went with it. Never mind.

Wednesday: TQ Day 353.

Dinner in a gaggle, then spend the evening reading. I felt like calling, so I did. There's really not that much to talk about, but it was nice to hear your voice. I am very ready to get back to the real world, even if it means a lot of foofurraw checking out of the Hospital, moving, checking into San Antonio, and starting the new job. I imagine that I won't have much spare time for a while. We will really need to get a hot tub.

Thursday: TQ Day 354.

Up at 0400 for an incoming patient, which turns out to be an Army tanker who fell off his tank onto his hip. Despite all the yelling and screaming (mostly his), it turns out to be an "owie" and I send him back. Back to bed until 0830.

I take Brian on a personalized tour of the base. In his six months here, he has never seen any of the sights. He pretty much sticks to the "Brian triangle": DFAC, work, home. First stop is Brian's dream spider hole, the huge Iraqi bunker complex that almost no one knows about. Then coffee at "the Black Sheep," which has really run down since the new Army unit took over. Then pics with the palm tree, the lake, the MiGs, and so on, then home. At least now he has a few pictures of "been there, done that."

Go running by myself while everyone heads off to lunch, and then sit on the Beach doing crossword puzzles. Dinner at 1700. Work on some turnover briefings after that. An exciting day, all told.

Saturday: TQ Day 356.

Since it's a gorgeous day with unlimited visibility, I go up to the Crack House for some photos of the base and the SSTP from the air. As I'm admiring the view, I see a helo come in fast and hot to Flight Line Post 1, which is where casualties are usually dropped off. Hmm. I make my way over to the SSTP and, as I walk in, we get a call for an incoming patient, by air, ETA unknown. I prognosticate that the patient will be here in a couple of minutes and, lo! And behold! I'm right.

An unusual case, flying in from another surgical unit. A surgeon had operated on the guy and he was being flown to Baghdad when he became "unstable" and was diverted to us. However, when we look at him, he is quite stable. I suspect that the guy was not well sedated when he was put on the helo and started "bucking" the ventilator, which freaked the corpsman out, so they came to us. While I do not think that you need to be a special "ERC" nurse to do this, you do need to have a corpsman trained to handle a portable ventilator and push drugs, which is what the Army and the Air Force have.

Anyway, he was hit by an IED, has frags to his back, both legs, and one arm. The surgeon had opened his belly and found minor liver, kidney and spleen injuries, which did not require anything. He washed out the extremity wounds. He notes that there is "vascular compromise" to his right leg, which has shattered bones in the calf, ankle and foot. This is a bit odd — he notes a vascular injury, but does not treat it and instead washes out the soft tissue injuries, which could wait. Without blood flow, anything else is irrelevant. We look his leg over and get to work on it. Once we have an ex fix on the leg so it's straightened out again, blood flow is restored. The problem was that with the bones all broken, the blood vessels became kinked and consequently there was no blood flow; holding the bones out straight fixed that problem. All of that said, we probably get similar consternation and criticism from the surgeons we send our patients over to...

During the case, there are people everywhere. No one who works in the OR has arrived from the new crew yet, but we have over 20 people in the OR, everyone wants to watch. I'm not in charge; otherwise I would insist that, for the RIP, the only observers should be the people who actually work in that area. I also note that there are several people wearing the t-shirts from a year ago, the ones that have the motto, "Damage Controllin', Death Cheatin'." I think back to what our sage, "Joe-be-wan," said a year ago when he saw this motto: "You never cheat death, he always comes to collect."

We are finishing up with this guy when we hear of another one coming in. This patient is billed as an EPW with a GSW, no other details. I go to the COC and hear "Witchdoctor" say that the guy is shot in the chest. I get the OR set up for "badness." The Iraqi (who, it turns out, is Iraqi Army and not an EPW after all) arrives looking pretty dead. Rush him to the OR, see that he has a bullet wound at the bottom of his ribs on the right. No pulse. Knife. Slash open the chest, in between the ribs. He does not bleed from the incision, that's never a good sign. Get out the BIG chest retractor. Open the chest, heart is stopped. Snip the pericardium which surrounds the heart, start manual cardiac compressions. At this point I see the new ER and FP guys nearby, and I show them how to do manual cardiac compressions. While the boss opens the other side of the chest, I clamp the aorta. The right side of the chest has blood in it, but the bullet has gone through the chest into the liver. The guy stays dead so we stop; enough futility for one day. Sew up his chest and we are done. About 20 minutes all told, and only 2 minutes from the time he's in the room to the time we had everything open.

The boss tells me that one of the ER guys had followed me into the OR, and he looked like he'd dumped a load in his pants when I opened the chest. (Well, first he started to run the other way but the boss called him back.) Since I have done this here a few times before, and our good OR tech was there, we have this routine down pretty well. No time for a prep, just slash and go (you have to be alive to get an infection). She hands me the knife, then the big Mayo scissors (my favorite trauma instrument, I can do most anything with them), then the retractor, then the aortic clamp, and we are done. I'm glad the ol' trauma surgeon is still able to impress people. Actually, it's only because most Navy docs see essentially no trauma and so they're not used to this. Me, I love it. Which is not to say that I revel in human tragedy, merely that if it's going to happen, I'd like to be there to try and do something about it.

Rumor is that the rest of the FNGs show up on Monday or Tuesday. Great planning: dribble the new guys for a surgical unit in over a week, and send the OR personnel last. Not a single person who actually works in the OR has arrived yet, no surgeons, gas passers, or any other OR people.

Sunday: TQ Day 357.

Up for mass at 0930. Afterwards, we had planned another "Sunday with Psych," but a casualty comes in, an Iraqi soldier shot in the head. I'm the duty doc today. We take him straight back to the OR but there is nothing to do — his brain is dead, his heart just doesn't know it yet. I declare him "expectant" and he dies in a few minutes. I had cleared the room of most of the spectators for this, because when we do this, the patient sometimes makes some fairly distressing breathing noises as he goes, and a lot of the new guys (and some of our own kids, for that matter) may never have seen this before.

...Then back to the coffee. We invited all the new docs to come by, the ones who are here, so there were about a dozen people all told. They seem for the most part a nice enough bunch.

After dinner, we watch *Bicentennial Man*, the Robin Williams movie about the robot who becomes human. Since we've moved out of the old hootch and I've packed everything up, I'm really on the back side of the deployment and am starting to count the days. I miss you a lot, and knowing that the time is growing shorter is making it worse. Hard to get excited when it's months away, but now that it's weeks, oh baby!

At 2300 the radio says we are getting one U.S. military casualty by ground. This becomes three by air. It turns out that a Humvee was hit by an IED, no injuries. The reaction force that went out to get them ran into the back of a tank at 40 mph; we get three guys complaining of all sorts of pain. Eventually, all are cleared. Since we had rousted a lot of the new guys out of bed for this, the boss decides to do a "hot wash" for them to discuss how we do things. We go back to bed around 0230. One guy with back pain we put on the ward for the night. Even though we had agreed two days ago that their guys would already be shadowing our guys, when asked which of their corpsmen will be looking after the patient, we get, "Oh, they are all off already, we are not taking duty at night yet." Uh huh.

Monday: TQ Day 358.

Up at 0930 for yet another casualty. A grenade went off near a turret gunner; he has a small puncture wound in the side of his head but looks okay. However, we sent him out for a head CT. The boss, who yesterday was telling me not to hover over the new guys, keeps going in the ER tent and hovering. Told you so, boss. But eventually they get the guy packaged and he leaves.

Go grab some coffee and then run with Pat at 1300. We are into our fourth mile when we hear of another incoming casualty, so Pat and I run back to the STP. It's a guy with a broken leg. Mike does an ex fix on him with Jose, the PA from the ACE, who wants to do the ortho PA program. I head over to the Beach to cool off, and a few minutes later, we get another guy coming in. This one is quite remarkable in that he's our first Air Force trauma patient I have seen in my year here — and of course it's a non-battle injury. The guy stood up under a forklift and ripped his scalp open on the forklift blade.

He walks in from the Humvee that brought him. The boss and I bet a near beer on how long it will take for them to unwrap his head. I say 4½ minutes, he says ten. At four minutes, we walk in and they are just finishing pulling the bandage off. Damn, I'm good. It's easy, actually. The new ER doc is pretty typical; I knew that he would go straight to the injury without checking for other, more lethal, things first. After a few minutes of letting them dick around, we take the guy back to the OR to sew him up. Since it is a very large laceration, there's a large flap of scalp lifted up and his skull is visible under it. Our Marines think it is pretty cool, though.

Tuesday: TQ Day 359.

Chat with the new guys that have shown up about how we've done things, suggestions, and so on. They seem like a reasonable group; the problem is that they have absolutely no medical plan. The boss had asked them who their top doc is — they don't know. Who is in charge of their ER — they don't know. The answer to almost everything is either they don't know, or they will figure it out when the Big Boss gets here in a month. As new waves of them arrive, they are uncertain who is supposed to go to Fallujah and who stays here. One guy arrives who is not even listed anywhere, which makes you wonder how he got here in the first place. A complete Charlie Foxtrot. The boss, as current OIC and the senior officer present, has given the general surgeon and his twig their marching orders, and has told our CO that he has serious misgivings about whether they will be able to meet the turnover date two days from now. We may have to keep control for a few more days while they unscrew everything, especially since some of their people are not here yet and their surgeons have yet to see a single casualty.

Since the transfer is in two days, their guys are supposed to be taking things over today with us assisting, then tomorrow we watch over them, then on Thursday it's all theirs. So who is getting radios, the handoff of which was supposed to occur at 1200 today? What are their duty sections? Unit "Camp Commandant"? And so on and so on.

I go running at 1600. Have barely made it back when we hear of incoming casualties, three U.S. military, no other details. We all head up to the STP, where there is a lot of milling around. We learn that their guys still are not taking duty at night, WTF? After an hour, we stand down, no one has heard anything else and we are tired of waiting.

It's about two hours later, while Brian and I are chatting, that the radio goes off again. New voice from the COC. "Ridgeway 22, have the duty crew come to the STP." So I, as duty surgeon, call the COC. Is this an "All Ridgeways" call? Are we getting casualties? "I just called 'All Ridgeways,' we have three patients up here now." Well no, you didn't. A few seconds later: "Attention all Ridgeways. We have three patients at the STP now." Yup.

I head up there and am the first doc to arrive, so I start right in on seeing these guys, all of whom are minimally injured. In about three minutes I figure that between the three of them, there is maybe one broken hand. All three are from a rolled Humvee on a convoy about seven hours ago; the same casualties, in fact, we had been called for much, much earlier in the day.

After about forty minutes, the boss and I go back to the SWA hut. He says that they do not plan on giving the Marine drivers or the generator techs radios. Their twig, who insisted on getting a radio first, refuses to answer it. When will it end?

14. March 2006: The Turnover

Wednesday: TQ Day 360.

At 0900, the "veterans" meet at the chapel to discuss the turnover. The consensus: the FNGs are not ready. Their key players only showed up two nights ago, and have had no real opportunity to work together. Hell, a lot of them don't even know where they will be working or what their jobs are supposed to be.

The Catholic contingent (the boss, Brian, Gerry, Joe, and me) had planned to go over to Lakeside for Father Tim's 1130 Ash Wednesday service; but as we drive out of the parking lot, the radio goes off. The boss and I head back to the STP while the rest carry on. We stand around for a while, waiting.

Eventually the patient arrives, an Iraqi with multiple frags from an IED. The boss, after yesterday's aggravations, decides to stay out for the most part. He has me shadow them. One look tells me that the guy will probably live, but needs to go back to the OR. The ER guy takes him to the ER tent instead. The new surgeon did not get up there in time; but I let them, they need to learn these things. Over the next thirty minutes they try to get vital signs. They can't get IVs. He has a hole in his head and needs to fly out. I am constantly standing behind their surgeon, pushing her like she's a resident: what are you going to do now — not what is your differential, but what are you going to DO? You want to fly him out, what are YOU doing to make it happen? YOU have to drive this bus, so start driving. Eventually, she can't stand it any more and moves the guy to the OR, where we can clear everyone out. We find the source of his low blood pressure: too large a blood pressure cuff— that's cured. Eventually, he flies out.

The boss has a "hot wash." The key is organization and leadership. Get organized, and figure out who is in charge. I state bluntly that I believe that the surgeons should drive this bus. It has worked for us for a year, and only the surgeons can call the surgical shots. Not a popular view, but it's the truth. Name one trauma thing a non-surgeon can do that a surgeon can't do possibly better and faster? The new ER doc looks unhappily at me and says nothing.

The boss has a meeting with the new officers to discuss the turnover. They all feel, to a man, that they are completely ready to take over. He disagrees. So the turnover will be delayed for one or two days; hopefully by then they will have their stuff together.

Thursday: TQ Day 361.

After the conference, some words from the boss to the vets. We leave in 9 days, hopefully, but be prepared for changes. Leave Kuwait two days after that, get to the States the next day, and then supposedly no more than four days at Lejeune and then home. The Hospital will give everyone a "96" (4 days off) on their return, as long as it coincides with a weekend (what sort of crap is that?). Everyone who still has a radio, turn it in to the COC after the conference, so the new guys can redistribute them. The official medical turnover will be in one to two days.

Unencumbered by a radio for the first time in a year, I go running for a while and then back to the hootch where the topic of conversation is the new signs on the toilets: "Plumbing is a problem, it has to stop." Huh? "From now on, only toilet paper is to be flushed." Good thing I was issued a folding shovel, I guess I will have to bury my stool. Yuck.

Finishing dinner when we hear on one of the new surgeons' radio that there are two patients "on the pad," so we all walk over. I tell them not to run as it's dark and you'll just hurt yourself on the loose gravel road.

When we get there, it's obvious that a convoy drove through the gate and dropped off the patients. Truck hit by an IED. Ronnie just happened to be up at the STP when they rolled in so he got things going. I walk into the tents and look around to check it out. One guy has obvious facial burns, they are planning to intubate him, good. The other looks better but seems to have a shoulder dislocation. They seem to be moving along, albeit erratically, so I stand back. The duty surgeon seems very reluctantly involved in their management, but doing it nonetheless.

At one point I hear that he plans to take the face burn to the OR to debride him — huge mistake, which the boss points out to him. You rarely debride facial burns; it's usually not necessary, and the results are cosmetically horrible. In addition to which, debriding burns in general produces massive blood loss, which you really do not want to do here with our limited resources. Fairly early on we had had four burns show up at once; the boss had wanted to take them to the OR for escharotomies (to prevent pressure from the tight burned skin injuring nerves and blood vessels). I had convinced him that this would not be a good idea, that they would all start to crump within the hour, and he had followed my advice and we had sent them all out immediately. I was right, two of the four crumped on the helo and had to be hand-ventilated. We would never have been able to send them if we had kept them, and they would probably have died. (One eventually did, the other three are doing well at BAMC in San Antonio. I plan to look them up when we move there.) The boss had taken this lesson to heart, and was now passing it along.

I have tried to hang back, as has the boss, and we have reined in Mike, too. At one point I head off to the bathroom. I come back with my hands held together and say to the boss, "So if all I can flush is toilet paper, what am I supposed to do with this?" and I drop a scrunched up cardboard toilet roll onto his arm. He freaks and jumps backwards, as if I were dropping a turd on him. Gotcha. Laughed our asses off; perfect timing and good stress relief.

The duty surgeon then wants to send two helos, because one patient is ready to fly out and the other is not, he will need more time. How much more? "They told me 15 minutes." So your problem is not that you need two helos, it's that one group is working too slowly. You don't need a second helo, you need to walk in there, tell them they have three minutes to be done, and then stand there and make them do it.

About ten minutes later, both patients are being put on the ambulance, and they head out. A slight delay when they have to take another monitor down to the helo, as the battery is dead on one. Oops. The new guys then do a "hot wash," which the boss, Ronnie, and I stay out of. This was orders of magnitude better than the first one they did, they still have a lot of problems, but they will get it eventually. They have to. Like we had to.

Friday: TQ Day 362.

We are supposed to muster daily at 1000, PT gear and bed-heads permissible, for accountability and to pass info. At 0955, the boss, Pat, and I head over to the muster area, which is about twenty feet from our hootch, only to discover that the Chief, our senior enlisted, has already had it and dismissed everyone. Another classic boss/chief interaction: "Did you pass the info on the training schedule?" "No." "Did you account for everybody, like, for example, me?" "No." "Chief, 1000 means 1000, not 0950. If your watch is fast, which we both know it isn't, you can synchronize it with mine. We are not doing this 'muster creep' like you did at Camp Lejeune."

At 1100, we have a formation, the new guys want an official "transfer of authority" ceremony, don't ask me why. I go up at 1045, to see that almost everyone is already formed up, muster creep once again. I know that the boss will be showing up at 1100. I walk by the Chief and our twig and, as I pass them, say, "If you think that I'm going to stand around for fifteen minutes waiting for nothing to happen, you are nuts. 1100 is 1100, not 1045." The twig opens his mouth, I look at him, and he shuts it again. The good thing about all of this is that, with everyone mustered, no one was in the COC and I managed to check my e-mail without having to wait for an open computer.

At 1058, I am out there in formation, and at 1100 the boss comes up and we start, just like we should. His speech is very brief: we're all going home, good luck to the FNGs. We are done.

Not much else goes on for the rest of the day, no surprise. The last radio was turned in to them, the torch was passed, and we are no longer in the loop. Call us if you need us, and we all know that they will not call.

Saturday: TQ Day 363.

Despite the lack of things to do today, we managed to entertain ourselves somehow. We are up for the 1000 muster, and we're supposed to start "redeployment training" at 1030. Of course, "redeployment" is actually Marine-speak for "going home," and we are doing this while we wait for our plane to leave in a week because it will supposedly shorten our time at Camp Lejeune. More boxes to check...

As we sit around drinking coffee before going to the chapel for the training, Brian makes the mistake of joking that it's his birthday (it isn't). "Oh, Brian, it's your birthday? We need to get you a cake and some presents." "No, you don't. It's NOT my birthday." "But Brian, you NEED a cake and presents..." And so it begins, again.

At the start of the training session, Pat gets up and announces to the entire unit that it's Brian's birthday, so we all sing "Happy Birthday" to him. Once the training is over, Pat and I go off to run a few miles, and we hatch further plots. Not much else happens for the afternoon. I get together the various unit pics and stats that we will distribute to the officers. Then off to dinner. During dinner, we stuff our pockets with as many apple cinnamon muffins as we can. I have a plan. On the way back, the boss and I stop at the exchange, where we buy a "Happy Birthday Grandpa" card (Brian is 55), a can of shaving cream, and *Dr. Phil's Guide to Weight Loss* (Brian can't stand Dr. Phil, and commented yesterday that he looked fat on the cover of his own diet book).

Brian tends to eat dinner late, so he heads out around 1930. I get to work. Get the card signed by everyone in the hootch. Wrap the book in paper with a nice colorful bow on it (leftover from the medal-making). The boss had a leftover red-and-white striped elf hat from Xmas; I put a cardboard cone into it so it's pointy and stands up straight. Then the *pièce de résistance*, the cake. I cut the bottom off a disposable bed pan to make

After Brian fibbed about his birthday as an excuse to get out of making a speech, what choice did his hootchmates have but to make him a cake? The recipe: ten Otis Spunkmeyer muffins smushed into a bed pan as a mold, coated in shaving cream, with a cigarette as a candle.

a shallow, squarish pan. Smush up about ten muffins into muffin paste, and mash it into the bottom. Flip it over, it's a reasonably firm square. Top it off with shaving cream for icing and a cigarette for a candle and, Voila! A birthday cake.

The unsuspecting Brian returns around 2100, and is ceremonially sat down and presented with his gifts. He even wears the hat. We almost pee'd our pants laughing, it was absolutely hysterical. Brian could not keep a straight face the whole time, he was laughing so hard he was crying. It was the best non-birthday he had ever had.

Sunday: TQ Day 364.

I am entering this a few days after the fact, not much to report. Went to Mass at 0930, then "Sunday with Psych." Running. Nothing else of note.

Monday: TQ Day 365.

We did more "redeployment training" today at 1030; it was fascinating. The twig read us slides for thirty minutes while my cerebral hemispheres took it in turns to fall asleep. I skipped running as I was a bit under the weather. Thirteen illness-free months in Iraq, and the week I expect to leave, I catch a cold!

The other thing I did today was turn in my laptop. Apparently everything that goes wrong for the new crew is blamed on us. For example, they lost a radio and then accused us of stealing it, even though they had eyeballed each one and signed for them all. So, even though I never signed for this computer, I turned it over to our twig and suggested that he have his counterpart sign for it from us.

Tuesday: TQ Day 366.

Tried to sleep in, no luck. The tents of the old HQ Battalion BAS, behind where we now live, were torn down this morning. So "beep beep beep" from bulldozers and trucks all morning. The sandbags around them remain, though, so it's the perfect paintball course, if only we had paintball. At 1030, mandatory motorcycle safety classes, even for those who have no motorcycles. Tomorrow, it'll be "Spouse Abuse Awareness," even for those with no spouse. Gotta check those boxes.

Another frighteningly tedious day, otherwise.

After dinner ("Arabic Bar," again remarkably similar to the "Indian Bar" and "Asian Bar") we watch the first of the *Lord of the Rings* trilogy, the first disc anyway. As you can imagine, the comments were flying. Something about "elf poontang..." Maybe they shouldn't make a movie of the Sci Fi novel *Grunts*. It's about a war from the Orc perspective...

My eight-year old laptop has finally died and, with it, my attempts at diary-keeping.

With the RIP, I have turned in my government laptop, and must resort to borrowed laptops and a thumb drive. What can I say — war is heck.

We spend 17 days waiting for our ride to Kuwait, the first leg of the trip home. We are fortunate in that at least we can stay at TQ for this, which is sort of like home, as opposed to sitting around forever in transient tents in Kuwait. Still, it gets very old very fast. We find things to do, though. Most of the FNGs don't come and socialize and we have abandoned HESCO beach to them as well; but using cocktail umbrellas I build a nice "HESCO beach for flies" outside our temporary hootch, complete with a little pond.

It's a beautiful day when we finally leave. I don't recall what the weather was like, but it was still a beautiful day. We marched out onto the runway perimeter and wait, looking more military than we've looked in months; full cammies, helmets, body armor, backpacks, weapons. To look at us, you'd almost believe we are in the Military, instead of a bunch of docs, nurses and corpsmen. Watch more FNGs march off and, just like when we had first arrived, we stare at them as they pass and say nothing. I bet it's been that way in every war. March out to the C-130, strap in, wait for what seems like forever, and finally take off. The cheering commences.

Only spent a day in Kuwait, mercifully, and then take the charter back to the States. We stop to refuel in Shannon, Ireland. The Irish clearly are used to us: at the pub facing the terminal gate, the innkeeper has already lined up the pints of Guinness. Of course, none of us would dream of violating CentCom General Order #1, no drinking while in or in transit through the CentCom area of operations...

We eventually land back at the Marine Corps Air Station at Cherry Point, from whence I had left over 13 months ago. Climb aboard the chartered tour buses and head back to Lejeune. On the way back, we do our final two postdeployment briefings. We file onto two buses and deliberately split up our psychologist and our psychiatrist so they can each give us the final stress briefing on the way to Lejeune, thereby complying with the letter of the law: that we are permitted to accomplish some of our postdeployment briefings in theater but must finish them after we return to the U.S., before we return home. Well, on the highway to Lejeune is the U.S., donchaknow. Brian is once again in stand-up comic mode: "If you are feeling stressed after you get home, try what I do. It works well for me, and it may work for you. Drink heavily, and if that doesn't work, try drugs."

Upon arrival at Lejeune, we are housed in exactly the same barracks we had been in when we left. To our surprise, the General is there to welcome us home, but he knows that some people's families have come down to meet them and so he keeps his welcome short. But it was a very nice gesture on his part and much appreciated.

The remainder of our welcome is less cordial. We are told by people who have never left the warmth of Camp Lejeune that we must repeat all of our postdeployment briefings because if they weren't done at Lejeune then they don't count. We refuse. A representative from the Hospital has come down to streamline our return to our parent command. She tells us that we must return to the Hospital and then file leave papers with our departments if we want time off after our return. Again, we refuse — we saw this coming, and have had our leave approved by the Marines before they officially give us back to the Navy. I ask if the Hospital plans on sending real buses for us to go home in, or will they insult their "returning warriors" with the same child-sized school bus they sent us down in; she assures me that it's all taken care of. We make the rounds, returning our gear, weapons, and so on. I am told to return gear I was never issued, for which they have no receipts, and again I refuse — show me the papers I signed for it and I'll give it back to you (assuming that I even have it). Finally, they leave us alone for the day and we head over to Mike, the Orthopod's, house for a welcome home bash.

The next day we are out in front of the barracks, anticipating the long-awaited ride home. Look, here come some nice tour buses. Oh, that's for the Marines in the next barracks over, for their 45-minute ride to Cherry Point. Wait, here are some more. Nope, it's for the enlisted Marines going 30 minutes to New River. Finally, in the distance, the white school bus. Yup, our ride for the next four hours, courtesy of the Hospital.

Again, a bunch of us refuse. We find a way to cram everyone into the vehicles of the families who have come down to Lejeune, and head north. We are finally heading home, and we are doing it in a little more style. The luggage can ride in the bus without us...

Epilogue

When I came home after a year in Iraq, many people asked me what I thought of my time there. To this day, I don't know how to summarize the experience. The Dickensian "It was the best of times, it was the worst of times" seems a little too pat, and it really wasn't either. It couldn't have been the best of times, I missed my family too much and we lacked indoor plumbing, two things I have come to appreciate much more as I have grown older. It certainly wasn't the worst of times, as I was doing what I had spent years training to do and no one was trying to kill me (at least, me in particular) on a daily basis. I think I'd best summarize it with the purported Chinese curse, "May you live in interesting times." Not every day was interesting, but there were many interesting days. Some of those days I was very interested in, and to some I was forced to pay particular interest, whether I wanted to or not (it is a curse, after all). I didn't learn a lot about surgery—I practiced a lot of what was previously just theory to me, but I may not have learned so much. But I did learn a lot about people, about people under pressure, and about the resiliency of both the human body and the human spirit. I may also have become a better carpenter. My wife assures me that my taste in clothes is no better, as I still wear the same Hawaiian shirt.

As I write this, it is just over five years since I returned from Iraq. In the interim, I have stayed Navy, traveled the world, and deployed to the war in Afghanistan and the earthquake in Haiti, and soon I will deploy again to Afghanistan. Despite the many tragedies that I have witnessed, I have neither insomnia nor flashbacks. I have noticed though, as I'm sure others have noticed about me, that my tolerance of imaginary crises is even lower than it once was. My sense of what is and is not important has changed. Life and death are important. People and families are important. Paperwork and busy work, not so much.

But I also have no delusions that I did more, or did it faster, or better, than anyone else. All of us medical types do what we are trained to do, and do what we have to do, as did those who came before us. And as those who come after us must do. From the field corpsman or medic, to the Battalion Aid Station, to the forward surgical unit, to the theater hospital, and all the way back home, we must form an unbroken chain of medical care—so either we all get the credit, or none of us does. And as the students of military history will point out, compared to our predecessors, we have it easy.

ZTS

Index